Ethics & Journalism

Ethics & Journalism

KAREN SANDERS

SAGE Publications
London • Thousand Oaks • New Delhi

SAGE Publications Ltd
1 Oliver's Yard, 55 City Road
London EC1Y 1SP

SAGE Publications Inc
2455 Teller Road
Thousand Oaks, California 91320

SAGE Publications India Pvt Ltd
B-42 Panchsheel Enclave
PO Box 4109
New Delhi 100 017

British Library Cataloguing in Publication data
A catalogue record for this book is
available from the British Library

ISBN 0 7619 6966 7
ISBN 0 7619 6967 5 (pbk)

Library of Congress Catalogue Card Number: 2002104220

Typeset by Mayhew Typesetting, Rhayader, Powys
Printed and bound in Great Britain by
Cromwell Press Ltd., Trowbridge, Wiltshire

For my parents, Terence and Dolores Sanders.

Contents

Acknowledgements

I wrote this book in the spring and summer of 2001 in the city of Pamplona. I would not have been able to write it without the study leave granted by the Department of Journalism of the University of Sheffield and the generosity of my colleagues in the department. I have learned an enormous amount from them over the past six years.

I am also grateful to the University of Navarra and to Professor Rafael Alvira of the Department of Philosophy who ensured I had ideal working conditions. Concha del Prado provided constant encouragement and laughter.

So many conversations with so many people have contributed to and inspired much that follows. Speaking and listening to journalists such as David Hencke, Mark Skipworth, Donald Trelford, Bill Hagerty, John Ryley and Peter Preston was particularly valuable. I am especially grateful to Linda Sanders, who read the manuscript and to the editors at Sage. They saved me from some major errors; any that remain are my responsibility. Linda is the most loving sister and friend. My thanks also to Jo Caseby for reading the manuscript and for all those conversations about journalism and ethics throughout the years. Ana Marta González was also very helpful in discussing some of the finer points of ethical theory.

I remember with deep affection Maureen and Andrew Tighe, my grandparents, both of whom died as I was writing this book. I wish to remember too the Cruzado family and especially Augusto Cruzado. They are exceptional people and Augusto was *un amigo muy querido*.

Maria de la Viesca is, and has always been, a tower of strength. I could not wish for a better friend.

Finally, my thanks to my parents who are examples to me in so many ways. To them I dedicate this book.

LIST OF TABLES

LIST OF BOXES

A reporter is 'a man without virtue who writes lies . . . for his profit.'
Dr Samuel Johnson

THE REPORTING BESTIARY: WATCHDOGS, VULTURES AND GADFLYS

In polls conducted in 1993 estate agents received the lowest rating in British public esteem; journalists were just above them. And yet the lure of a career in the media is stronger than ever. Reporters repel and attract; they are the twenty-first century equivalent of Dr Jekyll and Mr Hyde, the 'hack' for whom, in the words of foreign correspondent, Nicholas Tomalin, the only necessary qualifications are 'a plausible manner, rat-like cunning and a little literary ability (26 October, 1969).'

Little trusted, little loved (but often secretly admired), the reporter is seen as the cynical, ruthless figure parodied in the Channel 4 series *Drop the Dead Donkey* (1990–98) and films such as *Broadcast News* (1987) and *Network* (1976). Described by the satirical magazine, *Private Eye*, and the Royal Family as 'the reptiles', compared to jackals and vultures feeding on human carrion, this image of the journalist reached its apotheosis at the time of the death of Diana, Princess of Wales in 1997. The presence and behaviour of the paparazzi at the scene of the accident and Earl Spencer's public accusation that 'editors have blood on their hands – I always believed the press would kill her in the end,' was a low-water mark for British journalism.

Earlier that same year, the white-suited Martin Bell, a former BBC correspondent, won election to Parliament as the unofficial, anti-corruption candidate against the discredited Conservative contender, Neil Hamilton. Here was the journalist as figure of integrity, crusader for truth, exposing evil to the discomfit of the powerful, exemplifed by the *Sunday Times*' campaign for justice for victims of the thalidomide drug and John Pilger's coverage of East Timor.

Surveys in Britain show a more favourable perception of broadcast journalists than journalists in general, findings which are reversed in the rest of Europe and the United States. A Harris Poll conducted in the United States in 1998, using virtually identical questions to those asked in a 1997 UK MORI survey, showed that in the United States only 44 per cent of adults say they would generally believe newsreaders, while in Britain 74 per cent would trust newsreaders to tell them the truth. However, only 15 per cent of the British population would trust journalists to tell them the truth compared to 43 per cent of Americans (www.mori.com/polls/1998/harris.html). A MORI survey carried out in February 2000 for the British Medical Association confirmed the British public's ambivalent attitude to its journalists: 78 per cent of us believe that journalists do not tell the truth, although 73 per cent believe that news readers

Q: For each of these different types of people would you tell me if you generally trust them to tell the truth, or not?

	Tell the truth %	Not tell the truth %	Don't know %
Doctors	87	9	4
Teachers	85	10	5
Television News Readers	73	18	10
Professors	76	11	13
Judges	77	15	8
Clergymen/Priests	78	16	6
Scientists	63	25	12
The Police	60	33	8
The ordinary man/woman in the street	52	34	14
Pollsters	46	35	19
Civil Servants	47	40	14
Trade Union officials	38	47	15
Business Leaders	28	60	12
Politicians generally	20	74	6
Government Ministers	21	72	7
Journalists	15	78	6

Source: MORI poll in February 2000 on behalf of the British Medical Association. A total of 2,072 adults aged 15 and over were interviewed face-to-face during the period February 3–7 at 156 sampling points throughout Great Britain. Data was weighted to the known profile of the British population (www.mori.com/polls/2000/bma2000.shtml).

do (see Table 1.1). And yet we have one of the highest newspaper circulation figures in Europe (see Table 1.2). On an average week-day twelve million copies of national newspapers are sold in Britain, compared to almost two million in France, just over seven million in Germany and about 1.6 million in Spain.

As with most caricatures, there is something of truth and much distortion in the Janus-like image we have of journalists. And our continued, although declining, newspaper buying habits point to more ambivalence in our attitudes than the polls would indicate. Nevertheless, few would disagree that British journalists have, in the words of *Sky News'* political editor, Adam Boulton (1997), 'a slightly more Grub Street underbelly' than their American and continental counterparts, reflecting the vigorous traditions of the popular press (see Engel, 1996; Williams, 1998). Partly for this reason perhaps, they have been less prone to make claims to be a Fourth Estate acting in the national interest. According to this peculiarly British, unromanticized understanding of what journalists do and the impact they can have, journalism is a trade not a profession, journalists are 'reporters' and are more gadflys than watchdogs, reptiles than rottweilers.

Scepticism about journalism's aims and means does not lead to a quiescent industry. The *News of The World*'s reporters who, in April 2001 exposed the blurring of royal and business affairs in the Countess of Wessex's PR activities by posing as rich Arabs, could not be further removed from their Spanish counterparts whose own Royals are treated with extreme deference. Journalism in Britain is anything but boring.

However, scepticism exacts a business as well as an ethical price. A resistance to reflection, a permutation of the anti-intellectualism which runs through much of British culture, serves no one. Journalists and editors lose their jobs, people's lives are badly damaged, share prices are hit and circulation and viewing figures can fall in a climate where reflection on the practices and principles of journalism is actively discouraged.[1] As The Times journalist, Raymond Snoddy, put it, 'talking about and encouraging high standards and ethics in newspapers . . . is not some sort of self-indulgence for amateur moral philosophers or journalists with sensitive psyches: it is a very practical matter, involving customer relations, product improvement and profit' (1992: 203). This statement stands for all media, although it is undoubtedly the print industry which has been most loath to contemplate the larger implications of what it does.

THE HACK'S PROGRESS

Thinking about ethics is to think about what journalism is and what journalists do. One of the cherished beliefs of most British journalists is that their calling is not a profession nor ever should be. Professional status requires command of a specific area of knowledge which partly determines entry into the profession. Lawyers must know the law. But what body of knowledge is required of the journalist? Journalism, it is said, is more akin to a craft or trade, learned by doing. It should be open to all those who show the right aptitudes, usually summarized as a nose for news, a plausible manner and an ability to write and deliver concise, accurate copy to deadline.

This approach to journalism has meant that journalism training in Britain has been primarily trade-based. Unlike counterparts in the United States and the rest of Europe, training standards have traditionally been set by industry bodies: the National Council for the Training of Journalists (NCTJ) for the print industry and the Broadcast Journalism Training Council (BJTC) for the broadcast industry. Training in skills and knowledge of the law and the workings of government are fundamental. Ethics is not a compulsory separate subject. Training bodies stipulate that ethical reflection be addressed throughout training and that students be fully acquainted with industry codes of practice (the Press Complaint Commission's Code for the print industry and the BBC's Producer Guidelines and Codes of the Broadcasting Standards Commission, Independent Television Commission and Radio Authority for the broadcast industry). These training requirements have been incorporated into a variety of diploma courses at non-university institutions. Increasingly they form part of university courses which range beyond the immediate constraints of the traditional industrial training bodies.

The 'Columbia-Journalism-Review-School of Journalism', as it has been disparagingly described, arrived in Britain in 1970 when Cardiff became the first university to offer journalism courses (Thomaß, 1998). By 2001 there were 31 undergraduate journalism degrees and six had industry accreditation. This

Title	2000	2001
Spanish daily nationals		
El País	562,821	
La Vanguardia	244,644	
El Mundo	379,657	
ABC	378,965	
Diario 16	48,512	
TOTAL	**1,614,599**	
UK daily nationals		
The Mirror		2,203,815
Daily Star		591,392
The Sun		3,487,015
Daily Express		960,543
The Daily Mail		2,427,464
The Daily Telegraph		1,015,906
The Guardian		401,519
The Independent		225,496
The Times		710,709
TOTAL		**12,023,859**
UK Sunday newspapers		
News of the World		3,980,544
Sunday Mirror		1,855,258
Sunday People		1,404,313
Sunday Sport		195,220
Sunday Express		914,360
The Mail on Sunday		2,367,529
Independent on Sunday		247,544
The Observer		454,462
The Sunday Telegraph		802,483
TOTAL		**12,221,713**
French daily nationals		
Le Figaro	367,595	
France Soir	125,462	
L'Humanité	55,113	
Liberatión	171,336	
Le Monde	402,444	
Le Parisien/Aujourd'hui en France	492,518	
La Tribune	104,359	
La Croix	90,232	
Les Echos	153,968	
TOTAL	**1,963,027**	
German national newspapers		
Deutsche Tagespost mit ASZ		14,478
Die Tageszeitung, Berlin		58,738
Die Welt		255,159
Financial Times Deutschland		72,433
Frankfurter Allgemeine		408,641
Frankfurter Rundschau		192,182
Handelsblatt		155,660

Title	2000	2001
Hürriyet		81,219
Neues Deutschland, Berlin		57,743
Süddeutsche Zeitung		436,051
Abendzeitung		183,899
Berliner Kurier		165,506
BILD		4,396,309
B.Z.		259,018
Express		310,680
Hamburger Morgenpost		119,140
Morgenpost f. Sachsen, Dresden		110,342
T.Z.		149,500
TOTAL		7,426,698

TABLE 1.2 *(Continued)*

Sources: Audit Bureau of Circulation, Oficina de Justificación de Difusión, Informationsgemeinschaft zur Feststellung der Verbgreitung von Werbetägern (IVW) and Associacíon pour le Côntrole de la Diffusíon des Média.

represents an important and not universally welcomed shift in the educational background of journalists.[2]

Some fear that the shift to university-based education might blunt the edge of hard reporting in the same way that journalism schools are said to have done in the United States. The legendary publisher of the *National Enquirer*, Generoso Pope, was said to prefer British journalists to American ones because they hadn't forgotten that they were in the business to sell newspapers and not simply to right the wrongs of society. This gave their reporting bite so that, according to one journalist, an American reporter sent to a plane crash would write, 'I wept over the funeral pyre of 199 people,' whereas his/her British counterpart would write, 'Dead, that's what 199 people were last night' (Taylor, 1991: 59). But (and this will be the central contention of this book) being a reflective journalist isn't inimical to good reporting. If we consider what skills and knowledge journalists should have, the reverse is likely to be true.

SKILLS AND KNOWLEDGE

In 1996 US newsroom supervisors were polled to see what importance they gave to different knowledge and skill areas for the potential journalist (Medsger, 1996: 25). The ten areas which received most approval were:

1 Basic newsgathering and writing skills – 98%
2 Clear writing skills – 97%
3 Understanding that accuracy and truthfulness are essential in journalism – 96%
4 Interviewing skills – 95%
5 Analysing information and ideas – 94%
6 Ability to organize complex stories with clarity and grace – 86%
7 Writing on deadline – 82%

8 Well-informed about current events – 78%
9 Ability to recognize holes in coverage – 77%
10 Ability to develop story lines on your own – 76%

The American editors' list of qualities falls across several of the categories of understanding of knowledge identified by Aristotle as (i) *episteme*: scientific knowledge; (ii) *tekne*: art – making knowledge; (iii) *phronesis*: practical knowledge; (iv) *sophia*: philosophical knowledge; (v) *nous*: intuitive reason. They can help us to structure and understand the kind of knowledge journalists should have.

(i) *Technical knowledge*: The aim here is to learn how to *do* something. And, of course, the best way of learning how to do something is by doing it. Providing you with a theoretical book on how to ride a bicycle will be of little use in riding a bicycle. You will only learn how to cycle by *cycling*. Learning shorthand is an example of this kind of knowledge.

(ii) *Practical knowledge*: Ethics, politics and rhetoric, the art of persuasion, all require practical knowledge, knowing how to act, how to apply one's intellectual capacities in order to achieve the right outcome in the area concerned. A good doctor must not only know how to use a stethoscope but also have acquired intellectual habits of judgement and discernment which allow him/her to discriminate between chicken pox and what is just a particularly mottled complexion, and then prescribe the appropriate remedy.

Practical knowledge is about the correct application of acquired intellectual habits to one's chosen field for the attainment of particular goals. A journalist has to know what the story is and then know how to tell it. This involves technical knowledge but also powers of judgement and analysis: decisions about use and credibility of sources, appropriateness of tone, story interest, none of which are givens. Getting a story right, as the *Sunday Mirror* editor, Colin Myler, found over the Leeds football players' trial in spring 2001, can be critical to job security, a paper's reputation and share prices (see note 1).

(iii) *Philosophical knowledge*: In third place on the American editors' list of qualities was the awareness that accuracy and truthfulness are essential to the journalist's task. To understand why this should be considered so is to enter the realm of philosophical knowledge. Questions about what a journalist is and what reporting is for, are the often unexplored assumptions underlying practice. The view of one tabloid editor that, 'Information is only a commodity, like bread' will almost certainly influence the kind of stories printed in his paper.

Reflecting on ethics and journalism is about acquiring philosophical knowledge which is of intrinsic interest, self-sufficient, complete in itself. It is to say that education is more than training.

In this sense, reflection on ethics and journalism is distinctly out of tune with the temper of our utilitarian times. For it requires us to move beyond what the political philosopher, Michael Oakeshott (1993), has spoken of as the condition of worldliness, the thought that what matters above all is success understood as the achievement of some external result, usually striving to have a successful career as evidence of achievement. Of course, there is nothing wrong with having a successful career. Oakeshott's point is that an excessive concern with reputation can mean that the present is sacrificed to the god of the future; he suggests that it is preferable that: 'Ambition and the greed for visible results, in which each stage is a mere approach to the goal . . . be superseded by a life which carried in each of its moments its whole meaning and value' (1993: 32). Lofty words and, some might say, unrealizable aims yet they express what many have felt to be true about human existence.

Episteme and *nous* have been left outside this account: the first, because there is no knowledge area (although it is possible, but not wise, to be a reporter without knowing any law) which a journalist *must* master (unless of course he or she is a specialist correspondent); the second, because intuitive knowledge is just that: it can be tutored and nurtured but either you've got it or you haven't. Technical and practical knowledge have been traditionally taught in industrial training courses and philosophical knowledge is the dimension which university-based courses seek to add so that, in the nineteenth century ideal of John Henry Newman:

> It is the education which gives a man a clear, conscious view of his own opinions and judgements, a truth in developing them, an eloquence in expressing them, and a force in urging them. It teaches him to see things as they are, to go right to the point, to disentangle a skein of thought, to detect what is sophistical, and to discard what is irrelevant. (1852/1987: 197)

Does the shift to the university mean that journalism is acquiring professional status? And is such status desirable? It might be argued that professionalism, with its concomitant requirement for self-regulation, would exercise a healthy ethical pressure on journalists. Evidence from an extensive survey-based study of newsroom cultures in twenty-one countries suggests that this might be so (Weaver, 1998).

Weaver's study showed that there is no consensus about professional roles or ethical values. Respecting source confidentiality is a generally shared rule but using personal documents is not: 92.5 per cent of Spanish journalists, for example, considered this to be wrong as against 51 per cent in Britain. The level of agreement about ethical norms within a country was highest in Spain and at its lowest in Britain and interestingly, the UK is the country with the lowest proportion of its workforce in possession of university-based journalism qualifications: 4 per cent as against the highest world figure of 92 per cent for Spanish journalists (Canel et al. 2000: 101–2). Of course, opinions expressed in surveys are not synonymous with ethical behaviour and divergent views about controversial practices may express genuinely different understandings of what journalism is for. Journalists in Britain are also obliged to negotiate a number of legal quagmires which may make them more relaxed about certain practices. At the present state of play, we can say that journalism is not a profession in Britain despite its shift to the university. In sociological terms professions are thought to have four characteristics (Donsbach, 1997):

1 primary orientation to the community rather than to self-interest
2 a high degree of generalized and systematic knowledge
3 a high degree of self-regulation through codes of standards absorbed through work socialization and associations operated by the professionals themselves
4 a system of rewards which are symbols of work achievement so that professionals usually have a high degree of freedom and high income levels

Most of these criteria are not fulfilled by British journalism. As *The Times* columnist, Simon Jenkins, put it:

> . . . to apply the word profession to what appears in newspapers is pointless. Since the 17th century, the best guide to journalism has been to 'find out what the bastards are up to and tell the world'. A profession adheres to codes of practice, rules of fairness and confidentiality. Such constraints may apply in some reaches of journalism including, I pompously hope, my own. But the business of newspapers is so overwhelmed by market competition that most constraint has gone by the board. News is mixed with comment. Campaigning distorts coverage. Anonymous (that is, made-up) derogatory quotes are everywhere. Feeding frenzies consume all in their path. To their victims, reporters are a lynch mob in full cry. (11 April, 2001)

However, Jenkins would change little, concluding in the same article that he prefers 'the occasional stomach-churner to avoid the corrupt, establishment press of most of Europe and the bland local monopolies of America'. Although this is a little strongly stated, it expresses the dilemma when thinking about journalism and ethics. How can lively journalism be encouraged which at the same time is not blind to the very real damage that can be done by unethical practices? Without advocating professional status, neither feasible nor – in my view – desirable, it is possible to see how the university can provide a forum for a more considered reflection on journalism that is virtually impossible to achieve in the newsroom.

WHY JOURNALISM MATTERS

There is a view that journalism matters very little. Many journalists have remarked on the humbling experience of seeing yesterday's newspaper as today's waste paper. Studies of television news show that we barely retain information from one bulletin to another let alone from one day to the next (Gunter, 1999). This 'limited effects' understanding of the media is countered by an extreme view, sometimes advanced by journalists, of the media's power. The campaigning Victorian journalist, William Thomas Stead, declared:

> I have seen Cabinets upset, ministers driven into retirement, laws repealed, great social reforms initiated, Bills transformed, estimates remodelled, programmes

modified, Acts passed, generals nominated, governors appointed, armies sent hither and thither, wars proclaimed and wars averted, by the agency of newspapers. (cited in Snoddy 1992: 46)

It is notoriously hard to *prove* media effects, despite the prodigious industry spent in the attempt. But journalism matters not because we know it changes anything; it matters because in giving the news, journalists arbitrate, frame and amplify events and issues. They help create the map by which we understand the world beyond our immediate purview and by which we situate our fears, desires and aspirations. Public reaction to the *News of the World*'s 'name and shame' campaign against paedophiles in the closing months of 2000 provided a vivid example of how communities' desires and fears are engaged by journalism. Editor Rebekah Wade did not invent those fears but she provided the narrative context for them. As American journalist, H.L. Mencken, explained, all journalists aim 'to please the crowd, to give a good show; and the way they set about giving that good show [i]s by first selecting a deserving victim, and then putting him magnificently to the torture' (1918: 53).

Journalism matters. Journalists sketch in the contours of our moral landscape. They contribute to the business of telling us who we are, interpreting the world for us, making it intelligible.

JOURNALISM AS STORY-TELLING

It can be illuminating to compare reporting with other ways of interpreting the world – literary fiction, for example, or history, anthropology and biography. The latter deal with real events and literature with imaginary ones. Fiction narrates events that did not happen. History, biography and journalism tell of events that did. The distinction might be put very simply: 'The writer of fiction must invent, while the journalist must not.' When we examine the notion of truthfulness in journalism in Chapter four, we'll see that matters aren't quite that simple. However, to the judge who asked a journalist, 'So a novelist is the same as a journalist, then. Is that what you're saying?' I would categorically maintain that he or she is not.[3] Reporting has an exterior reference, a reference to the world of events about which it provides information to others. Fictional literature refers to creations of the imagination. A novelist wholly creates a world and indeed the hallmark of fine literary achievement is the credibility of the characters and universe summoned into existence by the artist. Jane Austen's *Emma* is a living, breathing, imaginary being. But literature and reporting do have one thing in common: they share a commitment to the 'story'.

The similarities with historical writing are even greater. In a certain sense, the so-called Father of History, Herodotus, was also the father of journalism. He understood his craft to be that of investigation, finding out, the production of eye-witness accounts – *hyster* means 'witness' – as opposed to the creation of mythological accounts. Historian and journalist, Paul Johnson, has drawn out the similarities between journalism and history. Their objects of study are distinct, for where the historian stands on the bow of a ship, looking back as the waves recede and the wake left by the ship indiscernibly merges into the sea, the journalist looks at the churned-up ocean just below. However, their methods and subject matter are similar: they must both have the ability to use and correctly evaluate sources; they must adopt a scientific approach to knowledge, testing hypotheses, rejecting those that cannot be corroborated through source or documentary evidence; their subject matter is events which happen in the world. Whether it is putting together a docu-drama, writing for *The Drudge Report* (the Internet magazine which broke the Lewinsky story) or reporting from Jerusalem for the *Independent*, there is a shared assumption by journalist and audience that the reports have a connection to events which have in fact taken place.

Journalists are story-tellers. In so doing they act as an interpretative community, providing texts, working within certain conventions and traditions, which become our understanding of events: the assassination of John F. Kennedy, the life and death of Princess Diana – our understanding of their lives is forever mediated by the interpretations of the journalists who told their stories.[4]

Plato was the first to point out in *The Republic* that the artists act as mediators of cultural symbols and values. He wanted to banish from his utopian republic those who told 'bad', 'corrupting' stories. In the same way, the journalists of today, unconsciously and sometimes consciously, are the equivalent of a contemporary priestly caste: they are the mediators of values – their scandalized headlines tell us what is right and what is wrong – and they are the guardians of language.

Aristotle said that a well-told story teaches us something. Narrative can provide practical wisdom and it always has an implicit moral intentionality. Journalism does this too, although its general shallowness compared to other genres can be measured by contrasting the experience of reading Tolstoy's *Anna Karenina* to reading the *News of the World*'s account of the adultery and suicide of a Russian countess. The subjects are similar – although one is real and the other imagined – both tell a story, but there's no doubting which is the most profoundly truthful of the two. Good reporting does not have to aspire to the condition of great literature; its techniques and constraints are different.[5] But at its best reporting also reveals something to us about the world (Carey, 1989).

COMFORTABLE BED-FELLOWS

There are many people who believe that journalism or work in the media is an intrinsically unethical calling. According to one American journalist, 'Every journalist who is not too stupid or too full of himself to notice what is going on knows that what he does is morally indefensible. He is a kind of confidence man, preying on people's vanity, ignorance or loneliness' (Malcolm 1990: 3).

And indeed some reporters would seem to believe they inhabit a different ethical universe. In his lament for American broadcast news, James Fallows (1996) gives one example of such thinking from the 1980s television show 'Ethics in America' in which soldiers and reporters were asked to talk about the ethical dilemmas of their work.

The law professor conducted the show in Socratic fashion, asking increasingly difficult questions to which the soldiers responded by thinking through and reflecting upon the issues, offering reasons for particular courses of action. The two journalists were asked what they'd do if they'd been allowed to go with enemy troops and then realized that they were planning an attack on home troops which would result in the deaths of all their 'own boys'? The response of the first reporter was to say he'd try to warn the home troops. The other argued that most reporters would have a different reaction: 'They would regard it simply as a story they were there to cover. You're a reporter. You don't have a higher duty'. In Fallows' view the second reporter's reply spoke volumes about the values of the journalists' craft and about the unreflective way reporters sometimes operate. The second reporter offered no arguments for his position. It was simply presented as a given.

This is a good example of the disingenuousness of those who argue that journalism and ethical practice are incompatible or that reporters are somehow exempt from thinking about the broader implications of their work. Questions about values, principles, right and wrong behaviour, are an inescapable part of journalism, as they are of any other human practice. Journalists themselves justify their decisions and actions by appealing to moral principles. They talk about 'the people's right to know', reporting in 'the public interest', 'giving the people what they want' and the importance of 'the story'. There are also all kinds of tacit rules underlying the day-to-day practice of reporting. So, for example, it is normally the case that 'dog don't eat dog' – journalists don't prey on one another. *The Sun*'s photograph of murdered *Sunday Times*' journalist David Blundy on a mortuary slab brought a storm of criticism from other newspapers. Thinking about right practice is inescapable in working as a journalist and the claim that journalists inhabit a different moral universe where one ethical code would apply say, to miners and another to those who work in the media, is in itself an ethical argument.

The attempt to put critical distance between journalism and ethics by arguing that journalists are simply in the business of selling newspapers or getting larger viewing figures in the same way as you'd sell a brand of soap, won't work either. Quite apart from the objection that reporters engage in practices that can directly affect the lives of their fellow human beings, even soap selling can raise questions about right and wrong practice. The possible contradiction posed by the chapter's title has a clear answer: good journalism is good journalism.

This book is about ethics and journalism: it focuses on the practice of reporting across the media on the assumption that it is possible to identify a set of core activities germane to the work of all journalists. Similarly, these core activities share key normative assumptions and raise common issues which will be explored in subsequent chapters. It is the practice of journalism I'm interested in and for that reason the particular challenges raised by the practice in related fields – the entertainment industry or the fields of advertising and public relations, for example – will not be examined.

Nor is the book intended to be an ethics handbook. It is hoped that it will help to expand the moral imagination, making the case that moral choices constitute a significant and not indifferent part of human existence. In doing this I focus on human agency. This doesn't mean I ignore or dismiss the role of ideology in shaping, constraining, and even at times, extinguishing the possibility of choice. But these are issues which have been comprehensively explored in the literature on media and journalism.[6] Questions of value, of what we mean by good and bad journalism and of whether the distinction matters anyway, are areas that have received comparatively less attention by British scholars.[7]

I hope the book will also assist in identifying the lineaments of ethical issues. This is a problem for all of us but it is particularly acute for those, such as politicians, editors and reporters, who are assailed by many competing pressures and temptations not to do the right thing. Finally, it is intended as a contribution to the debates about ethics and journalism which will also act as a spur to the difficult and rewarding practice of good journalism.

The book's contents cover three main areas: Chapters one to three explore the main approaches to ethical enquiry in the Western tradition; Chapters four to eleven examine in detail the ethical challenges facing journalists and Chapters twelve to fourteen set out ways of achieving ethical journalism. The key issue of the ethical responsibilities of the audience is not explored. That would require another book.

NOTES

1 The *People* editor, Wendy Henry's misjudged publication on 19 November, 1989 of a front-page photograph headlined 'The Royal Wee' of Prince William urinating, captioned 'Willie's Sly Pee in the Park', as well as the publication in the same edition of a colour picture of Sammy Davis Jr. showing the ravages of throat cancer, earned her the sack. The *Sunday Mirror*'s decision to publish an interview deemed prejudicial by the trial judge of Leeds football players led to the resignation of its editor Colin Myler on 12 April 2001. Predictions that the paper could face a massive fine hit the share price of the parent company Trinity Mirror, wiping £30 million pounds off its value.

2 An article in *The Guardian* typified the industry's suspicions and misgivings about journalism degrees, particularly those which had not gained industry accreditation. It was entitled 'Media Studies? Do yourself a favour – forget it,' 3 September, 2001.

3 A question asked by Judge William J. Rea during the MacDonald–McGinniss trial on 7 July 1987 cited in Janet Malcolm's *The Journalist and the Murderer* (1990).

4 See Barbie Zelizer's *Covering the Body* (1992) for a detailed examination of how the American media became the privileged tellers of the Kennedy assassination. Also see Michael Schudson's book *Watergate in American Memory* (1992) about the construction of a journalistic myth which has become central to the American profession.

5 This was, of course, the aspiration of 'New Journalism' as represented by the work of writers such as former *Washington Post* reporter, Tom Wolfe and journalist Hunter S. Thompson. Their technique is to interlace journalistic accounts of real people and events with composite tales and scenes, rearranging events and creating conversations in order to attain a greater psychological truth. In the hands of gifted writers it can work well but there are clear dangers in this approach, not least because it can erode the reporter's integrity and the public's trust.

6 McQuail's work (2000) provides a thorough and reliable guide to all media research, including the areas of political economy and ideology.

7 Two useful review articles of media ethics scholarship can be found in Christians (1995) and Starck (2001). There is a great deal of American work in the area of media ethics. British pioneers are Belsey and Chadwick (1992), Kieran (1997, 1998), Frost (2000) and Keeble (2001). The American scholar, Kenneth Starck, published in 2001 a valuable review of scholarship in the field of journalism ethics research. Starck concluded among other things, that 'a disquieting aspect of journalism ethics – in practice or research – is the disconnection between application and theory' (2001: 144). He also remarked on the gap between media ethics scholars and philosophers (2001: 144). One encouraging example of an attempt to bridge the gap was the philosopher, Onora O'Neil's discussion of press freedom and responsibility in the 2002 BBC Reith lectures.

2 Thinking about ethics

Ethics? As far as I'm concerned that's that place to the east of London where people wear white socks.

Kelvin MacKenzie, former editor of *The Sun*

WHAT IS ETHICS?

Ethics or moral philosophy, as it is also called, asks serious and difficult questions about how we should live our lives. Thinking about ethics is one of the oldest intellectual traditions of humanity and, in the western world, begins with the Greeks in the thought and writings of Socrates (c.470–399 BC), Plato (427–347 BC) and Aristotle (384–322 BC). In the fourth century St Augustine (354–430 AD) provides a Christian perspective which reaches its full flowering in the towering achievement of St Thomas Aquinas (1224?–1274). Immanuel Kant (1724–1804) is the great figure of the Enlightenment who attempted to frame an impregnable foundation for choosing the good based on the fact that we are rational creatures.

John Stuart Mill (1806–1873) provides the most complete Victorian statement of utilitarianism. In the modern period, the basis and sense of ethical inquiry itself is called into question in the work of Cambridge philosophers such as G.E. Moore (1866–1925) and A.J. Ayer (1910–1989). Ludwig Wittgenstein (1889–1951), the outstanding philosophical figure of his time, considered that ethics can not be explained but only shown. Reflecting the fragmentation of our postmodern times, it is no longer possible to point to an overarching, dominant framework for ethical reflection. Instead this chapter will provide a survey of the principal traditions of ethical thought which continue to inform discussions of how and why we should act in one way rather than another.[1]

Ethics has traditionally been considered a branch of philosophical study. Aesthetics is the study of the beautiful; political philosophy examines issues such as justice and legitimacy; epistemology is the study of the science of knowing; logic examines the structure of thought and argument; metaphysics explores notions of being and causality. And ethics? For some, particularly modern philosophers, it is the study of certain types of judgements, or evaluative words, such as 'good' and 'bad'. For others, such as Kant, it examines the relationship of actions and practical reason. For David Hume (1711–1766), it is an exploration of emotion, sympathy and motive. In Plato's Socratic dialogues we are invited to examine our ordinary opinions about morality. For Aristotle, ethics pertains to character, virtue and moral training. In its original sense, expressed by the Greek word *ethikos*, ethics is precisely this, something pertaining to character. *Moralis* is the Latin translation of the Greek word and the term from

TABLE 2.1	Tradition	Principal thinkers	Ethical focus
Approaches to	Virtue Ethics	Aristotle, Aquinas	Agent
ethics	Deontologism	Kant	Action
	Consequentialism	Bentham, Mill	Outcome

which we derive the more restricted notions of morals and morality centred on the notion of obligation. Ethics might be said to imply all these things. In its most general sense, it has usually been taken to be the study of the grounds and principles for right and wrong human behaviour. It examines values such as courage, self-control and generosity; looking at them as conceptions of the good that function as criteria in making choices and judgements. Ethical judgements, then, focus on standards of right and wrong and discussion and controversy arise in the clash of different values or principles. This traditional focus of ethical discussion has been complemented in recent years by an approach which takes virtue as its central notion (Slote, 1992). This will be explored more fully in the following chapter.

Key to all these understandings of ethics is the view that in a sense we are free to act in one way or another. Breathing would not count as an ethical act; a severe psychological disorder would affect the ethical quality of an action. In other words, we can speak of the ethical character of actions only to the extent that we posit that they are actions which we could to a degree choose to do or choose not to do.

A number of ethical approaches have been particularly influential. They can cut across each other but, for the purpose of clarity, I'll divide them into *deontological* ethics where the emphasis is placed on the notion of duty; *consequentialist* ethics where the consequence of action is underlined; and *virtue ethics* where good character is emphasized (see Table 2.1).[2]

THE ARISTOTELIAN TRADITION

Aristotle's major discussions of ethical questions can be found in the *Eudemian Ethics* and especially the *Nichomachean Ethics*. He asks how should I live now? He seeks practical knowledge so that we may know how to live well, developing all those capacities which are distinctive to us as human beings and thus achieving *eudaimonia*, happiness or 'flourishing'.

His question is an eminently practical one: what dispositions should I acquire? These dispositions – virtues – become settled and moulded over time through education and habit. They are a source of power which allow us to master skills. Aristotle identifies dispositions corresponding to our nature as rational beings: there are those appropriate to theoretical intelligence (summed up in wisdom or *sophia*); those corresponding to practical intelligence (practical wisdom or *phronesis*) and the virtues of character which organize our desires (virtues such as temperance, justice and fortitude).[3] The virtues are considered to be character traits, excellences of character which, through the exercise of practical wisdom, mean we get things right.

15

To every virtue corresponds two vices: one of excess and one of deficiency. This is Aristotle's doctrine of the golden mean. It has often been wrongly equated with a kind of safe moderation, almost a species of mediocrity. The opposite is the case: the virtues ensure that we live life to the full and have the healthy tension of a well-tuned violin with taut strings giving out the right note. Thus, says Aristotle, between meanness and profligacy, lies the virtue of magnanimity or great-heartedness; between cowardice and foolhardiness, courage. These are not fixed qualities. The journalist who crosses enemy lines to get a story may, according to the circumstances (what precautions were taken? How significant was the story?) be courageous in one instance or fool-hardy in another. The master, governing virtue is *phronesis*, practical wisdom, which allows us to judge correctly.

Thinking about the connection between virtue and happiness from a third person perspective – for example, how we'd want to educate our children – can be helpful in clarifying the link between them. Why do good parents wish to educate their children to restrain their selfish or violent instincts? The answer is that if we are good parents we do it for their own sakes because we want them to be happy. The right thing to choose is what the virtuous person would choose and indeed the fully virtuous person acts well and does so with joy. In Aristotle's words, 'virtuous conduct gives pleasure to the lover of virtue' (*The Nichomachean Ethics*, 1099a: 12) because their desires are in harmony with their reason.

The cultivation of all these virtues will produce the happy man or woman, the state of *eudaimonia* usually translated as either 'happiness', 'flourishing' or occasionally 'well-being'. The notion of happiness is notoriously subjective and for some it might be considered to consist simply of the attainment of pleasure. But for Aristotle it is akin to 'the sort of happiness worth having.' It is not, for example, that of the lobotomized patient who is content to sit in a chair all day staring out the window; nor is it that of the rich and powerful who seem happy but who lie and use others for their own ends. We may wonder whether we have a sufficiently stable notion of what or who the human being is in order to know which virtues should be cultivated. These, and other issues specifically applicable to the practice of journalism, will be taken up in the next chapter.

NATURAL LAW TRADITION

Aquinas brought Aristotle's thought into the Judaeo-Christian tradition, finding sources of philosophical renewal in the thirteenth century re-discovery of Aristotle's work. Aquinas took from him the notion that there are immanent purposes in nature so that human beings' aims and goals will flow from their specific nature. Aquinas understood the natural law as the participation of the rational creature in the eternal law which can be discerned by reason.

For human beings natural law is moral law. It is discovered not invented and concerns the person striving to achieve fullness of being in accordance with what they are. In following the natural law, human beings realize their nature, achieve *eudaimonia*, the flourishing that Aristotle considered to be the aim of moral life. This is of universal application: all humans possess the same essential constitution and therefore the same goals. Aquinas argues that natural law is known to all human beings and is discerned first in the principle that the person must do good and avoid evil. From here he derives further principles such as a concern with the transmission and preservation of life, the modification and development of the riches of the material world, the quest for truth, the practice of the good and the contemplation of beauty. The self-evident goods and values known to human beings and generally agreed upon form the basis of what is developed by later thinkers as a doctrine of human rights.

The natural law tradition is absolutist in that it posits the constant application and primacy of certain principles: there are certain actions which can never be a response in conformity with the dignity of the human person even though there are circumstances in which the precise course of action is not entirely clear. In other words, there are certain actions which are considered intrinsically bad whatever motives or consequences you might adduce. For example, the killing of an innocent person would never be considered good. This thinking holds that there are basic moral requirements – values – which should be respected in every act. This approach begins with an analysis of what it is to be human. To make a crude comparison, the natural law can be likened to a set of instructions for the correct functioning of something. Acting in accord with the moral law is to achieve the purpose of the human being.

The *Thomist* tradition, as moral philosophy inspired in Aquinas' thinking is called, continues to exercise great influence in part because Aquinas continues to be the Catholic Church's theologian and philosopher of choice. His thought was taken up in modern times by the French philosopher, Jacques Maritain (1891–1965) and his rational grounding of ethics and his understanding of the purposiveness of nature have proved to be of enduring relevance to discussions of ethics. Aquinas' view that life has meaning and that this meaning is in part available to human reason is a key tradition of thinking about ethics not yet overthrown by twentieth century ethical nihilism.

HUMEAN SENTIMENT

The Scotsman, David Hume was the great critic of ethical rationalism. He advanced two major objections. First, he maintained the impossibility of deriving an 'ought' from an 'is', sometimes known as Hume's law and taken up with a vengeance by certain modern philosophers. In this view, it is impossible for example, to make the statement 'if war is declared, I ought to enlist in the army' or 'if my daughter is murdered, the murderer ought to be punished.' Second, he argued that emotions – or 'passions' – not reasons, can provide motives for action. In *A Treatise of Human Nature* (1739) he emphatically declares that 'Reason is, and ought only to be the slave of the passions'. Reason alone never moves us to action. We are motivated by our emotions or 'passions'.

These are of two kinds: those based on self-interest and those based on sympathy. Emotions based on sympathy lead us to put self-interest aside and be moved on behalf of others. These moral sentiments can be found embodied in law and custom.

Hume's account is of a piece with his empiricism. It was an account that many have found attractive, especially those of a practical, Anglo-Saxon cast of mind. Yet it seems ultimately to be of little help in finding an objective basis for moral action. This certainly seemed so to the great Prussian thinker, Immanuel Kant, who wanted to find a way to set morality on an objective footing.

KANT AND THE CATEGORICAL IMPERATIVE

The British philosopher Roger Scruton described Kant's system of ethics as 'one of the most beautiful creations that the human mind has ever devised' (1997: 284).[4] His thought provides one of the principal ways of thinking about ethics and is also known as 'prescriptivism'. At the heart of his system is the view that moral beings are free, rational agents. Individuals should act on the premise that the choices one makes for oneself could become universal law. The famous 'categorical imperative,' governing all others, states the principle that one should 'act only according to that maxim by which you can at the same time will that it should become a universal law for all rational beings'. The test of a moral act – and he puts emphasis on action – is that it is of universal application. The maxim that 'a person must always be treated as an end and not merely as a means' is one such example, and another example of a categorical imperative. These categorical imperatives do not claim their force from empirical conditions or from our own desires. Our wish to make lots of money through paying our workers low wages is irrelevant. If we are rational beings, and Kant says we are, then these principles – as precepts of practical reason – would be seen to be the right and in fact the only grounds of action. Categorical imperatives tell us how we ought to act irrespective of our inclinations. They are compelling because they describe the structure of reason in action.

On a Kantian view of things, journalists could claim no privileges because categorical imperatives are not subject to circumstances. The maxim, 'Act to treat human beings always as an end and not merely as a means' would create huge difficulties for journalists who think only of getting a good story. The absolute prohibition against lying would also constitute a severe difficulty for those engaged in subterfuge, even if the justification was the strongest public interest defence that could be mustered.

Kant's system has sometimes been described as duty ethics or a *deontological* approach but this oversimplifies his achievement and aims. Kant's ethical system was seeking to find support for fundamental items of belief – 'do unto others as you would be done to', for example – which seemed vulnerable to the kind of philosophical scepticism expounded by Hume. Against the Humean view that we act only out of desire and that we can find no grounds for deriving an 'ought' from an is', Kant wanted to show that there were objective reasons for acting morally, basing ethics on reason considered independently of empirical experience. In attempting to understand the structure of what he called 'practical reason', Kant wished to establish morality's domain without reference to individual needs and desires but only to the concept of rationality itself. Thus, the categorical imperative would be considered as much a fundamental law of practical reason as the laws of thermodynamics are for physics.

However, this magnificent rational edifice appears to envisage human beings as angelic creatures of pure reason removed from the realm of nature, leaving the moral significance of the emotions insufficiently explained.

BENTHAM, MILL AND UTILITARIANISM

Utilitarianism has proved one of the most vigorous traditions in the English speaking world. Its key idea is that the consequences of actions are the key to assessing whether they are ethical. Jeremy Bentham (1748–1832) was the first to coin the term 'utilitarianism' and to work out a systematic statement of this approach in his *Introduction to the Principles of Morals and Legislation* published in 1789. His concern was more with legal reform than ethics. However, he set out the principle that the greatest happiness of the greatest number is the measure of right and wrong. The straightforward moral fact for Bentham was that human beings seek pleasure and avoid pain. He formulated a 'felicific calculus' which he claimed could be used to calculate pleasures and pains. This, he believed, was the whole basis of morals and legislation. Moral questions themselves were objective, scientific and calculable, and happiness and pleasure were considered equivalent.

John Stuart Mill shared the view that the greatest happiness of the greatest number should be the determining principle of human action. However, he argued that not only quantity but also quality of pleasure should be considered. Mill explored these issues in *On Liberty* (1859) and *Utilitarianism* (1861). The principle of utility establishes that the action which promises the most happiness is right. But whose happiness? I might ask why should I consider it reasonable to take other people's happiness other than my own into reckoning?

And how are we to judge a pleasure's quality? Who is to say that the pleasure of eating an ice-cream isn't as great as listening to Mozart? Furthermore, what motive do we have for adopting the principle of utility? Are we ever entitled to sacrifice a person's happiness for the sake of a greater number? And is happiness, anyway, measurable? Mill wasn't sure whether the principle of utility (that which produces the greatest good to the greatest number is right) should be understood to apply to individual acts ('act-utilitarianism') or rules governing individual acts ('rule utilitarianism'). Rule utilitarianism is invoked to overcome some of the difficulties act-utilitarianism can raise, such as the example that it would be legitimate to execute an innocent man in order to avoid greater evils. Rule utilitarianism claims that it must be simply shown that rules laying down the protection of innocent lives possess positive utility over the alternatives.

This moral theory is a kind of *consequentialism*, the belief that morality is judged by its beneficial effects and that principles should always be weighed against consequences. Thus, we adjust and amend our moral behaviour in accordance with what we perceive are its effects. Public interest arguments might be considered to be a species of consequentialism where no exceptions are made for practices such as subterfuge or entrapment on any grounds other than the public interest.

Moral absolutism, as it is termed by the consequentialists, where certain actions are always considered to be wrong whether or not their consequences are beneficial, is considered dogmatic adherence to prejudice. In other words, consequentialism doesn't allow one to say any actions are intrinsically good or bad, just better or worse. But a number of philosophers have pointed out that this way lies moral corruption. Bernard Williams has even argued that if utilitarianism is true, it is better on utilitarian grounds that people should not believe in it because of its tendency to debase the moral currency (1993: 96–8). In order to avoid worse consequences – the spread of a terrible disease, for example – the utilitarian is justified in taking pre-emptive action which in itself might be quite abhorrent (elimination of all the infected) and, in all likelihood would lead to an escalation of pre-emptive action and 'the total consequences of this, by utilitarian standards themselves, will be worse than if it never started' (Williams, 1993: 96).

Of course, examining an action's consequences is something we all do in assessing the rightness of an act, but there are some difficulties with this as an absolute ethical principle.

MODERN APPROACHES

The linguistic turn

In the English-speaking world modern philosophers have tended to focus on the examination of the logic of moral discourse. They have concentrated on the mechanics of language, the logical inferences we make, of whether, for example, it is valid to infer an 'ought' from an 'is', what the word 'good' means. This focus derived from the view that all philosophical problems could be solved by linguistic analysis, later to be called the 'linguistic turn'.

G.E. Moore's *Principia Ethica* (1903) is taken as one of the first modernist works of ethics. It was particularly influential with the Bloomsbury circle centred around Virginia Woolf, because of what they took to be its advocacy of the aesthetic sensibility and the primacy of personal relations. Moore identified what he called the 'naturalistic fallacy,' which says that the good cannot be defined in terms of natural properties, properties which are part of the natural world. Aristotle, for example, says that the good is *eudaimonia*, that is happiness or flourishing. If we say good is happiness, says Moore, we are simply saying that good is good. Thus, Moore claimed that 'good' is indefinable in terms of a set of properties. In Moore's view, 'good' is a non-natural, simple property like the colour 'red' which cannot be defined. Statements in which something is said to be good are 'intuitions' which are incapable of proof from whence the ethical theory he outlined has been called *intuitionism*.

There are various responses to Moore's argument that 'good' is a non-natural, simple property. We might say, for example, that while it points to the need for further investigation of the word 'good', it doesn't succeed in ruling out the possibility that happiness is involved in the meaning of goodness. Just because we can define something in terms of something else (a bachelor is a single man, for example) doesn't rule out that it also means something else.

Moore's work re-focused ethical discussion on questions of language, helping originate the view that moral philosophy should be concerned with 'meta-ethical' questions such as the nature of moral judgement and the possibility of moral knowledge. This approach, ruling out the discussion of ethical issues which confront us in daily life (Should I lie? Should I give money to that charity?), was fashionable for a time but has been superseded by the recognition that the view that moral philosophy is about meta-ethics is in itself a commitment to a specific ethical understanding. First-order ethical issues are back on the agenda. Philosophers are discussing matters such as the rights and wrongs of animal rights, just wars and abortion.

While Moore himself maintained the universality of 'good', his analysis contributed to developments in ethics such as emotivism. The most provocative statement of this approach is contained in A.J. Ayer's *Language, Truth and Logic* (1936). When you make statements such as 'Stoning an adulterous woman to death is bad', you're saying 'I disapprove of this action'. Moral judgements become completely subjective, the 'boo, hurrah' theory of ethics. Ethical statements don't describe anything; they are expressions of emotions and thus can be neither true nor false. C.L. Stevenson (1908–79) went a step further. He argued that to say, 'This is good' is more or less equivalent to saying, 'I approve of this; do so as well'. In other words, he argued that our moral judgements are expressions of attitudes aimed at influencing others.

The focus on the language of morals has continued in the work of R.M. Hare, whose Kantian-derived prescriptivism claimed that moral judgements are a special class of universalizable imperatives; against this, moral realism claims that moral judgements do indeed describe features of moral reality. However, there has also been a resurgence of work in the area of virtue ethics and the application of ethics to contemporary moral issues.

OBJECTING TO ETHICS

Relativism

Relativism is one of the most enduring ways of thinking about ethics. It is sometimes confused with saying that I should be equally well-disposed to everyone's ethical views. In fact, this is to espouse a non-relativistic morality of universal toleration. This is sometimes taken to be the morality of *The Guardian* newspaper but even *The Guardian* would probably draw the line at child sacrifice. It was certainly not the approach taken by MacKenzie's *Sun* where moral judgements had the sharpness of the pub conversation.

Relativism argues that ethics is what each person dictates for themselves. It is subjective, personal and unable to furnish absolute and universal norms. If we are a relativist, faced with someone who believes in the rightness of child sacrifice, we would have no way of advancing an argument in our favour. We would have to maintain that they have as much right to believe that child sacrifice was acceptable as I to say that it was wrong. In a certain sense, relativism extinguishes ethics because it maintains that neither right nor wrong exist apart from the opinions we adopt about them. No opinion has any authority apart from the point of view of the person who adopts it.

This approach, so characteristic of much modern thinking, is in fact an age-old debate going back to the ancient Greeks. Plato explores it in *Thaetetus* to show that the attempt to hold relativism as a principle is undermined by the very fact that it is relative. Bernard Williams has described relativism as 'possibly the most absurd view to have been advanced even in moral philosophy' (1993: 20). He shows that it involves trying to establish a non-relative principle (a morality of toleration) as a means of justifying ethical relativism. We will return to this subject at the end of the chapter.

Talking nonsense

Ludwig Wittgenstein in his *Tractatus* propounded the view that value was not in the world but outside it, which was tantamount to saying that to try to speak of or explain ethics makes no sense because it refers to nothing which is in the world. In this phase of Wittgensteinian thought, his philosophy of language ruled out the possibility of a theory of ethics. Nevertheless, he spoke about the realm of the mystical to which all that having authentic value – aesthetics, ethics and religion – belonged (Black, 1964: 374). Paradoxically, he claimed that it was inexpressible. In other words, Wittgenstein's position was very different from that of the thorough-going logical positivist who would claim not only that trying to speak of ethics was nonsense but that ethics itself was nonsense.

In a lecture he gave to the Cambridge 'Heretics' society, he explained his view that ethics cannot be expressed in the language of facts because its value lies beyond the world of facts. In his own words:

> My whole tendency and I believe the tendency of all men who ever tried to write or talk on Ethics or Religion was to run against the boundaries of language. This running against the walls of our cage is perfectly, absolutely hopeless. Ethics, so far as it springs from the desire to say something about the meaning of life, the absolute good, the absolute valuable, can be no science. What it says does not add to our knowledge in any sense. But it is a document of a tendency in the human mind which I personally cannot help respecting deeply and I would not for my life ridicule it. (cited in Monk, 1990: 277)

At the time he gave the lecture he scribbled a note which said, 'What is good is also divine. Queer as it sounds, that sums up my ethics' (cited in Monk, 1990: 278).

Nihilism

Friedrich Nietzsche (1844–1900) described himself as an 'immoralist' and yet the problems of morality were a central part of his philosophical thought. He considered that various 'moralities' had emerged in human history in response to specific social and psychological needs. His investigation of their 'genealogy' revealed two major types: slave and master moralities, the former characteristic of the 'herd' and Christian morality. After declaring that 'God is dead', he argued in *Beyond Good and Evil* (1886) that there were no moral facts and that evil made no sense. Good could be contrasted with bad and what was good for human beings was 'enhancement of life'. His ideal of excellence was the 'Übermensch', the Superman, who embodied the 'will to power' and the aim of dominion over himself and others.

It's not clear whether Nietzsche was himself a nihilist. But his unflinching recognition of the consequences of the alleged 'death of God', revealed the abyss of meaning which would mark the major ideologies of the twentieth century. His legacy colours the work of many whose thought came to dominate the lecture-halls of western universities. As Scruton has observed, 'from Marxism to deconstruction, the modernist philosopher has occupied himself with the proof that there is no authority, no source of law, no value and no meaning in the culture and institutions we have inherited, and that the sole purpose of thought is "liberation"' (1997: 460).

Institutions, laws and traditions are to be understood in terms of the interests they advance. For Jean Paul Sartre (1905–80) and Michel Foucault (1926–84) institutions are structures of power. Sartre proposed an ethics of personal freedom based on the notion that we are what we want to be: freedom is the basis of all value and we must seize it by authentic living, by which we also make our own morality. This, says Sartre, is achieved by 'commitment' but given his rejection of objective morality, he cannot be in a position to recommend this as a course of action.

Foucault's work centres on the character of institutions as power structures with strategies that produce the forms of life of different eras. Like Sartre he rejected the notion of a stable human nature and advocated self-transformation, including a critical response to the present, as the realm of ethics. The work of Sartre and Foucault contributed to the modern and postmodern view that the world is devoid of value and meaning. The ruin of meaning was carried one stage further in the deconstructionist work of Jacques Derrida. His strategy was to use the work of Ferdinand de Saussure, which emphasized the arbitrariness of the signs used in language, to undermine the stable meaning of texts. He uses the term 'undecidability' to describe the situation of being faced with multiple readings of a text, all of which are as justifiable as each other. The endless process of 'différance' found in the text creates what has been called 'hallucinatory thinking'. Deconstruction ultimately undermines meaning for, in claiming that a text can be interpreted to say anything, it becomes hard to maintain that it in fact says anything. As Derrida himself says:

> Reading, in the broad sense which I attribute to this word, is an ethical and political responsibility. In attempting to overcome hallucinations we must decipher and interpret the other by reading. We cannot be sure that we are not hallucinating by saying simply 'I see' ('I see' is, after all, what the hallucinating person says). No, in order to check that you are not hallucinating you have to read in a certain way. I have no rule for that. Who can decide what counts as the end of hallucination? It is difficult, and I have difficulties with my own work also. (cited in Kearney and Dooley, 1999: 78)

The abdication of meaning, the collapse of value brings us to the nihilist position where it may be said that there are no longer any limits and therefore no morality.

CONCLUDING THOUGHTS

This summary of ways of thinking about ethics is self-evidently incomplete. Like all maps it simplifies and schematizes a complex reality. Furthermore, it deals with the subtle and difficult work of powerful thinkers for whom there is no adequate substitute other than to read what they wrote. Of course, moral philosophy is not the only way to think about ethics. Literature and history provide an alternative way of considering ethical issues. There is, for example, no better depiction of the exercise of different kinds of virtue and vice than that found in the novels of Jane Austen.

However, this is not the same as reasoned reflection on ethical issues. *The Sun* photo editor who attempted to resist his editor's demand to publish a front-page photograph of a rape victim, tried a feeble appeal to 'Ethics'. Faint as it was, his was an acknowledgement of the truth that other principles besides selling papers come into play in journalistic decisions. The failure to see this was a moral failure. Thinking about why this was so is the subject matter of ethics.

There are two other major points worth making. It is clear that in the heat of the newsroom no journalist will painstakingly weigh up whether Kant's categorical imperative or Humean sympathy should apply to a given case. Ethical reasoning is as much an art as a science and getting things right is not about being an expert in moral philosophy. However, knowing what others have thought can help sharpen reasoning and enrich the moral imagination. Second, in discussing each tradition, weaknesses have been identified in each one. This can prompt the very moral nihilism which this book is at pains to deny. The counterpoint to this is to state that the accounts given function to some degree as ideal-types of ethical outlook and for that reason it is all too easy to find flaws in them. However, as will become clearer in the next chapter, I maintain that some of these approaches do indeed yield greater insights into our moral condition than others, while some are ultimately barren. In other words, I argue that it is possible to adumbrate ways of thinking about ethics which are truer than others.

Finally, I want to tackle a number of objections to the very notion of thinking fruitfully about ethics. Some of them have already arisen in the course of this chapter but I'll outline them in more detail here (see Elliott in Patterson and Wilkins, 1991: 15).

Conflicting ethical traditions

One of the major difficulties in contemporary ethical discussions is the range and sometimes apparent incommensurability of ethical traditions which come into conflict. How, for example, do those who adopt utilitarianism argue with those who derive their ethical principles from a natural law tradition? But isn't this the point of ethical thought? With careful reflection it is possible to identify the precise grounds of the disagreement and reflect on the strengths and weaknesses of each approach. It may be argued that no rational resolution of disagreements is possible because the moral rationality of each is internal to it and distinct from the other. But, as MacIntyre argues, 'if two moral traditions are able to recognize each other as advancing rival contentions on issues of importance, then necessarily they must share some common features' (1997: 276).

Every opinion is equally valid

This position was advanced in our account of relativism. But what does it mean? If we take it to mean that everyone may express an opinion on a moral issue, then its triteness makes it hardly worth stating. If it means that every opinion is of equal value, this is itself an ethical principle which needs further explanation. If, on the other hand, it means that all opinions make equal sense, then it is clearly untrue.

Discussion about ethics is all very well but the fact is that people always act out of self-interest

Ethical dilemmas arise where values clash or where values other than self-interest come into play. Going to prison to safeguard a source requires considerable stretching of the self-interest principle and seems a less plausible explanation than that there appear to be occasions when we believe it is necessary to take decisions which don't benefit ourselves.

Thinking about ethics is futile because scientific knowledge is the only reliable knowledge we can obtain

This is the dogma of scientism that only information yielded by the scientific method provides knowledge. It ignores the fact that even science must make a commitment to the intelligibility of the world which rests on a non-scientific assumption. On the other hand, it is true that there is a contrast between fact and value. But in Williams' words:

... morality is not just like science or factual knowledge, and it is essential that is should not be. The point of morality is not to mirror the world, but to change it; it is concerned with such things as principles of action, choice, responsibility. The fact that men of equal intelligence, factual knowledge, and so forth, confronted with the same situation, may morally disagree shows something about morality – that (roughly) you cannot pass the moral buck on how the world is. But that does not show . . . that there is something wrong with it. (1993: 33)

I will now turn my attention to a specific way of thinking about ethics that can be of particular use in the practice of journalism.[5]

NOTES

1 This chapter offers an overview of some of the main schools of ethical thought. There is no one account of ethics which might be recommended. Useful summaries of the various approaches can be found in Roger Scruton's *Modern Philosophy* (1997), Bernard William's *Ethics and the Limits of Philosophy* (1995), F.C. Copleston's *History of Philosophy* 12 volumes, (1950) which is to be preferred over Bertrand Russell's entertaining but unreliable *History of Western Philosophy* (1944).

2 To give an instance of this overlap, Aquinas argues that the morality of an act depends not only on the intention of the person who carries out an act (*finis operantis*) but also the objective end of the act (*finis operis*). In other words, in the natural law tradition consequences matter too.

3 Much of our moral vocabulary has become restricted to narrow and impoverished understandings of what words such as 'virtuous' and 'pious' once meant. 'Temperance' is another good example. It is often today understood as 'being teetotal'. In fact, temperance is about so ordering our desires and emotions that we live life to the full. So, it is, for example, not talking incessantly or not being obsessed about keeping the house clean.

4 Kant's principal texts dealing with ethics are *Critique of Practical Reason*, tr. L.W. Beck, New York, 1965. *Groundwork of the Metaphysics of Morals*, tr. H.J. Paton, New York, 1964; *Lectures on Ethics*, tr. L. Infield, New York, 1973; *Die Metaphysik der Sitten* translated as *The Metaphysical Elements of Justice*, tr. J. Ladd, New York, 1965; *The Doctrine of Virtue*, tr. Mary J. Gregor, New York, 1964.

5 I am conscious that I have said nothing in this discussion about whether the existence of God is relevant to ethics. This was something debated by Plato in *Euthyphro* and the argument there, as characterized by Geach (although he didn't agree with it), was as follows: 'If what God commands is *not* right, then the fact of his commanding it is no moral reason for obedience. . . . And if what God commands *is* right, even so it is not God's commanding it that makes it right. . . . So God has no essential place in the foundations of morals' (Geach, 1994: 117). However, as Geach points out, while it may not be a prerequisite of having any moral knowledge to have knowledge of God, it may be that to have certain knowledge such as 'one may not do evil that good may come of it', it is necessary to have a certain conception of God. In others words, our moral code will be greatly affected by what view we take of God.

In Chapter one I argued that the practice of journalism necessarily involves thinking about ethics. In this chapter I will outline an approach to ethical thinking which I believe is helpful and right. Before I do this, I would like to address two issues: first, why is journalism, like medical and legal practice, an area where questions about values and principles constantly arise? And second, how is ethical practice thought about by those working in the media?

THE TEMPTATIONS THAT JOURNALISTS ARE HEIR TO

Journalism and the market

Journalism is big business and Britain has one of the most competitive news markets in the world. According to the Labour government's White Paper, *A New Future for Communications* (2000), the communications industry is growing at a faster rate than any other part of the UK economy. In 1999 television companies raised over £4.9 billion through advertising, subscriptions and programme exports. The creative industries generated revenues of around £60 billion in 1999 and telecommunications around £31 billion (2000: 15). Britain is a centre for world-wide news operations such as Reuters and Sky News as well as providing the European operational base for media companies such as CNN. Internet news portals and services, also available on mobile phones, have expanded the choice of information outlets and the journalistic marketplace has never been so crowded.

What does this mean for journalists? In a sense, it simply further underlines an issue which has always been the case: they are not autonomous moral agents. They must work within business enterprises whose owners and managers are concerned, as much as anything, with profits, increased circulation, audience figures and, in some cases, disseminating propaganda.[1] Rupert Murdoch is the archetypal media baron whose commercial ambitions have been key in moulding the character of the different outposts of the News International empire. *The Sun*, for example, took 'the tradition of British popular journalism – sometimes proud and sometimes tawdry – and turned it into a financial platform for domination of the electronic media' (Chippindale and Horrie, 1999: 487).

Nothing wrong with making money except where the drive for profits and audience become the only determinants of what reporters can do. So that, to cite a real example, the news editor of a local paper would veto a front-page photograph for a story showing someone from the black community in a positive light on the grounds that it would not go down well with the white, blue-collar readership. Journalists and editors can be placed in an invidious situation where the wish to act well is thwarted by the demands of the bottom-line. All too often the result is cynicism about the very possibility of ethical behaviour because of market pressures, an issue we'll return to in Chapter eleven.

Journalists are in many ways far less powerful than we would sometimes imagine. Except for the privileged few, most journalists have precarious working conditions and even star reporters and journalists are cast aside with ruthless ease (Franklin, 1997; Glover, 1999: 295). These are undoubted difficulties. Nevertheless, we would never accept the reasoning 'I could not have done otherwise' as justification for performing a bad action. The former Conservative minister, Alan Clark, often the subject of media attention himself, put it more graphically: 'it is impossible to overestimate the level of crude vindictiveness that reporters are encouraged to apply. Little regard need be paid to their protestations that, like concentration camp guards, they were only acting under orders' (1999: 284).

Sex, crime and rock'n'roll

Journalists' work often leads them into areas which raise particular ethical difficulties. Any kind of work can provide an arena for developing personal integrity or not. But there are few trades or professions in which such an array of thorny dilemmas can arise. Journalists cover crime, disasters, war; more often than not they're engaged in digging out stories that powerful interests would prefer left untold. They must frequently consider questions about whether the means justify the end. When is it legitimate, if ever, to lie or mislead another in order to obtain information? Where should the line be drawn on the broadcast of upsetting images of torn bodies and grief-stricken victims of war? How much detail of a murder case or rape trial should be given? Where does prurience begin and good reporting end?

Reporters are also prey to the sometimes unscrupulous efforts of sources to manipulate news. Indeed an entire lobbying industry exists to obtain favourable coverage or prevent unfavourable coverage for their clients and this is particularly true for soft news such as show-business, lifestyle features and art reviewing (Wilson, 1999: 32). Financially high-octane areas like sport and business news are notorious for the kinds of pressures that can be brought to bear on reporters. Football managers have been known to ban reporters from their grounds because they've written critical pieces. Politicians and their publicists are also well known for the black arts they employ to ensure positive coverage. Some such as the Labour politician, Roy Hattersley, believe they are helped by the parliamentary lobby which, by encouraging journalism based on gossip and innuendo, had a corrupting influence on British political reporting.

Occupational routines

The news business is about getting stories out as quickly and as accurately as possible. News isn't news if it isn't fresh and being first to a story is part of what drives journalism. News production is also precisely that: it is about producing information to the limits of length and subject categories prescribed by the media outlet the reporter works for. Newspapers usually have sections on Home, Europe and International news but they might, as a journalist friend once suggested to me, have sections determined by the Seven Deadly Sins: Gluttony, Lust, Sloth, Anger, Pride, Envy and Avarice. Often a particular culture of what makes a good story for a particular news programme or newspaper also constrains what a reporter can do. At its worst, this culture will manufacture news to a preconceived formula. As Randall explains:

> On mass-market papers in particular, editors are determined to have stories of certain types – light, frothy ones or breathless dramatic ones. Executives hear of a story in its early stages, decide the kind of headline or treatment they want and then they (or the reporter) organize the facts or the treatment of them to force the story into a formula. (2000: 18)

It is inevitable that reporters work to time and space limits and that they are encouraged to produce stories of certain kinds. But what's worrying is when these pressures undercut a reporter's or editor's commitment to fair and accurate coverage of issues which go beyond a 'frothy' or 'breathless' agenda.

Every day reporters and journalists are faced with multivarious moral dilemmas including:

- conflicts of interest: so-called 'freebies' – gifts, free meals and drinks, promotions, free trips – can be a source of gentle corruption or an acceptable way to obtain information.
- treatment of sources: is the use of unattributable material legitimate? Is it fair to print or broadcast a story about someone who has been unable to comment? How to treat bereaved relatives?[2]
- methods: when are deception, fakery, lying, ambush interviews acceptable?
- level of publicity: do the gruesome details of a suicide need to be spelt out? Should we be told about the sexual lives of politicians? Plumbers? School-teachers? Where are the limits and who decides?

ETHICAL APPROACHES TO JOURNALISM

There is no escaping the question of ethics in journalism. Deception, invasions of privacy, treatment of suffering, payment of criminals, the use of sexually explicit material are all areas in which controversies have arisen in the last twenty years. On the other hand, the media's self-proclaimed role as society's watchdog, exposing corruption and ill-doing for the public good, raises the question of how sound the media's own practices are? Indeed their all-pervasiveness and apparent power has placed the spotlight on the journalists themselves (see O'Neill, 2002). Those who act as a kind of contemporary priesthood have seemed at times to respect no higher authority than themselves, believing that they are accountable to none. In Balfour's celebrated phrase they have 'power without responsibility, the prerogative of the harlot throughout the ages'. So what moral codes govern the behaviour of journalists in practice? Who's guarding the guardians? How do people in the journalism business approach ethics?

The cynic

One possible approach is to treat ethical questions with indifference or cynicism. The Cynics of Ancient Greece sought to live with the simplicity of animals. One of their most famous figures, Diogenes, lived in a tub and called himself 'the dog', the Greek term for which gives us the word 'cynic'. It is said that when Alexander the Great asked Diogenes if there was anything he could do for him, he replied, 'Yes, get out of the light.' Cynics claimed to see through all conventional values which is the link with our modern conception of cynicism.

In journalism the cynic claims that ethical practice doesn't matter or is impossible. In fact, thoroughgoing cynicism is quite rare, probably because it is unsustainable. Even the editorial director of the soft-porn newspaper *Sunday Sport* found there was a limit to the level of journalism readers and advertisers would accept when he was appointed editor of the *Star*. Mike Gabbert's publication of a photograph of a topless, large-chested, fifteen-year-old schoolgirl was the last straw and got him the sack (Chippindale and Horrie, 1999: 271–2). H.L. Mencken's view that nobody went broke underestimating the taste of the public in this case was proved false.

The PR executive

Ethical practice may be treated as a way of keeping the audience sweet. In other words, provided there is no protest, there's not a problem. In the view of American scholar and journalist, Philip Meyer, 'If there is one consistent motive in the way that the people in the news business approach ethical problems, it is a desire to please. So ethics is treated not as a striving towards integrity, but as a public relations problem' (1991: vii). Thus, unless there is a popular outcry or the threat of legislation, nothing will be done. This was distinctly the impression given by the statement put out by newspaper editors on their decision to adopt a common Code of Practice under the auspices of the Press Complaints Commission:

> We, having given due consideration to criticism of the Press by Parliament and public, accept the need to improve methods of self-regulation. Accordingly, we declare today our unanimous commitment to a common Code of Practice to safeguard the independence of the Press from threats of official control. (PCC first annual report, 1991)

The PR principle might provide a useful rule of thumb but it has serious drawbacks as a way of providing quality journalism.

The deontologist

Professional codes of practice setting out duties have proliferated in the last twenty years. Deontologists take their ethical bearings through strict adherence to them. Again, they are undoubtedly useful, providing general guidance on some of the most contentious areas of journalistic practice. But they cannot contemplate every eventuality nor can they resolve hard cases.

The professional dogmatist

Professional codes regarding speed, exclusivity and objectivity or appeals to the public interest, the public's right to know or freedom of expression all form part of the craft lore which is especially influential in journalism practice. The importance of getting a story out can override the imperative to check sources. A 'spoiler' – a story copying and 'spoiling' another publication's exclusive – can be considered perfectly acceptable in keeping with the view that being first to a good story is one of the highest journalistic accomplishments. Objectivity, particularly in broadcast media, can be deified to the extent that the pursuit of truth goes out the window in the wish to be impartial and get both sides of the story.[3] Appeals to principles such as the right to freedom of expression can be made which exempt journalists from the normal ethical behaviour of their fellow citizens. In all these examples a strong case may be made in their favour. But it must be made and not presumed.

The lawyer

Some in the media business might be tempted to apply the principle if it's legal it's right, illegal wrong. Certainly laws and statutory regulation can ensure the outer boundaries of ethical behaviour. However, at best the law provides the skeletal minimum to ensure right practice. It is in the position of the Old Testament Ten Commandments. 'Thou shalt not kill' is a basic requirement for civilized society; the New Testament 'Blessed are the peace-makers' describes the ideal of right behaviour. Thus, even if we accept that a law is ethical (not always necessarily the case as the Nazis' Nuremberg laws showed),[4] the right way to report court cases would still need the fleshing out of ethical principles.

The *Daily Mail*'s reporting of the case against the alleged murderers of the teenager, Stephen Lawrence, and the front-page headline naming them as 'MURDERERS' (14 February, 1997) can be considered with the *Mail on Sunday*'s subsequent publication of undisclosed evidence at the trial of Colin Stagg in 1996 who was accused of the murder of Rachel Nickell. In both cases the accused were acquitted and in both the newspaper concerned very publicly pointed the finger of guilt at them. No law was broken but was the press action ethical? MacKenzie's action in publishing a front-page photograph in *The Sun* in which a rape victim is clearly recognizable was one his picture desk tried vainly to resist. As Chippindale and Horrie tell it:

> They all knew of the unwritten agreement by all the papers [that they wouldn't publish identifiable photographs of rape victims], and took it for granted that it would be followed. But, as MacKenzie kept demanding them to tell him a reason why not, all they could say was that it was a matter of ethics. Legally, they had to admit, there was nothing to stop him.[5] (1999: 364)

All these approaches, save the first, aim at encouraging 'right' journalistic practice. They may all play their part in achieving this. But how does the journalist or editor at the coal-face making split second decisions about whether to go to air or publish a story weigh up the claims of each? Ground-rules might be set, general principles accepted but the problem arises where matters are less clear and time is short – always the case in journalism.

This was brought home to me when Sky News executive, John Ryley, conducted a workshop with Sheffield University MA students. He used a video prepared by Sky News for the 1999 Edinburgh Television Festival showing actors playing the parts of journalists reacting to the unfolding of a news story. Decisions about credibility of sources, reliability of material and news values had to be made in a matter of seconds. Abstention was not a choice as Ryley made clear to a group of doubting students. Good judgement and what can only be called good instincts were the key.

How can they be attained and what measure can be applied to assess them? In Chapter two I referred to the approach known as 'virtue ethics'. This, I believe, can provide a valuable perspective for assessing and achieving ethical journalism and I will now give more detailed consideration to its distinctive contribution.

VIRTUE ETHICS

Broadly speaking, three traditions have been particularly influential in the discussion of ethics: ethics which emphasises rights and duties (*deontology*); ethics which emphasises the consequences of actions (*utilitarianism* or *consequentialism*) and ethics about character or what has become known as *virtue ethics*. As I noted earlier, in some respects, the three overlap. For example, any consideration of the goodness or badness of an action will always take into account its consequences and the intentions with which it is carried out.

From being the least regarded of the ethical traditions, there has been something of a revival of virtue ethics at the end of the twentieth century (Hursthouse, 1999; Foot, 2001; Oakley and Cocking, 2001). This may be partly because it deals with issues neglected by other traditions such as happiness, character and the education and the role of the emotions in moral life.[6]

Rehabilitating virtue

Earlier last century the French poet, Paul Valery, gave a speech to the French Academy where he declared, 'Virtue, gentlemen, the word "virtue" is dead or at least is on the point of being extinguished. . . . I've only heard it mentioned in conversations as a curiosity or as a subject of irony' (cited in Pieper, 1990: 14).

The word 'virtue', like so much of our moral vocabulary, has come to be seen as old-fashioned, almost emptied of meaning. It is associated with priggishness, sanctimoniousness, correct behaviour, chastity. In moral philosophy it refers to none of these. As we saw earlier its classical roots link it to notions of strength, force and the power of something to fulfil its specific function. In the Aristotelian and Thomist views human beings have a specific nature which means that they have particular aims and goals. Virtues are those qualities the possession of which allow one to achieve one's *telos* or end. Aristotle considered this to be *eudaimonia*, happiness, flourishing, well-being blessedness, the sort of happiness worth having.

Virtue in the Christian tradition later came to mean good habits of behaviour. At the heart of these habits are the so-called four cardinal virtues (from 'cardes' – hinge), the lynchpin virtues: justice, wisdom (or prudence), temperance and courage (or fortitude). Of these practical wisdom – *phronesis* in Aristotelian terminology – is considered the mother of all virtues, the touchstone because doing good requires knowledge of the truth. Justice is considered the virtue which enables one to live in truth with one's neighbour; fortitude the ability to bear and overcome difficulties in pursuit of worthwhile goals and temperance refers to achieving interior harmony and peace.

Virtues are in part good habits and a habit is a stable disposition which inclines us to specific acts. A good habit is a virtue and a bad one a vice. Thus, the habit of leaving my house-key in a specific drawer relates to the virtue of order; the habit of eating ten chocolate bars after every meal refers to the vice of gluttony.

Habits of these kinds refer to action, conduct, character. They can be strengthened by repetition and always have repercussions. We're changed – improved or worsened – by our actions. The virtues imply the acquisition of a power one did not have, a conquest of time and growth in freedom. Thus, being orderly allows one to do sooner, better and with less difficulty, the different tasks one must do.

Virtues are, however, more than just tendencies to act in certain ways. For Aristotle they are also excellences of character or 'irreducibly plural intrinsic goods', valuable in themselves and not reducible to one single good (Oakley and Cocking, 2001: 9). As Hursthouse puts it, 'Each of the virtues involves getting things right, for each involves *phronesis*, or practical wisdom, which is the ability to reason correctly about practical matters'. And of all the virtues practical wisdom is the one which always operates as a virtue term, that is 'it always picks out something that makes its possessor good' (1999: 12–13).

This expresses one of Aristotle's insights namely, that moral wisdom comes with experience. A child can not be expected to have the virtues of an adult. A fresh, young reporter can't be expected to have the fund of wisdom of a senior journalist. When journalists get stories wrong, it is often because of a lack of judgement based on experience.

One such example was the publication in the Sheffield University student newspaper of a story about a student who had hanged himself. The coroner recorded an open verdict, leaving it unclear whether his death was the result of suicide or auto-erotic asphyxiation. The student reporter's diligent research tended to support the latter explanation and a story was duly published on these lines provoking student outrage and a coroner's complaint. The issue was whether the importance of detailing the dangers of auto-erotic asphyxiation (assuming that this was the true cause of death) outweighed the intrusive character of the report. Speaking to a former *Birmingham Post* and Press Association court reporter about the case, she remarked that a more experienced reporter would have weighed up these factors and probably come down against publishing explicit details. Her reasoning was grounded on her court experience which had shown her that the practice was sadly not uncommon, especially among lonely young men. On both counts the story could not be considered sufficiently newsworthy to override the invasion of privacy reporting it would entail (Caseby, 1998).

Virtue ethics highlights the key role of judgement and its basis in experience, and for this reason, also underlines the fact that depending on our experience, we will sometimes need to seek advice. Aristotle believed practical wisdom to be the presiding intellectual virtue which ensured that our natural dispositions could function as virtues. He thus considered that practical intelligence and excellence of character should go together. Practical intelligence without virtue is mere cunning and a stupid, good person is not virtuous at all. The role of judgement is crucial because circumstances play their part in deciding what is virtuous behaviour: for example, talking about your own or someone else's private life can, in some circumstances, be a form of laudatory sincerity (if one speaks to a doctor or priest about the psychological and spiritual problems caused by a spouse's infidelity) and on other occasions, it would be foolish indiscretion (to tell all on the *Jerry Springer* show, for instance). Indeed, it is possible that someone might have a natural disposition to be sincere but this would not be the same as virtue which requires the exercise of judgement.

Two criticisms might be aimed at virtue ethics. First, it might be argued that virtue ethics is similar to a have it all, nebulous third way where no absolutes apply. Its certainly true that it does not lay down rules for action as other ethical approaches do; there are no rules of utility or categorical imperatives. Nevertheless, considerable precision can be given, and of course, virtue ethics does not claim there is only one true account of what a virtuous person would be and do. As we have seen there is a teleological dimension to virtue ethics: the virtues are *for* something and, as we explore what this might mean for journalists, we will discover that what one should or should not do can be made reasonably clear. Each choice about what to do is also a choice about who to be. In acting we not only do something, we also shape our own character. To the question 'what should I do?', virtue ethics replies 'be loyal, truthful etc'. Second, it is said that virtue ethics pays no attention to consequences. This is not true. Virtues aren't just about having certain dispositions and motives; they also involve bringing about in action what the virtue indicates. However, virtue ethics does not make consequences the sole criterion of right action.

THE EDUCATION OF THE EMOTIONS

To act virtuously is to act from inclination as well as for the right reason. For example, a well-trained soldier may act courageously from fear of his officers but a genuinely virtuous person acts on the basis of a true and rational judgement and because he or she wants to. The Aristotelian account allows that the emotions are morally significant. What does this mean? It means, as Hursthouse puts it, that the virtues and vices are not only dispositions to act but also to feel emotions as reactions and also impulses to action (see 1999: 108). Thus, faced with someone who is suffering (because of the death of a child, for example) we will *act* to ease their grief, spending time with them, but also 'such comfort and assuagement as we can offer, as we should, springs solely from our emotional reactions. If we can't come up with the right ones, we fail them, and it is a moral failure' (Hursthouse, 1999: 118). In the virtuous person emotions and actions are in harmony.

This view of the moral significance of the emotions highlights the importance of the education of the sentiments. Moral education is in part education of the emotions. To illustrate this Hursthouse gives the example of racism as a paradigm case of bad training where 'it is hard to think of a single emotion that is immune to its corruption' (1999: 114). Disgust, fear, distrust and hatred are the stock in trade of the racist. None of this is natural. It all has to be inculcated and it shows the importance of encouraging the right feelings for the right things from infancy because it's very difficult later to re-train people. Even where we labour under the disadvantages of a corrupting moral education or allege ingrained character traits ('I'm naturally untidy, rude, lazy' etc), if we want to be better people, and thus happier, we may still seek to cultivate the springs of virtuous behaviour in action and feeling.

Highlighting sentimental education as a requirement for ethical practice points to two conclusions: first, rules are not sufficient guides to ethical practice. In its upholding of a complaint against the *Bucks Herald* for harassment of the bereaved parents of a girl found hanged, the Press Complaints Commission makes it clear that it was the reporter's judgement and her insensitivity to the parents' grief which were at fault. 'In this case,' reads the adjudication, 'regardless of whether the complainants had explicitly told the journalist that she should leave and not return to their house, the Commission considered that common sense should have indicated that the repeated approaches over a short period of time were not appropriate' (Report No. 53, 2001: 12). Second, if rules are not enough, thinking about how to cultivate the right kinds of emotions for the right occasions should inform the education and training of journalists.

ACTING VIRTUOUSLY

What is it to act virtuously or well? Hursthouse outlines four conditions, the first three of which satisfy the conditions for acting morally while the four together satisfy the conditions for acting virtuously (1999: 123–5).

1 Performance of a certain kind of action.
2 The agent must know what he or she is doing and for a reason rather than from inclination.
3 The agent acts for a right reason.
4 The agent has the appropriate feeling or attitude when he or she acts.

As Williams has pointed out this can involve us in an apparent catch-22 situation where 'the philosophical understanding of the various virtues will require some, at least, of the understanding that comes from having the virtues' (1995: 130). In other words, in order to know how to act virtuously we already need to have some virtue. We could also say, as the German philosopher Robert Spaemann has written, that thinking about ethics at all pre-supposes some kind of moral experience (1987: 10).

We couldn't even begin to speak about good, bad or better if we didn't have the experience of, for example, feeling ashamed of how we'd treated someone or gladness because of the joy our kindness had produced. These kinds of experiences, even if the exact forms of them can be culturally divergent, do seem to be universal and are the necessary starting-point for understanding what it is to act virtuously.

Most of the time ethical practice is called for on the ordinary occasions of our working life. For these situations the question about how one should act is answered by saying one should act as the virtuous person would act. However, there may be occasions when hard cases or even what philosophers describe as 'irresolvable' dilemmas arise in which there are no moral grounds for preferring one action over another because they're both equally bad. A hard case might, for example, be a judge's demand in a terrorist trial for a journalist to reveal a source who has information which could be vital for the conviction of the accused. What should the journalist do? Can virtue ethics provide guidance when we are faced with problems of this kind?

In a way it cannot because it does not provide a decision-making procedure as other ethical approaches do. Instead we would need to ask ourselves what is it to be just, honest, loyal in these circumstances? And, most importantly, it would require the application of practical judgement to get the measure of the hierarchy of goods governed by each of these virtues. In all likelihood we would also need to ask advice about the best course of action. If all these circumstances applied, we could say that we had acted virtuously without prescribing that such and such an action was necessarily the one to take.

What about an action in which it is apparently necessary to do something wrong to avoid a worse evil? The classic example is where an axe-murderer runs into your house and demands to know where your mother is hidden. Lying certainly seems to be the best alternative. In Geach's view, 'if you can see no way out but a lie, the lie may be the least wicked of the alternatives you can discern: it is still wicked, and you should blame yourself that you lacked the wisdom of St. Joan or St. Athanasius, to extricate yourself without lying' (1977: 121).[7] Even if we don't entirely go along with Geach on this, I think we can certainly see the point of Hursthouse's comment that, 'A too great a readiness to think "I can't do anything but this terrible thing, nothing else is open to me" is a mark of vice, a flawed character' (1999: 87). Hard cases and irresolvable dilemmas are thankfully rare in a journalist's life. However, they can be the acid test for virtuous behaviour which goes to the extreme of being prepared to lose one's life rather than commit certain wicked acts.

WHY ACT VIRTUOUSLY?

The example of whether it would be preferable to lose one's life rather than commit an evil act poses the question of 'why act virtuously?' It is probably the toughest nut of all to crack in ethical accounts. Why should I be good? Why should I act well when I might lose my job, my life? There are various possible responses. One is to say that being virtuous benefits the person. If I'm truthful, work hard, try to be loyal and generous, I will be a loved and respected member of the community. Virtue is its own reward. It represents the most reliable guide to living a happy, fulfilled life. R.M. Hare (1981) argues that the benefits of virtue can be formulated as empirical claims about what works well, providing reasons of a non-moral sort to be virtuous. Hursthouse, however, argues that it is useless to attempt to justify morality from the outside 'by appealing to anything "non-moral", or by finding a neutral point of view that the fairly virtuous and the wicked can share' (1999: 179). The rewards of virtue can in a sense be only understood by those who have a minimum of virtue.

However, even if we're able to accept that virtues benefit their possessor, we might object that this is not always the case. What about the situation in which we have the courage to express our disagreement with the editor about a story and subsequently lose our job? One response is to argue that for the virtuous any loss occasioned by the exercise of virtue is no loss. But this is plainly not true. The loss of my life is a loss indeed from a purely non-religious viewpoint. However, if we think about the connection between virtue and the attainment of a happiness worth having, we might see why acting well, even when this appears to prejudice us, is worth doing. Acting badly may bring a certain kind of satisfaction but it would not be the kind of happiness that those who try to be kind, generous and loyal would want.[8]

KEY FEATURES OF VIRTUE ETHICS

To summarize this necessarily brief overview of virtue ethics, we can point to several features of virtue ethics that provide it with its distinctive approach to ethical practice. These include:

Character. Character is essential in the virtue ethics account of right and wrong action. As we have seen, virtues are character traits that we need to live flourishing lives. This means we need them to be good human beings and to carry out good human actions. The criterion of the rightness of an action is that it is what a virtuous character would do in the circumstances.[9] This means that we can explain what is right only by what is good or of value in the agent's action. The criterion of acting rightly is not, as is it in utilitarianism, the maximisation of the good. Being unjust to maximise the good could never be acceptable on this basis. Meilaender explains this well:

> An ethic of virtue seeks to focus not only on such moments of great anxiety and uncertainty in life but also on the continuities, the habits of behaviour, which make us the persons, we are. Not whether we should frame once innocent man to save five – but on the virtue of justice, with its steady, habitual determination to make space in the life for the needs and claims of others. Not whether to lie to the secret police but on the steady regard for others which uses language truthfully and thereby makes common life possible. (1984: 4–5)

Practical judgement. Practical judgement or *phronesis* is the presiding virtue. It deals with uncertainty, contingency and the unknown. It has been called 'good sense . . . in the service of good will' (Comte-Sponville, 2001: 32). It is the disposition that allows us to deliberate correctly, not in general but in a given situation. It can be seen as a virtue for the present and for the future and in this sense is linked to what Weber called an ethic of responsibility (*Veranwortung-sethik*) which, without disregarding principles, looks at foreseeable consequences of action. It is an overarching regulative ideal which governs all action (Oakley and Cocking, 2001). In other words, it is not possible to provide a priority ranking of virtues; practical judgement must examine all the factors in play, weigh them up and then decide.

Experience. The exercise of practical knowledge is linked to the fact that moral wisdom comes with experience.

The education of the emotions. To act virtuously is to act from inclination as well as for the right reason.

Teleological ethics. Virtue ethics does not lay down rules for action as other ethical approaches do; there are no rules of utility or categorical imperatives. However, there is a teleological dimension to virtue ethics: the virtues are *for* something.

PROFESSIONAL AND OCCUPATIONAL GOALS

The teleological approach of virtue ethics knits well with the notion of professional or occupational goals acting as a regulative ideal. The virtues are for something and so, it might be said, are the occupations or professions we pursue. A good profession or occupation will be so inasmuch as it contributes to a key human good. What acting well means in a professional role will be judged by how it contributes to achieving the goals of the profession. So, for doctors it has been suggested that the substantive human good aimed at is health, for lawyers justice (Oakley and Cocking, 2001).

Without entering into arguments about the professional status of journalism, it could be argued that the content of the regulative ideals of a good
journalist will be determined by a model of what reporting or journalism is.
There are limits to what a doctor can do and still be said to be a doctor. If
making money becomes a journalist's governing regulative ideal we say that they
are something else – a good 'buisnalist' or 'infotainer', for example (see Oakley
and Cocking, 2001: 89) – but we wouldn't say the person was a good journalist.
If we know what journalism is for and, as I mentioned in Chapter 1, I would
suggest it has something to do with truth(s) telling, we can begin to describe the
ways in which journalists should respond to the daily ordinary and extra-
ordinary challenges of their work.

NOTES

1 The great 1930s press baron, Lord Beaverbrook, owner of the *Daily Express*,
declared to the 1945 Royal Commission on the Press that he owned newspapers for the
purposes of propaganda.

2 These interviews are known as 'deathknocks' and can be particularly harrowing for
both reporter and source. In 1999 a reporter from the *Stoke Sentinel* lost his claim for
unfair dismissal after he refused to carry out his editor's instructions to approach a
football manager for an interview after his son's suicide.

3 Former BBC correspondent, Martin Bell made this complaint about BBC reporting
of war: 'In place of the dispassionate practices of the past, I now believe in what I call the
journalism of attachment. By this I mean a journalism that cares as well as knows; that is
aware of its responsibilities; that will not stand neutrally between good and evil, right and
wrong, the victim and the oppressor' (italics in original; 1998: 16).

4 In 1935 the Nuremberg Laws were passed outlawing marriage and sexual relations
between Jews and Germans and barring Jews from employing German women as servants
under the age of forty-five.

5 The 1976 Sexual Offences (Amendment) Act did not permit media identification of
an alleged victim of rape from the time a defendant was charged. In 1987 *The Sun*
published the address and feebly disguised photograph of Jill Saward, victim of the Ealing
Vicarage rape. MacKenzie took advantage of the fact that media identification of a victim
was only banned from the time that a defendant was *charged*. The 1988 Criminal Justice
Act closed this loophole by severely limiting what could be published from the time a
complaint was made.

6 In the account that follows I'm greatly indebted to Rosalind Hursthouse's (1999)
lucid discussion of these issues where interested readers can find a more detailed analysis.

7 Geach (1977: 114–15) tells us that St Athanasius was rowing down a river when he
encountered his pursuers coming in the opposite direction. They asked him 'Where is the
traitor Athanasius?' to which he replied, 'Not far away' as he rowed off down the river.

8 Philippa Foot describes these difficult questions in chapter 6 of *Natural Goodness*
(2001). She discusses the case of Germans who defied Hitler and for this were executed.
In their case, she says, 'someone who is sacrificing his life for the sake of justice would not
have said that he was sacrificing his happiness, but rather that a happy life had turned out
not to be possible for him' (97).

9 Acting as the virtuous person means, for example, to do what is brave, generous,
honest and just and on the contrary, not to do what is cowardly, mean, dishonest or
unjust. See Hursthouse (1999) for a discussion of virtue ethics ability to provide action
guiding rules.

4 Lying to tell a story

Why, once Jakes went out to cover a revolution in one of the Balkan capitals. He overslept in his carriage, woke up at the wrong station, didn't know any different, got out, went straight to an hotel, and cabled off a thousand-word story about barricades in the streets, flaming churches, machine-guns answering the rattle of his typewriter as he wrote, a dead child like a broken doll, spreadeagled in the deserted roadway below his window – you know.

Evelyn Waugh, *Scoop*

'Truth?' said Pilate, 'what is that?'

John 18: 37

Many of us would accept the truth of the adage that 'there is no smoke without fire'. But we might be well-advised to apply this principle cautiously to the media. For journalists do sometimes invent, providing the appearance of fire where there is none. The journalist Peter McKay tells the following story:

> A former reporter, Malcolm Muggeridge, recalled that, short of a paragraph to fill out the column one day, he added that a certain prominent man was a great music-lover, present at all the great concerts. After this harmless fiction entered the newspaper clipping libraries, no future mention of the man appeared without reference to his love of music. (1999: 190)

In Chapter one we saw that truth-telling and story-telling are both integral parts of a journalist's craft. In this chapter I'll explore two related matters: first, I will examine the relationship between telling the truth and telling a story. Are there arguments to support the advice 'Never let the facts get in the way of a good story'? Or Rupert Murdoch's reported view, when told that 'Hitler's Diaries', published in the *Sunday Times* were in fact forgeries, 'Well, we are in the entertainment business'? In other words, I will examine the relationship of journalism to truth, truthfulness and honesty.

I'll then turn to the issue of whether lying can ever be justified as a way of obtaining the truth. The more specialized form of deception known as fakery will be examined in the following chapter.

THE VALUE OF TRUTH

The idea that we should tell the truth is deeply embedded in most cultural traditions. All of the great world religions exhort their followers to avoid falsehood. Judaism and Christianity trace the origin of disorder and evil in the world to the power of the lie which plays on human pride. 'And you shall be like gods', Satan tells Adam and Eve. In *The Nichomachean Ethics* Aristotle says 'Falsehood is in itself mean and culpable, and truth noble and worthy of praise' (4, 7). In a court of law we are charged to tell the truth and parents train their children not to lie. Mark Twain advised: 'When in doubt, tell the truth. It will confound your enemies and astound your friends' (cited in Bok, 1980: 145).

But, as Pilate asked Christ, 'What is truth'? In an earlier chapter we saw how relativism has become one of the chief dogmas of the modern age in the western world; we live in times in which the view that truth exists is constantly being challenged. A kind of 'epistemic relativism' is advanced 'namely the idea . . . that modern science is nothing more than a "myth", a "narration" or a "social construction"' (Sokal and Bricmont, 1998: x). This epistemic or cognitive relativism, as distinct from ethical relativism, has been a *leitmotif* of postmodern thought which maintains that there is no world of facts just our construction of them.

Such a view – a radical scepticism about the ability to know the real world – has a long history. And it is arguable that postmodernists have performed a useful service by bringing into relief some of the assumptions of the scientific world-view, one of which is the intelligibility of the world scientists explore.[1] Indeed, the notion that truth is possible, accepted in scientific endeavour, is what gives it its immense authority. If we accept a meaningful world, we will also accept the view that we can know and discover facts about the real world, explanations which explain the coherence of experience, and that truth does in fact exist.

As we saw in Chapter one, the facts that journalists report are of a particular kind. Rarely can they interrogate the world in the way a novelist can, but at their best journalists do reveal part of the truth about the world.

Truth is necessary for the possibility of truthfulness to exist and the latter is the virtue which refers to personal authenticity in our relations with others. For communication to take place at all, trust in truthful communication is necessary. The contagion of totalitarian societies by lies and their destruction of social bonds has been well documented in the work of Czech playwright and statesman, Vaclav Havel and the Polish writer, Czeslaw Milosz.[2] As we have seen, however, truth is not a straightforward matter: the yardstick for truthful communication in the confessional or the doctor's surgery differs to that which might be appropriate for a conversation with a colleague.

TRUTH AND TRUTHFULNESS

Journalists seek to tell us things which are true. However, our ability to discover the whole truth about any matter is severely circumscribed by our own intelligence, perspicacity, time and resources. This is no less true for the reporter. In the western tradition,[3] a number of practices have evolved to provide structural safeguards to the pursuit of truthfulness in the reporting of facts. They can be summarized as i) the striving for accuracy and, ii) the search for objectivity, with the concomitant removal of bias through getting both sides of the story.

The canon of objectivity

One of the chief dogmas of western journalistic practice is the idea of objectivity; namely the view that news reporting should seek impartiality and even-handedness in its reporting.[4] This objectivity is the BBC or Press Association ideal of reporting.[5] Chapter two of the BBC's *Producers Guidelines* deals with impartiality and accuracy. Its statement of editorial values underlines the importance of both:

> Due impartiality lies at the heart of the BBC. All BBC programmes and services should be open-minded, fair and show a respect for truth. No significant strand of thought should go unreflected or under-represented on the BBC. (www.bbc.co.uk/info/editorial/prodgl/chapter2.shtml)

The *Guidelines* further explain that 'due impartiality' doesn't mean just getting two sides to a story nor does it require 'absolute neutrality on every issue or detachment from democratic principles'.[6] It is a practice aimed at removing the distorting effect of prejudice from whatever source, ensuring that full and fair accounts are given of events. According to this view, the goals of objectivity and the related practice of impartiality would go some way to eliminating reporting filtered by the more extreme kinds of religious, racial or other types of prejudice.

The British newspaper industry is not bound to this convention in the same way as the broadcast industry which must be scrupulously impartial in political affairs. This is obviously not the case for the press which is famously partisan in its political views. Nevertheless, even the press has signed up to the notion of impartial and objective reporting (see PCC code Clause 1 Accuracy) and to the avoidance of negative stereotyping of social groups (see Clause 13 Discrimination).

Failure to abide by these commitments can have disastrous consequences as *The Sun* discovered when it published its infamous headline about the Hillsborough football stadium tragedy, 'THE TRUTH' (19 April, 1989). Its one-sided attack on the behaviour of Liverpool fans – 95 of whom died in Sheffield – provoked disbelief and anger on Merseyside and the paper's sales dropped accordingly (Chippindale and Horrie, 1999: 371). *Sun* editor, Kelvin MacKenzie, subsequently apologized.

Accuracy

Accuracy, getting the facts right, getting to the truth of the matter, is one of journalism's Ten Commandments. As the BBC puts it:

> We must be accurate and must be prepared to check, cross-check and seek advice to ensure this. Wherever possible we should gather information first-hand by being there ourselves or, where that is not possible, by talking to those who were. But accuracy is often more than a question of getting the facts right.

All relevant information should be weighed to get at the truth of what is reported or described. (www.bbc.co.uk/info/editorial/prodgl/chapter2.shtml)

Getting names, dates, ages right, attributing information correctly, not relying excessively on cuttings,[7] checking sources (especially important as the Internet becomes increasingly used as a source), and not making up quotes are all essential to the story's credibility.[8] Making an error of judgement on any of these matters can have very serious consequences as *The Sun* found to its embarrassment after it failed to check out the video apparently showing Princess Diana cavorting with James Hewitt (8 October, 1996). The following day the editor had to apologise to his readers and to Princess Diana, uncomfortably having to confess that: 'Today *The Sun* is in the unhappy position of admitting we fell victim to one of the most elaborate hoaxes of the decade' (9 October, 1996).

The journalism of attachment

The possibility of objectivity and accuracy has come under attack from many quarters. Against the idea of impartiality, Martin Bell (1998), former BBC journalist, has advocated the notion of a 'journalism of attachment'. His experience in the BBC tradition of a journalism of distance and detachment, what he terms 'bystander journalism', led him to believe that objectivity is 'an illusion and a shibboleth'. He doesn't argue for campaigning or crusading journalism, as practised by George Orwell and John Pilger, which has its place in polemical or political literature. His argument with objectivity is that it promotes the idea of morally neutral journalism. There is, he says, a time to be passionate and a time to be dispassionate. On these grounds, he argues for a more truthful depiction of the horrors of war for 'what is the justification,' he asks, 'for a disengaged journalism which would require its practitioners, as special people with special privileges, to close their hearts to pity?' (1998: 22).[9]

A different kind of objection to objectivity and accuracy is raised by those who believe that it is wrong to assume that there is a world of facts and a world of values and that such a view depends on a naively empirical view of the world. It questions the world of facts as ideological constructions which reflect the imperatives of power. I'll examine these criticisms next and show that, while providing a useful corrective to simplistic accounts of reporters who simply 'report', they fail to undermine the usefulness of certain conventions as a spur to journalistic truthfulness.

Truth-telling and story-telling

In Chapter one we saw how journalists tell truths as they tell stories about things which have happened. As such they act as interpreters. Now we can only interpret what is already there. Interpretation implies the existence of *something*. Interpretation involves disclosure.[10] Thus, journalism would seem to be about interpreting reality, disclosing its truth, and telling stories.

Interpretation is also an activity to which we bring premises, prejudices in the sense of prejudgements. We bring a set of assumptions and expectations to bear on the subject we're seeking to understand. Some are personal, others are a kind of implicit background knowledge. Watching and understanding films, for example, is a cultural practice which is learnt. All the ways of acting, thinking and seeing which seem to be a part of the ways things are – natural givens – form part of the 'platform of understanding' with which we approach all experience. In this sense, we are all subjective and journalists are no exception.

Some would then argue further that facts and fictions are also the products of interpretative communities and cultural categories. Thus, the notion of 'stalking', for instance, is a cultural construction. From this perspective, journalists are not only literally story-tellers, in the sense that their stories are narratives, but also in the sense that their stories are fiction. They are not reporting something 'out there.' They themselves construct the characters and story-lines so that, for example, 'Tory sleaze' and 'Labour spin' are as much the journalists' own creation as a reflection of reality. There is some truth in this. Subjectivity is part and parcel of the human condition and news stories have an intrinsic narrative structure. Many stories can be woven from the same material and they all partake of a lesser or greater degree of truth; they may all disclose reality to a lesser or greater degree. But to admit subjectivity, recognize our role as interpreters, acknowledge that we can never be complete masters of meaning, does not entail an abdication of a commitment to truth.

I would argue that it is possible to maintain a clear distinction between the notion of fact and fiction. Fiction, in the sense of making things up, has no place in journalism. The immediate referents of history, journalism and fiction are different. However, they do all share one quality: they narrate the human experience of time. Journalists bring together multiple events into a story which is complete and unified. A totality is constructed out of scattered events.

Stories narrate events about people. Historical, journalistic and fictional narratives are about human actions. They also contain an ethical commitment in the sense that the author is a moral observer, there is always an implicit intentionality. It can be more or less explicit – the story can be written or presented in a 'neutral' style or in a way which allocates praise or blame – but it is inescapable. For this reason, truly neutral stories do not exist and in this sense, I believe Martin Bell is right.

It is quite another matter to then say that because in all narrations there is a narrator or because reporting is subjective and the effacement of authorship is impossible, that practices aimed at truthfulness should be thrown overboard. Subjectivity is not antithetical to truthfulness but where it is not counteracted by conventions such as objectivity and accuracy, it may become so.

Temptations against truth

Where pressures are extreme, as occurs typically in wartime, the temptation to discard the commitment to truth is very strong. 'The first casualty when war comes, is truth' was the famous comment by American senator, Hiram Johnson in 1917.

Journalists who reported the war in Bosnia described how easily truth-fulness could fall victim to mediocre journalism. According to BBC reporter, John Simpson (1999: 450):

> Second-rate journalism is a herd activity. Editors want from their reporters what other editors are getting from theirs. The hunt was on in Bosnia for Nazi-style atrocities, and several reporters won major awards for reporting them, even though their sources were afterwards questioned. Atrocities certainly took place, and more were carried out by the Bosnian Serbs than anyone else. But a climate was created in which it became very hard to understand what was really going on, because everything came to be seen through the filter of the Holocaust.

Simpson's colleague at BBC World, Nik Gowing, was more explicit in his condemnation:

> Some of the strongly anti-Serb reporting in Bosnia is the secret shame of journalism. There is a cancer now which is affecting journalism: it is the unspoken issue of partiality and bias in foreign reporting. (cited in Simpson, 1999: 450)

This is true in wartime but it also occurs in times of peace. The presence of the stranger, the person different to us in language, colour, religion or even clothes, becomes the 'other'. And the history of humanity bears out Herodotus' observation that: 'Everyone with exception believes that their own native customs are by far the best'. Journalists here have a special responsibility to show sensitivity to groups who have often been represented in caricatured or stereotyped fashion. All UK media industry codes contain guidance on avoiding stereotyping. Nevertheless, as John Simpson puts it (2000: 323):

> . . . a great deal of what you read in the newspapers or see on television is not so much wrong as depressingly stylized. Journalists often only seem to think in terms of stereotypes: innocent victims, great leaders, evil killers, vicious dictators, tragic children, vengeful wives, love rats. Under this kind of treat-ment the complexity of life, which is its truth, evaporates almost instantly.

It may be true that the term 'objectivity' is a relic of scientism and should be discarded but while it continues to denote the struggle for fairness and impar-tiality in reporting, it is probably worth hanging on to.[11]

In sum, truth and truthfulness are at the heart of the journalistic enterprise. On the whole, journalists aim to be truthful. But there are times when in order to be truthful or to obtain information so that a truthful story may be told, reporters believe it necessary to lie. The *Sunday Times'* journalists who disclosed the 'cash for questions' scandal in 1994 lied to the twenty MPs to whom they sent letters purportedly from a company seeking their advocacy services for cash. The journalists were rebuked by Parliament but they also revealed to the public an unsavoury aspect of Parliamentary practice not widely known. If journalists set great stock on truth, what justified their lies? As Sigmund Freud said of his own profession: 'Since we demand strict truthfulness from our patients, we jeopardize our whole authority if we let ourselves be caught by them in a departure from the truth' (cited in Bok, 1980: 221).

LYING AND DECEPTION

We're all familiar with lies. We've all either told or been told a few. But what are they? First of all they are not false utterances. If I say, 'The programme starts at seven', when you've just seen in the newspaper that it starts at eight, you'd assume that I'd got mixed up. To know whether I'm telling a lie, you have to determine whether or not I know my statement to be false. I might even tell you something which I think is a lie (that is, I believe what I tell you to be false) and yet it turns out to be true. We can say that a lie is a statement believed by the person to be false and intended to deceive another. Or, in St Augustine's words 'every liar says the opposite of what he thinks in his heart, with purpose to deceive.'[12] American philosopher Sissela Bok, limits the scope of lying to 'any intentionally deceptive message which is *stated*' (1980: 13). However, we can also deceive others through disguise or silence or allowing others to understand words in one way when we mean something quite different.[13] We will take Bok's narrower sense here and look at the wider issue of deception when we come to examine fakery.

Journalism is about reporting the truth so what place does lying have? As we've seen, truthful reporting is by no means straightforward and indeed it is possible that the difficulty of providing a satisfactory response to Pilate's question of what is truth can have a paralysing effect. It simply isn't possible to communicate everything about a subject. If truthfulness is such a difficult matter, what does it matter if I'm sometimes a little 'economical with the actualité', as Conservative politician Alan Clark famously put it?[14] Or even that I should take liberties with the truth and tell the occasional lie?

Is lying objectionable? St Thomas Aquinas and St Augustine share Kant's absolute condemnation of all lies. However, they admit different gradations in the seriousness of a lie according to its intention and aim. Thus, 'jocose' and 'useful' lies – the former, lies told in jest and the latter, lies to help – are qualitatively different from lies which aim to harm. Utilitarians look to consequences and Jeremy Bentham held that if no negative consequences flow from a lie it is not objectionable. Mill, however, considered that there are strong utilitarian grounds for objecting to lying for, in undermining trust and credibility, lying has negative consequences.

Kant takes an absolutist line on lying and advances non-consequentialist reasons for finding lies objectionable. His categorical imperative stating, 'Act only on those maxims that you can at the same time will to be a universal law' rules out all lies. For if lying were universalized, communication would break down. Lying itself would become impossible because nothing would be believed. Thus, he admits no exceptions to his general prohibition on lying.

One way philosophers have attempted to allow for exceptions to this prohibition is to ask what is the deceit for? Is its principal aim to deceive or commit some other unjust act, or is it in fact to save someone's life? If we tell an untruth to an unjust aggressor, the main aim is to save life. Our intention, as it is when we use force against someone to defend ourself or our family, is to save ourself or others. The argument is that where the goal is good – saving life – and all attendant circumstances are good, the person who utters a falsehood is *not* a liar, just as the person who kills the attacker is not a murderer. If we accept that killing in self-defence is legitimate, then it would be strange to argue that telling someone a falsehood for the same reason was not. But doesn't this seem to suggest that Plato's noble lie is permissable? Plato argues in chapter 3 of *The Republic* that rulers may lie to their citizens in order to advance the common good. Attractive as it is, it is hard to see how this line of argument can draw a distinction between just and unjust deceptions or even separate out the deception from the principal aim of the deception. There may be good reasons for a deceptive communication but it is surely always a lie. Deceptive communication always prejudices the other and ourselves, even if there are good grounds for doing so.

Sissela Bok has strong consequentialist objections to lying. She argues that liars underestimate the harm and overestimate the good that results from a lie. Lies that can seem insignificant can cumulatively undermine valued institutions and practices. For example, if lying on CVs were to become common practice, they would no longer be of any use to us. She argues that not all lies should be condemned but that a negative weight should be attached to them. The liar bears the burden of proof that a lie is necessary as a last resort and that other alternatives have been explored. In other words, 'lying requires explanation, whereas truth does not' (1980: 30). Thus, in Bok's view, truthful statements are preferable to lies in the absence of special circumstances. If lies are contemplated, it should be possible to justify their use publicly to reasonable people in order to counterbalance the 'self-deception and bias inherent in the liar's perspective' and that found in a complacent professional group (1980: 92). This view introduces the all important principle of accountability into play, which is especially important where those who lie exercise power over others' lives and where there is a risk that deceptive practices become widespread in a given profession.

LYING AND THE PUBLIC INTEREST

So where does this leave the use of lies by journalists? Journalists do lie and deceive and the attitude to these practices, at least by print journalists, appears to be quite permissive (Weaver, 1998). However, most would propose substantial reasons to justify such actions. In all likelihood, the journalists who posed as doctors in order to try to enter a hospital ward and obtain photographs of dying television celebrity, Russell Harty, would be considered cunning but not admirable members of their trade. The high-tide of sensationalist journalism of the late 1980s appears to have receded and the presumption against the use of deception is now firmly enshrined in all industry codes (see Box 4.1). It would be strange it this were not the case since journalists routinely denounce others for deceit even if, in the name of the 'story', journalists may sometimes consider themselves exempted from the moral rules they apply in our name.

Much investigative journalism involves lies and deception. Bok notes that the paradigmatic American political scandal, Watergate, involved the weaving of 'a whole fabric of deception' by the reporters Woodward and Bernstein (Bok, 1980: 120). *The Guardian*'s investigation of the alleged wrongdoings of Conservative minister, Jonathan Aitken, involved it in a piece of deception for which its journalists were roundly censured by the House of Commons. Ironically they finally brought about Aitken's fall through proving that he had lied on oath in the libel case he'd brought against *The Guardian*.[15]

BOX 4.1   Deception

PCC Code Clause 11

(i)   Journalists must not generally obtain or seek to obtain information or pictures through misrepresentation or subterfuge.
(ii) Documents or photographs should be removed only with the consent of the owner.
(iii) Subterfuge can be justified only in the public interest and only when material cannot be obtained by any other means.

BBC's Producer Guidelines

Chapter 3 deals with fairness and straight dealing and states that 'contributors should be treated honestly, and with respect'. It specifies further that 'they should not feel misled, deceived or misrepresented before, during or after the programme, unless there is a clear public interest, with dealing with criminal or anti social activity'. The deception should, however, be the minimum necessary.

In all codes the duty not to deceive can be over-ridden by an appeal to the public interest, an exemption applied to Clause 11 of the PCC code (see Box 4.2). In the industry's own terms the public interest does not justify any lie or any kind of deception. The 'public interest is not', the PCC has made clear, 'whatever happens to interest the public' (Report 1, 1992: 11). Journalists must justify the use of subterfuge on specific grounds including the exposure of criminal activity. The print industry opens up this justification to include where there is a risk to public health or that the public will be misled by the words or action of an individual or institution. They must also show that they could not have obtained the information by any other means. The use of subterfuge by *Sun* journalists to investigate 'Sex in the Suburbs' was condemned as not having a sufficiently robust public interest defence (Report 22, 1993). The activities of *Sunday Times'* journalists in showing the practice of MPs accepting cash for questions was considered acceptable (Report 24, 1994).[16]

BOX 4.2 PCC Code – The public interest

1. The public interest includes:

(i) Detecting or exposing crime or a serious misdemeanour.
(ii) Protecting public health and safety.
(iii) Preventing the public from being misled by some statement or action of an individual or organization.

However, the fact that it is acceptable that journalists can be liars is far from ideal. The deception practised on the Countess of Wessex in March 2001 by a *News of the World* reporter dressed as an Arab sheikh undoubtedly highlighted Sophie's lack of judgement and the blurred lines demarcating the legitimate pursuit of business interests from the misuse of royal status for private gain. The case also illustrated the difficulty of judging when the public interest is in fact at stake: was Sophie's action a 'serious misdemeanour'? Was she misleading the public? At most she seems to have been guilty of arrogant, foolish and greedy behaviour. The newspaper's behaviour, apart from occasioning much merriment, some solemn discussion about the future of the monarchy and extreme irritation among the Royals,[17] did not add to journalists' reputation for honesty.

Even where the public interest argument is more clear-cut, can we argue that lying is right? I would say that we cannot. The best we can do is admit that it is the least bad action in the circumstances. In an imperfect world where powerful interests exploit and hurt others and where politicians and judges fail in their duty, lying and deception become acceptable and understandable journalistic practices. My lack of integrity may mean I can think of no better way in difficult cases but this does not mean I should accept that the 'end justifies the means' (which is what the codes seem to argue) and that lies are unimportant or do not matter. Bok expresses the issue well:

> These practices are not immutable. In an imperfect world they cannot be wiped out altogether; but surely they can be reduced and counteracted. . . . often the justifications they invoke are insubstantial and they can disguise and fuel all other wrongs. Trust and integrity are precious resources, easily squandered, hard to regain. They can thrive only on a foundation of respect for veracity. (1980: 248–9)

And how can the need to lie be reduced? First, the breaking down of structures of concealment and secrecy would do much to remove the incentives to deception. The Sophie sting arose from a legal injunction preventing a former employee from speaking out about alleged malpractice at her PR company.

Greater institutional transparency and a stronger culture of freedom of information would allow British reporters to investigate more easily (see Rogers, 1997). Second, more open discussion by the industry with non-journalists about the cases in which deception and lies are used would help ensure that 'public interest' justifications are not simply self-serving arguments from which the 'public' is in fact excluded. Third, training programmes which emphasize the centrality of an ethic of truthfulness in reporting could contribute to a presumption against lies in ordinary journalistic practice. Journalists, like all human beings, will continue to tell lies and, on rare occasions, they will be told for good reasons. But as far as possible it is preferable for a reporter not to be a liar.

NOTES

1 Scientism is the view that scientific methods yield the only reliable, genuine factual knowledge.

2 See Havel's *Living in Truth* (1987) and Milosz's *The Captive Mind* (1953).

3 Even the term 'western tradition' is probably too wide-ranging. However, if we take it to mean an understanding of journalism as a commitment to the provision of 'objective', detached reporting of what goes on in the world, we can contrast it with views of journalism which equate it with State-controlled news for propaganda purposes which was and is current in the communist world. Herman and Chomsky (1994) would argue that western news too is propaganda of a kind. However, even if you agree with their arguments, it is clear that at least lip-service is paid in the west to non-propagandistic models of journalism.

4 There is an extensive literature on this subject. Judith Lichtenberg (2000) has produced enlightening work. Also see relevant chapters in McQuail (1993) and (2000) and Harrison (2000).

5 The Press Association is the main domestic news agency for British media.

6 The BBC is itself 'explicitly forbidden from broadcasting its own opinions on current affairs or matters of public policy, except broadcasting policy' (Chapter two of the *Producers' Guidelines*).

7 The PCC warned about this practice in two editorials in 1992 (Reports 7 and 12). Over-reliance on clippings – through which errors and lies can be re-cycled *ad infinitum* – typifies practice in busy newsrooms. The PCC also warned of the practice of using information from brief telephone interviews to produce reports giving the impression that in-depth, face-to-face interviews had been carried out.

8 Cleaning up quotes is, however, acceptable journalistic practice. Ronald Reagan was asked in 1979 why he expected to be more successful in gaining the Republican presidential nomination in 1980 than he had been in 1976. He replied: '. . .uh. . .it's kind of encouraging that more of the people seem to be coming the same way, believing the same things'. In the AP quote he was reported as having said, 'It's remarkable how people are beginning to see things my way' (cited in Meyer, 1991: 59).

9 Martin Bell's advocacy of the 'journalism of attachment' sparked a lively debate among journalists, centred particularly on the rights and wrongs of war reporting in Bosnia in the 1990s. Many journalists were very critical of Bell's argument. See, for example, Hume (1997).

10 The science and art of interpretation is hermeneutics whose intellectual roots lie in 18th and 19th century scholars' wrestling with the meanings of Biblical texts.

11 See also Lichtenberg (2000) and Ward (1999). The latter tries to develop a more precise definition of what he calls 'pragmatic news objectivity'. He believes that

objectivity is 'a comprehensive ideal that can justify the more specific values of fairness, accuracy and accountability to the public.' (1999: 9).

12 St Augustine also defines lying as 'the expression of a false meaning with the intention of deceiving' ('*Mendacium est quippe falsi significato cum voluntate fallendi*') in *Contra mendacium*, chapter 12 & 16. This is a less satisfactory definition because it is possible that one may have the intention to deceive by communicating something which is in fact true. St Thomas Aquinas makes this clear in his discussion of lying in the *Summa theologiae* Second Part of the Second Part, question 110, article 1.

13 Geach gives a good example of how we might mislead others by allowing them to understand words in a way which is different to what we intend. He relates how St Joan of Arc sent letters to her commanders where the mark of a cross indicated that they should understand the sentences in the opposite sense to their normal meaning. Thus, anyone who should not read the letters would be misled by them. This is what happened. At her trial her English enemies, failing to unravel the code, accused St Joan of lying. According to Geach (1977: 115), 'surely she had a good defence; words get their meaning by convention, and her commanders, to whom the letters were addressed, knew the convention and were not misled; if English soldiers, who had no business to read her letters or to be in the country at all, read them and were misled, that was not her affair.'

14 Clark used this expression in his evidence at the Matrix Churchill trial for illegal exports to Iraq in November 1992. He effectively brought about the trial's collapse by acknowledging that his ambivalence had given exporters the impression that he would turn a blind eye to their illegal activities. A similar phrase was used by the then cabinet secretary Sir Robert Armstrong a few years earlier at the *Spycatcher* trial in Australia when he spoke about being 'economical with the truth'.

15 *The Guardian* concocted a letter on House of Commons' notepaper purporting to be a letter from Aitken requesting a copy of the Paris Ritz bill. The procurement of this information was to 'stand up' the paper's allegation based on Mohammed al Fayed's information about who'd paid for the stay. However, the Commons censured the paper's behaviour. In an interview the editor of the time, Peter Preston, defended his action to me on the grounds that it was a way of obtaining information while at the same time protecting the confidentiality of the source. Preston explained that he told al Fayed: 'I'll give you a cover story. We'll mock up the phoney letter from Aitken's office which we'll send to your office at the Ritz saying, "Can we have a copy of Aitken's bill?" You send it back. The Ritz keeps a copy of the phoney letter on file and then if I play you false and reveal something about the Ritz that lands you in the shit, you're in the clear because you can say "Look. The person is a liar".' Preston argued: 'There was nothing dissembling about the cod fax. It was on my own fax machine. In a sense it was a hostage in an exchange of documents. We sent it over. He sent the bill back. He was the owner of the hotel so he could say he was the owner of the bill. There was no intention at that stage of using it. It was a smoking gun and if it went off, it would shoot me in the foot. I knew that perfectly well which was why it was offered' (1999). As far as Aitken is concerned, the *Sunday Times* journalist, Mark Skipworth, described it to me as 'truly one of the great stories of the 90s. It's the kind of story you'll tell your children: "always tell the truth, you don't want to end up like Jonathan Aitken"' (1999). Aitken had begun his fight against *The Guardian* in 1995 with the immortal words: 'If it falls to me to start a fight to cut out the cancer of bent and twisted journalism in our country with the simple sword of truth and the trusty shield of fair play, so be it'. He was jailed for perjury in 1999.

16 Mark Skipworth was the deputy editor of the *Sunday Times* Insight team who suggested the sting which caught two Conservative MPs who agreed to accept payment for asking questions on behalf of the bogus company, Sigthin (an anagram of Insight). When I asked him whether they'd discussed the ethics of it, he replied: 'Oh yes. Absolutely. We went through the Code of Practice. It was greatly in the public interest so there was no problem on that level' (1999). However, there was a twist in the tale. The PCC decided to reopen the file on the case and, having considered the findings of the

Parliamentary committee that investigated the issue, concluded that there had been a discrepancy in the *Sunday Times*' evidence (Shannon, 2001: 192).

17 In a statement from Buckingham Palace it was said 'The Queen deplores the entrapment, subterfuge, innuendo and untruths to which [the earl and countess of Wessex] have been subjected in recent days' (*The Guardian*, 9 April, 2001). However, reports that the Queen was livid were played down by Palace officials who commented, 'She doesn't do furious – she is supremely detached' (*The Guardian*, 6 April, 2001).

> Modern life is heading to this strange place where everything is a representation
> of a representation and nothing is real.
>
> > Paul Attanasio

Plato pictured human life as a pilgrimage from appearance to reality. In his allegory of the cave in *The Republic*, prisoners are chained inside a cave facing a wall. Behind them is a fire and a parapet along which people pass carrying different objects. The prisoners can only see shadows cast against the cave wall by the light of the fire playing on those on the parapet. The flickering images aren't the reality. The shadow-bound consciousness of the prisoners isn't reality, although they take it to be. Reality – the world of Forms – can only be found in the sun-lit world outside the cave. Plato believed that artists produce an image-ridden illusion which gives only the faintest gleam of reality. Their view of the world is distorted by their own passions and prejudices. He was even suspicious of writing as interposing another symbolic layer between us and our perception of the true, the real.

Plato would probably not have liked television at all. In some ways television is an inherently deceptive medium. Like Plato's prisoners we are shown representations of reality, not reality itself. A critical version of the Platonic view was taken up two thousand years later by the heirs of the Frankfurt School. Forced into exile, Theodor Adorno and Max Horkheimer were not impressed by what they considered to be the 'bread and circuses' culture of their new American homeland and declaimed against what they believed to be the alienation produced by American popular culture exemplified by Hollywood and later television. The historian, Daniel Boorstin, declared (1971: 37):

> The American citizen . . . lives in a world where fantasy is more real than reality, where the image has more dignity than its original. We hardly dare face our bewilderment, because our ambiguous experience is so pleasantly iridescent, and the solace of belief in contrived reality is so thoroughly real. We have become eager accessories to the great hoaxes of the age. These are the hoaxes we play on ourselves.

Ironically, Hollywood itself has also explored the theme of television's shallowness. In the 1976 film *Network*, the broadcaster screams at his viewers: 'In God's name, you people are the real thing! We're the illusions'. And he continues, 'Television is not the truth. Television is a goddamned amusement park. Television is a circus, a carnival, a travelling troupe of acrobats and story tellers, singers and dancers, jugglers, side-show freaks, lion-tamers and football players. We're in the boredom-killing business'. *Quiz Show* (1994) explores the loss of innocence of the American people about the truthfulness of television quiz shows and *The Truman Show* (1998) depicts a topsy-turvy world where life itself has become television spectacle.

The Internet has fuelled the concern with what is authentic and inauthentic. Chapter four examined the reporter's commitment to truth-telling. This chapter explores practices which are part of the vocabulary of the reporter's craft – staged shots, reconstructions – that make us believe that what we see is true.

SEEING AND BELIEVING

In St John's Gospel the Apostle Thomas tells the others he will not believe that Christ has risen from the dead: 'Until I have seen the mark of the nails on his hands, until I have put my finger into the mark of nails, and put my hand into his side, you will never make me believe' (20: 25). The truth of an event cannot be gainsaid if we have seen it with our own eyes. Pictures presented in a news, current affairs or documentary context have traditionally had this special kind of authority. We believe what we see to be true. And yet the grammar of pictures, and especially of television, is shot through with artifice. Photographs are regularly cropped, documentaries use reconstructions and news programmes employ establishing shots of nodding politicians. Digital technology has made it even easier to manipulate text and image; the Internet has made it simpler to indulge in ever more sophisticated fakery. Can we still trust pictures to tell us the truth and where do the limits of fakery lie?

Picture manipulation

All pictures are interpretations of reality: they squeeze a slice of life into a small piece of celluloid or television screen. However, manipulating images in order to distort the reality represented is a different matter. Manipulation has a long history. From the days of Daguerre photographers have retouched, airbrushed or stage-managed pictures for ideological or artistic reasons. In 1857 Oscar Rejlander published a photograph entitled 'Street urchins tossing chestnuts'. It showed two ragged children, one of whom watched a chestnut fall though the air. However, at the time the photograph was taken, capturing a moving object in mid-air was an impossible technical feat; the image had been produced by using a fine thread (see Lester, 1991: 92).

Digital technology now makes picture manipulation easier and more difficult to detect than ever. Technicians can resurrect the dead and have them converse with the living: Steve McQueen advertises motor cars and a contemporary footballer meets Martin Luther King to advertise mobile phones. The face of the Conservative leader in the 2001 election campaign can be transformed into that of Margaret Thatcher with lipstick, earrings and a full head of hair. In May 1996 the London *Evening Standard* published a photograph of Labour politician, John Prescott, in which the beer in front of him had been airbrushed out and the bottle in front of his wife cropped to make it look like a champagne bottle. The caption to the picture was 'Champagne socialist' (NUJ, 1996). This technology could very well undermine the traditional authority of images, if electronic manipulation of pictures becomes widely practised. For this reason, Britain's National Union of Journalists launched a campaign to ensure that every time a digitally-manipulated picture is used, a little symbol or kite-mark appear with it. On 26 February 1998, the NUJ's Code of Conduct was amended to include a clause about picture manipulation, stating:

> No journalist shall knowingly cause or allow the publication or broadcast of a photograph that has been manipulated unless that photograph is clearly labelled as such. Manipulation does not include normal dodging, burning, colour balancing, spotting, contrast adjustment, cropping and obvious masking for legal or safety reasons.

Staged shots and reconstructions

Staged shots and reconstructions are an accepted part of televisual language. Whenever a producer asks someone to perform in any way for the camera, we enter the world of artifice. We see people walking down the road and into their home, politicians walking up stairs, an interviewee reading a book – so-called establishing shots – which constitute a low-level, acceptable degree of deception. Commercial and public service television have guidelines about their use (see Box 5.1) but they are so integral to certain programme genres that their use is rarely acknowledged.

Wildlife films, for example, regularly use reconstructions and staged scenes, mocking up scenarios, intercutting sequences shot in aquariums and zoos with real wildlife footage. David Attenborough happily admitted that footage of a polar bear giving birth was shot in a Belgian zoo. A producer working on a BBC wildlife programme told me of the lengths to which they had to go to get shots of a mass of fluttering butterflies. Their wings were extended with dental floss and a fan produced the necessary draught of air to provide the illusion of migrating butterflies. Attenborough argued that to label the scenes as 'recon-structions' would break the spell.

'Docudramas' or 'docusoaps' such as *Driving School* and *Airport* were all the rage in the 1990s (see Berry, 2000). They showed ordinary people – traffic wardens, airline staff, a learner driver – seemingly going about their ordinary business. It was fly-on-the-wall documentary converted into soap-opera and people assumed that what they saw on the screen was really taking place before their eyes. Of course, a moment's thought would have allowed the viewer to realize that the cameraman's presence just when Maureen wakes up in the middle of the night, terrified at the prospect of her driving test, was too fortuitous to be a coincidence. Nevertheless, there was genuine surprise and disappointment when it was revealed that some scenes were re-enactments rather than the real thing.

These techniques are used regularly on our screens. They risk planting the idea that if you think the overall message your images convey is true, then the difficulties of making natural looking television justifies you faking it.

BOX 5.1   Independent Television News guidelines

Reconstruction

The reconstruction or re-staging of events in factual programmes can be a great help in explaining an issue. It must always be done truthfully with an awareness of what is reliably known. Nothing significant which is not known should be invented without acknowledgement. Reconstructions should not over dramatize events in a misleading or sensationalistic way.

Reconstructions should be identified clearly so that no-one is misled. Repeated labelling may be necessary to achieve this.

Cheating the viewer

Staged scenes and reconstructions, not always labelled as such, are considered legitimate fakes by programme makers because, as a producer on a wildlife series explained, 'we were not trying to distort anything, our facts were correct, and "to break the spell" would have seemed ludicrous. Imagine a sequence in which a lion catches and kills a hyena and a sign on the screen says "reconstruction". Yet there are instances where such sequences have been "arranged"' (Weightman, 1999).

But how are these to be distinguished from 'illegitimate' fakes? Looking at the controversies of the 1990s, what has really caused anxiety among broadcasters is fakery in current affairs documentaries. One of the most serious cases was a programme shown on Carlton television in 1996 in the *Network First* documentary strand. The programme called *The Connection* was about supposed Colombian drug smugglers. It purported to reveal the activities of a drug cartel smuggling cocaine into Britain. It showed a 'mule' ingesting drugs before entering the country. In fact, the sequence was a reconstruction with an actor. The scenes of the 'mule's' apparently continuous plane journey from Colombia to Britain had been filmed in sections several months apart. The ITC ordered Carlton to pay a £2 million fine to the government and broadcast an on-screen apology. An inquiry concluded that the programme makers had used key personnel with little television experience.

In September 1997 there was yet another example of fakery in documentaries. Channel 4's *Too Much Too Young: Chickens* about the supposed activities of two rent boys in Glasgow, showing so-called clients negotiating for sex. The scenes were in fact staged, not signalled as such, with production staff and their friends. In February 1999 the Independent Television Commission fined Channel 4 £150,000 for these scenes in breach of section 2.12(i) of the ITC Programme Code. This allows that the use of dramatized 'reconstructions' in factual programmes 'is a legitimate means of obtaining greater authenticity, so long as it does not distort reality.' It adds, 'Whenever a reconstruction is used in a documentary, current affairs or news programme it should accurately reflect the known facts and be labelled unless there is no possibility of viewers being misled'. The *Daily Mail*'s shocked front-page headline asked 'CAN WE BELIEVE ANYTHING WE SEE ON TV?' (5 February, 1999).

Channel 4 itself stated that the staged scenes constituted 'an unacceptable breach of trust with the audience' and announced that the producer involved would not work again for Channel 4 until such time as she could show that she was trustworthy. It also announced that it was strengthening its guidelines on secret filming and fly-on-the-wall documentaries and that it would run seminars for its producers on their regulatory and ethical responsibilities.

Shortly after these revelations, the *Mirror* revealed that there had been fakery in so-called confessional television shows such as *Vanessa* and *Trisha*. The Mirror front-page headline which broke the story declared: 'VANESSA SHOW FAKED' with two subheadings explaining that '"Abused wife" was unmarried' and that '"Feuding sisters" had never met' (11 February, 1999).[1] Sisters who had appeared on the show turned out not to be sisters at all but a couple of actresses hired by an agency. They appeared as part of a warring family and in another incident, an actress appeared as an abused wife. In their eagerness to get the 'right' guests, researchers had been sloppy in checking credentials. *The Mail on Sunday* followed up this story a year later with the news that daytime chat shows were using 'professional guests' (5 March, 2000).

An interesting variation on the theme of fakery was the deception of journalists and programme makers by members of the public. In 1998 a Channel 4 documentary *Daddy's Girl* had to be withdrawn a day before transmission when it was discovered that the 'father and daughter' were in fact boyfriend and girlfriend. Later Channel 4 interviewed the couple, Stuart and Victoria, about their motives. 'They wanted a weird thing,' said Stuart, 'and when they came across us they got a weird thing'. They were amazed at how keen the production team was to suspend disbelief. As one *Guardian* columnist put it, 'It is hardly surprising that they had so little respect for truth in television, when they found that television had so little respect for itself' (Aitkenhead, 5 February, 1999).

'Legitimate' and 'illegitimate' fakery

Why was the fakery of wildlife programmes considered legitimate and that of current affairs documentaries not? Industry codes accept 'legitimate' fakery. As the ITN guidelines about staging scenes state (2001):

> Factual programmes should always present a fair and accurate picture of the situations they portray. Audiences should never be misled by what they see or hear in a programme. However, there are few factual films which do not involve some intervention from the director, even those which are commonly described as 'fly on the wall' or observational documentaries.
> . . . production methods, especially in television with single camera location shooting, sometimes mean that it is impossible to record all events exactly as they happen. Many of the techniques that are used to overcome this have long been part of the accepted grammar of programme-making.

They conclude: 'We should never be so embarrassed by the techniques that we use that we cannot share them with our audience.' So where did the makers of *The Connection* and *Chickens* go wrong? For *The Guardian*, who had exposed the fakery of *The Connection* in the first place, the issue was straightforward:

> The worst professional offence a journalist can commit is knowingly and deliberately to publish fiction as fact. That is what happened to Carlton Television's programme, *The Connection*, and that is why the story should be read carefully by everyone working in British television today. Journalism should be a process of searching for the truth. Once that process is poisoned the bond of trust between programme-maker and viewer is broken. (8 May, 1998)

But was it that simple? It seems more a case of having violated the stricter conventions surrounding current affairs as compared, for instance, to wildlife documentaries. Inserting episodes purporting to be something that they are in fact not (rent-boys soliciting, for example) is unacceptable for the former but not for the latter (a polar bear giving birth). In both cases, it is not disputed that the re-enacted event did not take place; it did, but was not captured on film. The issue seems to be more that the use of techniques to create verisimilitude in programmes like *The Connection* must be labelled as such while for other genres the conventions are less strict.[2] The appropriate use of televisual fakery would seem to be as much about knowing the rules of the game than a straightforward commitment to truthfulness.

BREAKING TRUST

Does it matter that *Vanessa* was hoaxed by actors? That a lot of what we see might be fake? According to some, it depends on the programme genre. As far as confessional television is concerned, some commentators maintain that everyone knows that this kind of programming is a kind of pulp fiction or light entertainment. In a sense they consider it heartening that British confessional television has been unable to find sufficient 'genuine' guests when compared with their American counterparts. 'I'm glad that we're bad at these shows,' newspaper columnist Alison Pearson (17 February, 1999), concluded in an article entitled 'Let's be glad that we're bad', 'and that we're struggling to find guinea pigs: it reflects well on us. We're not yet comfortable with the idea that emotions are just another branch of entertainment.'

Some media professionals justify deception on the grounds that most people are very media literate and understand that many programme genres such as quiz shows and wildlife programmes use fakery. Notwithstanding this view,[3] the industry itself considers the kind of practices exposed in *The Connection* and *Vanessa* with extreme concern. Industry regulators acted rapidly to punish these breaches. Former director-general, John Birt, convened a meeting of senior BBC executives and five members of the *Vanessa* programme team were formally disciplined.

Why does fakery matter when it is in any case part of the vocabulary of television? Because if we are shown rent boys soliciting with no rider, we expect that to be what we are seeing. If it is not, we are being misled and deceived: not about what does go on, but about the kind of evidence being presented. The conventions which have grown up around news and current affairs are that the images which accompany the text are not meant to be visual illustrations or interpretations of events. If we are told on the news that there has been a suicide bomb in Tel Aviv and are shown images of urban devastation and public grief, we expect this to be documentary evidence of the event. In programmes like *Chickens* or even *Driving School* what appears to be documentary evidence is not. As Warburton explains, what you see does not record an actual event, rather it is a reconstructed one. He describes this function of photographs and/or images as having a status analogous to relics.[4] Just as seeing Emily Bronte's dress displayed at the Haworth parsonage puts us in touch with the nineteenth century writer, so the photograph of Auschwitz in some way allows us to be there. Writing of our understanding of the Vietnam war, Warburton says:

> Malcolm Brown's [sic] image of a Buddhist monk's protest self-immolation, Eddie Adams' still of a police chief in Saigon executing a Vietcong officer with his pistol . . . Huyn Cong Ut's unforgettable photograph of a naked girl, burnt by napalm, running towards the camera; these and other images had a profound effect on how that war was understood. But their effect depended upon their being reliable as documentary evidence for what they appeared to depict. Without the causal link back to a real event, these images would simply have been manufactured propaganda and would not have their eyewitness status that they in fact did have. (1998: 124)

Of course this oversimplifies. Browne was an eyewitness because the AP office had received a call from Buddhist activists telling him where to go to witness the protest against government oppression of Buddhism rather than their prosecution of war (Arnett, 1994: 101–2). Nevertheless, the point is well-made. Where fakery is freely employed and not signalled, visual communication becomes increasingly problematic.

THE MENDACIOUS MEDIUM

However, some argue that anything which undermines the credibility of television is a good thing. Seeing is not believing and all that makes us question the authority of broadcast media is a helpful contribution to public scepticism. In an article entitled 'Television's guilty secret: it just can't stop lying', journalist Matthew Parris, argues just this. Television is, he says, 'inherently and unavoidably corrupt' and the sooner the public realizes this and broadcasters are cast down from their pedestal the better. He concludes (10 May, 1998):

> Nobody should rely on the printed word and few do: we are seen as witnesses for the prosecution or defence, not judge or jury. Television thinks it is both

judge and jury. And, because seeing is believing, the public believes. It should not believe now, nor ever in the future. This latest controversy [about *The Connection*] will undermine the credibility and status of television professionals and help destroy public trust. It is therefore very good news.

In Parris' view, the media denunciation of fakery is inconsistent. And the apparent increase in resorting to deception has little to do with financial motives but with the competitive urge to make gripping television. The journalist and writer, A.N. Wilson shares this view. In an article entitled, 'The television camera nearly always lies' he wrote (19 March, 2000): 'Television . . . is a medium in which truth-telling is all but impossible. . . . almost all television coverage – whether of natural history or current affairs – is in part faked.'

'The line between fact and drama in documentary has grown increasingly blurred' is also the view of television producer, John Willis, 'and in the struggle between journalistic truth and dramatic excitement, drama is winning' (18 May, 1999). However, his diagnosis, one shared by many industry professionals, is that it is the battle for ratings which is undermining journalistic integrity.[5] Corners are cut, inexperienced staff are used and projects are oversold to commissioning editors. The pressure to deliver becomes intense.

RESTORING TRUST

The logical consequence of Parris' view of television as the mendacious medium, echoed by writer A.N. Wilson, is that we must not trust television or broadcast journalists. This seems rather a counsel of despair. If we go down this road, we end up with a Cartesian-like supposition that all we perceive are the illusions and deceptions of an evil demon manipulating our perceptions to give a false sensation of engagement with reality (see Warburton, 1998). Seeing is no longer believing and one of the brakes on scepticism has gone. It also removes the onus upon reporters and programme makers to strive for integrity. What does it matter if you lie and deceive, it would appear to say, if the medium you work in cannot help doing that anyway?

However, the story A.N. Wilson's article refers to, shows why such arguments taken *in extremis* are dangerous. In 1992 ITN showed images of painfully thin Bosnian Muslims held in a Bosnian Serb prison camp, Trnopolje; the scenes were all too reminiscent of Nazi war crimes. International outrage forced the Serbs to admit the Red Cross and eventually close the camps. Subsequently a small radical magazine, *LM* (formerly *Living Marxism*), published a story in 1997 entitled 'The picture that fooled the world,' based on a German journalist's report that the pictures had been staged. He claimed that the barbed wire which appeared to surround the prisoners, in fact enclosed the reporters. ITN sued *LM* for libel and won the case.

Now surely this does matter. Just as it matters whether the historian, David Irving, is right to deny that Hitler's government carried out a deliberate policy of extermination of European Jewry. If the bond of trust between news and current affairs journalists and the public is broken, we could see documentaries go the same way as wrestling in the 1970s or quiz shows in 1950s' America.[6]

It is important to understand the limitations of the visual vocabulary of television and the extent to which artifice is used in programme making. In this sense a dose of healthy audience scepticism may be no bad thing. It is also possible that television professionals should be more honest with their audience about the conventions of different genres of programme making. However, suggesting that television is intrinsically mendacious is a step too far.

British broadcast journalists have enjoyed high levels of trust and credibility.[7] But it is a trust which could easily be squandered by a disregard for truthfulness. Television executive, Michael Grade, considers that: 'There is far too little training in broadcasting. There are a lot of new kids who have come in who really don't understand the seriousness of cutting corners.' And an ITN executive concluded after the confessional shows' controversy that: 'There are people making these shows who haven't got the first idea about ethics' (cited in Hellen and O'Reilly, 14 February, 1999).[8] Perhaps a less patronising attitude by broadcasters to its audience – a greater willingness to admit to the contrivances of the digital and audiovisual world – would go some way toward showing that truth really is their currency.

NOTES

1 There was a nice irony in seeing those beacons of truth and strangers to fakery, the tabloids, leading the campaign to uphold truth and integrity on television.

2 The following guidelines from the ITN (2001) set out precisely the requirements for current affairs documentary makers who must ensure that:

- programmes truthfully and fairly depict what has happened
- programmes never do anything to mislead audiences while it may, on occasions, be legitimate to re-shoot something that is a routine and insignificant action, it is not legitimate to stage or re-stage action which is *significant to the development of the action or narrative, without clearly signalling this to the audience*
- contributors should *not* be asked to re-enact *significant* events, without this being made clear in the film. (This does not preclude programme-makers arranging to record sequences at a particular time to fit in with the timetable of a shoot)
- if significant events have been arranged for the cameras (including the recruitment of contributors) that would not have taken place *at all* without the intervention of the programme-makers, then this must be made clear to the audience
- shots and sequences should never be inter-cut to suggest that they were happening at the same time if the resulting juxtaposition of material leads to a distorted and misleading impression of events.

3 This is by no means certain. A BBC 2 series in 1998 on television fakery featured a viewers' focus group. They were astonished at the extent of its use in programmes like *Driving School* and *Blind Date*.

4 The term 'relics' from the Latin *'reliquiae'* refers to some object, usually part of the body or clothes which remains as a memorial of a departed saint. Even in pre-Christian times it has had this religious connotation and for this reason, is perhaps not the most exact analogy.

5 This is the view, for example, of Martin Bell. Writing about the *Vanessa* controversy he said, 'The chat shows' carelessness with the truth is the inevitable outcome of a TV culture in which nothing matters but money and ratings.' (16 February, 1999)

6 This is not to defend the ITN's libel action which effectively put *LM* out of business. Many journalists, including the BBC's John Simpson, were highly critical of ITN and argued that the pictures were not what they seemed. According to Simpson, 'The ITN reporters were careful not to call Trnpolje a concentration camp; but when their pictures were shown around the world other television organizations were much less meticulous. Again, they thought they knew what the pictures showed. The judge in the ITN-*LM* case seemed to support the key point that the barbed wire ran around the camera crew not the prisoners, but he accepted the word of the reporters that they had not realized this.' (2000: 322)

7 This is borne out by opinion polls (see Chapter 1) and the continuing prestige of, in particular, BBC news services.

8 John Willis agrees: 'Media ethics should not only be part of training on the job, but also an obligatory course component for the thousands of media studies students currently enrolled in Britain' (18 May, 1999).

> Every act is an irrevocable selection and exclusion. Just as when you marry one woman you give up all the others. If you become King of England, you give up the post of Beadle in Brompton. If you go to Rome, you sacrifice a rich suggestive life in Wimbledon.
>
> G.K. Chesterton, Orthodoxy.

Our entire legal system is predicated on the notion that we are free, that we can be held responsible for our actions. Praise and blame only make sense where we consider that people could have done otherwise. Awards for bravery recognize that in very challenging circumstances somebody has chosen a highly courageous course of action, for if she had no choice but to save the child, then she couldn't be considered courageous.[1] In other words, for our actions to have a moral quality, they must be considered in some sense free.

Freedom is of immense importance. It is a core value of the western tradition. People will die for it and the way we choose to punish people is to deprive them of their freedom.

It is also one of the central principles appealed to by the media in Britain, and particularly the United States, to give it an exceptional status in the pursuit of its task. 'Freedom of the press' and 'freedom of expression' have been the clarion calls of those who have sought to resist the oppressive powers of the State. The struggle for freedom of the press, taken so much for granted when it exists, has been long, difficult and still unachieved in many parts of the world.[2] But what does freedom of the press mean? What grounds do we have for supporting it? What, if any, are its limits? These are the questions I will explore in this chapter.

UNDERSTANDING FREEDOM

One of the paradoxes of the modern era is the great store set by the notion of individual freedom and the simultaneous denial by much contemporary thought that we are in fact free.[3] Determinism, for instance, claims that things could not have been otherwise. And yet you are unlikely to accept that as an excuse if I punch you on the nose. So what do we mean by freedom?

Hamlet's 'infinite space'.

At one stage Hamlet declares, 'O God! I could be bounded in a nutshell, and count myself a king of infinite space' (*Hamlet*, Act II, scene 2). This is the most intimate freedom we possess. It is inner freedom at the most radical and profound level, an interior space which no one else should possess if we don't want them to. One of the horrors of torture is that it seeks to crush this most intimate freedom of all, the freedom which allows us to have a sense of self, the possession of our desires, thoughts and feelings. The torturer or the despot aims to destroy this autonomy, and in extreme situations can succeed. But even in very difficult circumstances human beings, can manage to hold on to this inner realm.[4]

The existentialist philosopher Søren Kierkegaard (1813–55) described the human experience of anguish or anxiety as the experience of freedom. Anguish is different from fear, which is fear of *something*: I experience fear when I see a spider or when I'm confronted by a man with a knife. Anguish, he says, is dread or anxiety at the possibility of something. The feeling I have as I must decide whether to break up a relationship is a tension which arises from my experience of freedom. Inscribed in this feeling of anxiety is the experience of existential freedom. This kind of thinking is core to the creed of existentialism which places the exercise of freedom at the very heart of what it is to be human, arguing that moral standards can only be chosen. I am what I choose to be.

Hobbes' choice

Thomas Hobbes (1588–1679) characterized freedom as choice so that in a given situation one could have done otherwise. Thus, you ask me what I'd like to drink and I choose a glass of red wine, where I could have chosen white wine. All the choices I make – the minor ones about which drink to have as well as the major ones about which university to go to or person to marry – reveal the contingency of my existence and the fact of my freedom. The Hobbesian idea of freedom as the absence of external impediments to the exercise of choice undoubtedly expresses three important truths namely, i) without choice one cannot be said to be free; ii) truth cannot be imposed on anyone without sacrificing their freedom; iii) authenticity, being true to oneself, is an important part of what it is to be human. We are, to a certain extent, in our own hands.

Taken to an extreme, this is the existentialist view which claims that my freedom is my essence. Without telling me how, existentialists urge me to create myself and my world by exercizing my freedom. Any encroachment on my freedom, any acceptance by me of given values, tradition or the demands of other people is to enter the realm of inauthenticity. This is the true and terrible sense of Jean-Paul Sartre's phrase that 'Hell is other people'. Freedom in this understanding leads to us into a moral dead-end and ignores the fact that none of us start from a zero point.

A milder view, echoing Hobbes' account, is that which characterizes freedom as the right to pursue one's self-interest bounded only by the freedom of others. This was formulated in Mill's famous 'harm' principle in his essay *On Liberty* which states (1859/1982: 119):

> . . . even opinions lose their immunity when the circumstances in which they are expressed are such as to constitute their expression a positive instigation to a mischievous act. . . . Acts, of whatever kind, which without justifiable cause do harm to others may be, and in the more important cases absolutely require to be, controlled by the unfavourable sentiments, and, when needful, by the active interference of mankind.

Actions should be permitted so long as they do not injure the interests of others. Here we find the quintessential liberal position where freedom is understood as the lack of external impediments to the exercise of choice insofar as harm is not caused to others.

But what kinds of choices? Should there be no external impediments to my ability to fulfil my desires, whatever they may be? Or is it assumed that our freedom is to make choices as rational agents? However, it is feasible that such beings only emerge in a society which, through the restriction of choices, moulds us into moral agents. In other words, by teaching your child not to eat the whole packet of chocolate biscuits, you show her what it is to be considerate, to think of others. Indeed, the kind of character of which Mill approved – truth-seeking, independent, not crushed by the weight of 'collective mediocrity' – is unlikely to be nurtured in an environment where she herself takes her autonomy to be the chief good. Second, if choice is esteemed above all things, how is the application of the harm principle ensured? What indeed does injury to the interests of others mean? These issues raise difficult practical questions for journalists and of itself Mill's account has no answers.

Growth in freedom

Can one be more or less free? Can one speak of being more or less oneself? We can think of paths we choose which enrich or impoverish us: developing a cocaine habit, learning to drive, being tidy. Using our freedom to develop habits which enlarge our capacities and potency, is to create 'virtues', strengths which increase the range of our freedom. On the other hand, if we choose, for example, never to get out of bed, we will quickly find our freedom is diminished, not only in the sense that we have circumscribed the scope of our activities, but also in the very real sense that we will lose the use of our legs. Freedom grows or decreases depending upon how we use it.

Political freedom

This realm refers to the value of freedom as expressed in community: what we are permitted to do and what we are encouraged to do. Various aspects of our social condition can act as spurs or restraints to our freedom. Thus, for example, the absence of family affection; the lack of a living wage; legal deprivation or political restraints are very real impediments to being free. In his *Two Concepts of Liberty* Isaiah Berlin (1958/1966) wrote of a dual notion of freedom:

a) Negative freedom: I am free to the extent that I'm unhindered by others, generating a sphere of negative rights. In this sense, freedom is liberty from; it is the absence of interference.

b) Positive freedom: I am free to the extent that I am my own master. Freedom isn't just the absence of restrictions, it is the presence of resources. Thus, for example, it's all very well to speak of Britain as a free society but if my social situation is such that I can never go to university then to what extent am I really free?

FREEDOM OF EXPRESSION

The value we give to freedom as such has an ancient lineage. The Greeks compared their free-born state to that of the servility of the Persians. However, the right to express freely one's opinions, views and beliefs, especially on political or religious matters, has a fairly short history. Socrates was condemned to death because of his refusal to honour the gods.

The history of the notion that the expression of dissident or subversive views should be tolerated and be neither censured nor punished by the law runs parallel to the development of the press itself. John Milton's *Areopagitica* was published in 1644 in response to Parliament's re-introduction in June 1643 of the government licensing of publishers. The earliest 'newsbooks' in Britain date from the 1620s, while the first daily newspaper, the *Daily Courant*, began publication in May 1702. Milton's impassioned plea for freedom of expression and toleration of falsehood has entered the Anglo-American canon:

> Give me the liberty to know, to utter, and to argue freely according to conscience, above all liberties. (1644/1946: 35)

It is not so often noted that his defence of freedom of expression and toleration has clear limits. He would not have tolerated 'popery, and open superstition, which as it extirpates all religions and civil supremacies, so itself should be extirpate . . .; that also which is impious or evil absolutely against faith or manners no law can possibly permit, that intends not to unlaw itself' (38). Milton's defence of freedom of expression was firmly grounded in a Protestant world-view according to which the English people had a providential mission to work out the truth of the Reformation for the enlightenment of the peoples of the earth.[5] It does, however, adumbrate the main features of future discussion about freedom of expression: what is its scope? How are we to define 'harmful' speech? His distinctive contribution was to argue against the principle of pre-censorship and in favour of tolerance for a broader swathe of views than was usual for his time.

Typical accounts of the history of the notion of freedom of expression establish a kind of apostolic succession of its defenders beginning with John Milton (1608–74), followed by John Locke (1632–1704) and culminating in John Stuart Mill.[6] Locke's work establishes the individual as the unit of value and action and the bearer of rights to life, liberty, property and the pursuit of happiness. These are considered true in virtue of human nature and not in the gift of government, which should protect such rights. This novel view was first enshrined in the American Constitution to which the First Amendment adds the guarantee that: 'Congress shall make no law . . . abridging the freedom of speech, or of the press.'

This was Mill's view: human freedom is a good because without it there can be no progress in science, law or politics, all of which require free discussion of opinion. J.S. Mill's *On Liberty* (1859) remains the classic text defending the principle of freedom of expression. His defence is grounded on the following principles:

- truth drives out falsity therefore there is nothing to be feared from the free expression of ideas be they true or false;
- truth is not stable or fixed but develops down the ages; much of what we once considered true turned out to be false and we should not, therefore, prohibit views because of their apparent falsity;
- free discussion is necessary to prevent the 'deep slumber of a decided opinion' and to allow the onward march of truth; considering false views allows us to re-affirm the basis of true ones.

FREEDOM OF THE PRESS

Freedom of expression now has the status of an almost unchallengeable dogma in democratic societies. It is written into the main international charters of rights (see Box 6.1) and in the United States it is Holy Writ where its constitutional status protects the media's freedom.

BOX 6.1   Right to freedom of expression

Universal Declaration of Human Rights
Article 19

Everyone has the right to freedom of opinion and expression; this right includes freedom to hold opinions without interference and to seek, receive and impart information and ideas through any media and regardless of frontiers.

European Convention on Human Rights
Article 10

1   Everyone has the right to freedom of expression. This right shall include freedom to hold opinions and to receive and impart information and ideas without interference by public authority and regardless of frontiers. This article shall not prevent States from requiring the licensing of broadcasting, television or cinema enterprises.
2   The exercise of these freedoms, since it carries with it duties and responsibilities, may be subject to such formalities, conditions, restrictions or penalties as are prescribed by law and are necessary in a democratic society, in the interests of national security, territorial integrity or public safety, for the prevention of disorder or crime, for the protection of health or morals, for the protection of the reputation or rights of others, for preventing the disclosure of information received in confidence, or for maintaining the authority and impartiality of the judiciary.

Britain and press freedom

In Britain the media enjoys no specific legal safeguards protecting freedom of the press as such. Legislation affecting freedom of information and freedom of expression extends to all those subject to the law, not just to journalists. And the law extends to limit freedom of expression in areas such as libel, defamation, contempt of court, protection of minors, blasphemy, race relations and official secrets. Indeed, the amount of legislation controlling freedom of expression, and thus of the media, has led to frequent criticisms that Britain is a secretive state and that more should be done to unravel the wealth of legislation constraining freedom of expression.[7] Former editor of the *Sunday Times*, Harold Evans, has been one of the chief proponents of American-style legislation, unsurprising in view of the struggle his newspaper had to publish the truth and obtain justice for the victims of the thalidomide drug.[8]

Is press freedom equivalent to freedom of expression?

Champions of press freedom argue that in a democratic political system, government exists with the consent of the governed. This consent must be informed consent and this can only occur where there is a free flow of information. Media freedom is considered the guarantor of democracy and, in a sense, equivalent to freedom of expression. Furthermore, it is argued that any restriction on media freedom produces a 'chilling' effect whereby the free flow of information is increasingly discouraged. If, for example, you force a journalist to reveal a source, in the future people will be less inclined to talk to journalists.

There is an argument, however, that freedom of the press is not necessarily a subset of freedom of speech. American academic, Judith Lichtenberg (1995), outlines conditions in which the freedom of the press can be considered a restraint on freedom of speech. Where the media, for example, suppresses information or stifles voices it is not, she says, serving the conditions for freedom of speech which is to permit expression and a diversity of voices. In fact, she argues that the oft-proclaimed freedom of the press is simply a form of property right summed up by the principle 'no money, no voice.'

There are three grounds upon which government regulation to constrain media freedom can be justified as a way to promote freedom of expression (Kelley and Donway, 1995):

1 *Argument from positive rights.* The public has certain rights to receive information and other goods. Where it is not receiving them, Government should intervene to secure these rights.
2 *Argument from democracy.* Government regulation may be necessary to ensure that the media provide the kind of argument and information that makes democracy possible.
3 *Teleological argument.* Freedom of expression is not an end in itself, nor is it a source of values, but rather an instrumental value for achieving higher

values such as truth and justice. Where these goals are not being achieved, intervention may be justified.

In Lichtenberg's view (1995) the freedom of the press should be contingent upon the extent to which it promotes certain core values. In circumstances where the media suppresses diversity and impoverishes public debate, the arguments for the freedom of the press turn against it and regulation becomes an option. This was, in fact, the view of Peru's left-wing military government in the 1970s (Sanders, 1990). The country's main national newspapers were expropriated and re-distributed to designated, marginalized social groups. The measures ended in failure and showed, albeit in extreme circumstances, how government intervention to ensure freedom of expression can all too easily end in state despotism to remove dissent.

Lichtenberg's distinction between freedom of expression and freedom of the press is also made by the philosopher, Onora O'Neil, in the 2002 BBC Reith lectures. In O'Neil's view we may support J.S. Mill's defence of individual freedom of discussion but for that very reason:

> A free press is not an unconditional good. It is good because and insofar as it helps the public to explore and test opinions and to judge for themselves whom and what to believe. If powerful institutions are allowed to publish, circulate and promote material without indicating what is known and what is rumour; what is derived from a reputable source and what is invented, what is standard analysis and what is speculation; which sources may be knowledgeable and which are probably not, they damage our public culture and all our lives. (Lecture 5, 2002)

AVOIDING HARM

Freedom's scope has been thought to stretch to the point where one can cause harm to others. But what does 'harm' mean? Throwing stones at someone can certainly cause physical harm but what kind of harm is caused by racist insults or the depiction of extreme violence? These issues mark the area of controversy in which liberal defenders of an untrammelled right to freedom of expression meet those who argue for a degree of censorship.

Understanding 'harm' is not as straightforward as it seems. Proving causality in human action is extraordinarily difficult. Did the broadcast of sexually explicit images of women turn some men into rapists? Did publication of a racist politician's views inflame racial hatred in Britain? Would unsanitized reporting of war save lives (see Bell, 1998)? If we examine cases where 'harm' is typically invoked as the reason why freedom of expression should be curtailed, we can see the difficulties of the arguments from harm.

National and public security

Most people would accept restrictions on war reporting to prevent information reaching the enemy which would endanger military operations. Reaction to the

Gulf War showed that the public favoured more not less control of journalists (Williams, 1992: 158). And, on the whole, editors and journalists themselves accept that a degree of self-censorship on such matters is sensible in order to safeguard national security. This is the purpose of the D-Notice (Defence Advisory Notices) committee, established in 1912, composed of four civil servants and fourteen senior journalists and responsible for issuing D-notices giving guidance to the media about coverage of ongoing security issues such as terrorism and nuclear arms.

In the build-up to the response to the attacks on the United States on 11 September 2001, the D-Notice committee issued an alert: '. . . we're now reaching the stage where informed speculation by well-connected journalists may actually be close to the truth. We would ask journalists to consider that they may be giving information to those who could use it to inflict harm on British citizens, military or civilian' (cited by Hodgson, 1 October, 2001). It would be hard to quibble with this reminder, and its implicit recognition that freedom of expression is not an absolute right where harm might ensue. However, inherent to the acceptance of this is agreement about the national aims being pursued. Avoiding harm to UK nationals may involve causing harm to Afghan citizens.

More obviously controversial is the use of censorship to shore up support for war either by not revealing setbacks or by sanitizing the conflict.[9] Journalist Philip Knightly, was alarmed at the latter development during the Gulf War in which the aim seemed to be to alter 'public perception of the nature of war itself, to convince everyone that new technology had removed a lot of war's horrors' (2000: 494).

This practice, aided and abetted by many journalists, was taken to new lengths during the NATO bombing campaign of Serbia in spring 1999. BBC correspondent, John Simpson, was attacked by the Labour government for his allegedly pro-Serbian stance. He'd written an article in the *Sunday Telegraph* in which he argued that the bombing didn't seem to be working and that one such attack had been on a column of Albanian refugees. He was sharply criticized in the House of Commons by Tony Blair for giving aid and comfort to the enemy. As Simpson himself wrote, 'it had to happen: when the going gets tough in wartime . . . the first instinct of British governments is to attack the people who are reporting the unpalatable' (2000: 267).

On a number of occasions, the media has found itself engaged in a battle with government about the boundary lines between the public's right to know and having proper regard to national security. In fact, as we've seen in war reporting, most journalists would accept that the 'public's right to know' is not absolute but subject to certain conditions. In particular, it is limited by the extent to which the revelation of something would cause unjust harm to someone else.

The difficulty arises when *failure* to report something would cause unjust harm to someone else and at the same time its publication would prejudice others. Many confrontations between the British media and government have involved cases of this kind. The leaking of secret documents in 1985 by the civil servant, Clive Ponting, revealed the truth about the sinking of the Argentinian ship, General Belgrano (Ponting, 1985). At the same time, it damaged the climate of trust and confidentiality necessary to the workings of government. However, in cases where harm to the national interest cannot be proven, there must be a strong presumption in favour of openness and transparency to safeguard honest and effective government.

Reporting terrorism

The coverage of terrorism is also a particularly difficult area, partly because one of the aims of terrorist activity is to garner publicity though media attention.[10] Terrorist incidents are fashioned in order to meet western media's criteria of newsworthiness (Carruthers, 2000: 170). Terrorists themselves, as Osama bin Laden and his al-Qaida organization showed during the US bombing of Afghanistan, can be consummate manipulators of the media.

In Britain broadcast reporting of 'the Troubles' in Northern Ireland has been the source of most tension between broadcasters and politicians (Miller, 1994). Interviewing IRA or INLA (Irish National Liberation Army) members and their associates,[11] filming terrorist incidents[12] and challenging official accounts caused immense official anger.[13] It culminated in the 1988 Broadcasting Ban prohibiting the direct broadcasting of the representatives of certain Northern Ireland organizations or those seeking support for them. They would be denied, in Mrs Thatcher's words, the 'oxygen of publicity.'

The ban did make broadcasters more cautious but it is questionable whether this was of any help in tackling the roots of the problems in Northern Ireland. As Carruthers puts it, 'bans on media reportage are most unlikely to suffocate terrorism altogether, for this prescription tackles only symptoms, not the underlying malady, and treats terrorism as essentially a problem for journalists, not for politicians' (2000: 190).

FREEDOM, TRUTH AND GOODNESS

Reporting on events which literally raise issues of life and death suggest that it is not freedom of expression as such which is the ultimate value. Where it is used to promote death and destruction, it is hard to defend. As Bok has pointed out: 'Internet sites for terrorism, criminal networks, bomb-making instructions, and violent pornography . . . pose special problems for all societies' (1998: 109). Freedom is a vital human capacity for the good it allows us to achieve in the service of truth. William Howard Russell's reporting of the Crimean War for *The Times* contributed to the improvement of nursing conditions for injured soldiers; George Orwell tried to tell us some of the truth about the Spanish Civil War and American war reporter, Martha Gellhorn, the truth about the civilian casualties of the Vietnam War (Knightley, 2000: 427–8). In all these cases the truth was served.

However, the difficult cases of war and terrorism also show that the fulcrum of all good practice, of all virtuous behaviour, lies in the application of practical wisdom. Virtue ethics cannot provide a decision procedure for what to do in the hard cases where reporting the truth may bring unpredictable consequences, both good and bad. It suggests instead that we need to bring our judgement to bear on the different circumstances with which we are faced.

Freedom and truth are of enormous value but there will be times when a prudent silence will be the course of action taken by the truly virtuous person. I am free to tell you that your entire family has just perished in a car accident. But if you were driving that car and are struggling to overcome your injuries, the kinder, better way is to break the news to you gently and gradually. Similarly, the details of bomb-making can be found on the Internet but it hardly seems a wise exercise of freedom to put them there.

UNDERMINING HUMAN DIGNITY

Some kinds of communication may be considered unwise because of the disproportionate harm they might cause. Others may be considered intrinsically contrary to respect for our fellow human beings. This perspective is founded on an understanding of humans as being more than the sum of either the colour of their skin, their gender, their body, sexuality, ethnic group or religion. From this viewpoint, certain kinds of coverage might be considered unhelpful, not necessarily because of any harm they might cause, which they may do, but because of the contempt they evince for the worth of other human beings.

Racism, homophobia and sexism

Stigmatizing an entire group of people on the basis of gender differences, ethnicity, sexuality or so-called 'racial' characteristics shows a singular failure in intelligence, a lack of moral wisdom. In Britain there are laws to prevent the worst manifestations of racism and sexism, once again demonstrating that we agree limits should be set to the exercise of freedom. But where do the limits lie?

In the 1980s and early 1990s newspapers like *The Sun* believed it acceptable to use pejorative terms for gay people. It would be unlikely to do so today. Twenty years ago racist jokes about people of Asian origin were acceptable. They wouldn't be now, although Irish jokes still are. Gentle teasing is distinct from outright abuse but how do we determine where teasing becomes insult? As *The Mirror* found in its coverage of the German football team during Euro 96, one editor's good-humoured re-run of the Second World War, is thousands of readers' disgust at xenophobic reporting. Again, good judgement is the key. Language and imagery which is demeaning, hostile, makes gratuitous reference to a person's religion, gender, sexuality, race or nationality is almost certainly an error of judgement. Reporters may be *free* to do this but it hardly reflects well on them if they do.

Violating the human being

Images of graphic violence – an execution, the aftermath of a bomb attack, a murder – raise special concerns. Journalists may be free to show or write about these incidents but when are they right to do so?

Similarly, it may be possible to use images or words which depict explicit sexual activity but when, if ever, it is appropriate to do so? The Obscene Publication Acts of 1959 and 1964 lay down that material is considered obscene, if it tends to deprave and corrupt those who encounter it. This sets down the outermost boundaries for the use of sexual material. However, like the debates about violence in the media, it frames the rightness or wrongness of obscenity in the effects it produces and media effects, as I pointed out in Chapter one, are extremely hard to prove.

Broadcast codes of practice, unlike their print counterpart, provide guidance on what is appropriate in matters of 'taste and decency,' as they are coyly termed.

The existence of the 'watershed' – the time (9pm) after which more 'adult' material may be shown – and the requirement to flag up beforehand the use of particularly graphic material, is a sensible acknowledgement of our differing sensitivities and experience. A friend of mine was, as a child, desperately upset by the scene in the Disney film *Bambi* (1942) in which the baby deer's mother was killed by a hunter. That is hardly a reason to ban *Bambi*.

Rather than considering depictions of graphic sex and violence from the point of view of their effects, a more helpful approach may be to consider what story it is we are telling about human beings in such coverage.

The *Sunday Sport* newspaper specializes in pictures of scantily-clad women in provocative poses. The *News of the World* delights in reporting in salacious detail the sexual lives of the famous and the ordinary and continues to be Britain's best-selling Sunday newspaper. What does such coverage say about women? About the reporters who produce it? About we who read it?

It may seem curious to bracket depictions of extreme violence and graphic sex but the link can be found in how both *violate* the intimacy of human beings in ways which undermine our wholeness, our integrity.

Naming of rape victims

In some US states this is legal. If it were legal in Britain, would it be considered right? It might be argued that freedom of expression should permit it. But wouldn't respect for another person's privacy, a privacy already violently invaded, favour restraint and self-censorship?

Giving offence

In May 1997 the England football team manager, Glenn Hoddle, was interviewed by a sports correspondent from *The Times*. In the course of the interview he allegedly said that disabled people were suffering the consequences of their sins in a previous life. Understandably this caused great offence and much of the press – including *The Sun* and *The Times* – and even the prime minister, Tony Blair, said he should resign, which he subsequently did.[14]

The case highlighted the ambiguities surrounding the issue of allowing free speech which gives offence. There seemed to be a certain irony in the fact that it was parts of the media, the champions of freedom of speech, who were outraged by the offence Hoddle's words had caused.

In the week after the attacks on the World Trade Center and the Pentagon, the BBC broadcast a live edition of 'Question Time.' Its anti-American tone deeply offended many viewers and it became the most complained about programme in BBC history. The BBC subsequently apologized (Bailey, 2000).

Blasphemy laws in England and Wales make language which tends to vilify Christianity in a way which is likely to cause resentment a criminal offence. Other religious groups have considered they should be brought within its purview.

Offensive speech is, however, hard to deal with because it depends on differing sensitivities and specific circumstances. Broadcasting passionately expressed critical views of American foreign policy was offensive because thousands of Americans had just been murdered. Mocking someone's religious beliefs may be considered the legitimate expression of different viewpoints by one person, and abusive or hurtful insult by another. Indeed, avoiding offence has probably far more to do with taste, good manners and mutual respect than the establishment of laws and the provision of censorship for speech we find offensive.

BEING FREE AND RESPONSIBLE

The notion of freedom raises the issue of responsibility, attending to the consequences of our actions. Freedom is a key value. But so is responsibility. I'm free to shout 'Fire' in a crowded night-club, cause panic and a riot but am I right to do so? This dilemma is well expressed in the following passage:

> The crucial moral characteristic of the human condition is the dual experience of freedom of the will and personal responsibility. Since freedom and responsibility are two aspects of the same phenomenon, they invite comparison with the proverbial knife which cuts both ways. One of its edges implies options: we call it freedom. The other implies obligations: we call it responsibility. People like freedom because it gives them mastery over things and people. They dislike responsibility because it constrains them from satisfying their wants. That is why one of the things that characterizes history is the unceasing human effort to maximize freedom and minimize responsibility. But to no avail, for each real increase in human freedom . . . brings with it a proportionate increase in responsibility. Each exhilaration with the power to do good is soon eclipsed by the guilt of having used it to do evil. (Thomas Szasz cited in Johannesen, 1990: xiii)

There are no easy answers to freedom's scope. But if we ask ourselves in controversial cases 'why am I doing this?' 'What do I seek to achieve?' 'What kind of human being do I want to be?', we may gain some clues as to how we should act. If we accept that we are, to a certain extent, free, we can accept too that we can be responsible.

NOTES

1 On the other hand, if she says she couldn't have done otherwise but save the child (she only acted as anyone else would have done in the circumstances), we may say that this is because she *is* courageous. In other words, courageous acts will come more easily to the person who habitually seeks to endure difficulty without complaint or overcome fear for the good of someone else; in other words, for someone who has acquired the virtue of fortitude.

2 As I write in the summer of 2001, opposition journalists in Zimbabwe continue to be subjected to a reign of terror by Robert Mugabe's governing party and the reporter, Martin O'Hagan, has been shot dead in Northern Ireland. In 2000 thirty-two journalists were murdered across the world (Castelló, 2001).

3 Evolutionary psychologists suggest that we are gene machines whose actions are determined by the innate biological imperative to perpetuate our genetic code. Apparently altruistic acts are genetically driven; 'love', 'generosity' are biological strategies. These explanations have a specious plausibility. They 'explain' everything and yet understand nothing, like the drawing used by psychologists which can be seen as a rabbit or as a duck depending under what aspect I look at it.

4 The British journalists, Brian Keenan and John McCartney, held captive in Lebanon for three years in the 1980s, sustained each other by sharing their dreams for the future. See Keenan's *An Evil Cradling* (1992). More extreme circumstances, however, can undoubtedly break the human spirit. See, for example, the account of the release from the dreadful conditions of captivity of an ETA kidnap victim in Pilar Urbano's *Garzón* (2000).

5 The English nation, Milton writes, is of a particularly 'quick, ingenious and piercing spirit' and 'Why else was this Nation chosen before any other, that out of her, as out of Sion, should be proclaimed and sounded forth the first tidings and trumpet of Reformation to all Europe?' He sees his turbulent times as a moment where 'God is decreeing to begin some new and great period in his Church, even to the reforming of Reformation itself: what does He then but reveal Himself to His servants, and as His manner is, first to His Englishmen' (1946: 32).

6 These accounts can give the impression that the development of freedom of expression was a purely Anglo-American project. It is true that for cultural and historical reasons Britain and the United States have founded their national identities in part on the sense of the distinctive place of freedom in their national traditions as compared to other countries ('Britons never, never, never shall be slaves'; 'America, land of the free') and our common law tradition appears to have been a better protection of personal liberties than its continental Roman law equivalent. However, the notion of freedom has also been central to other national traditions (the people of Aragon, for example and the Poles). It is interesting that in recent years British journalists have had to look to the Roman law tradition enshrined in the European Convention of Human Rights to protect freedom of expression.

7 Associations such as the Campaign for Press and Broadcasting Freedom have fought for many years for more official transparency and the introduction of legal rights to freedom of information. The 1999 Act was considered a step in the right direction but disappointed those who'd hoped that the Labour government would favour a more open, American-style regime.

8 In 1972 the *Sunday Times* began a campaign to bring to light the plight of children affected by the thalidomide drug. About 450 children were born in 1961 with serious

deformities after their mothers had been prescribed the thalidomide sleeping pill during pregnancy. Most had received no compensation from the manufacturers, Distillers who, it was later revealed, had known of the drug's risks and concealed the knowledge from the public. In the course of their investigation, the *Sunday Times* changed the laws of England and won compensation for the families affected, despite pressure from Distillers – the paper's biggest advertiser – who withdrew all advertizing after the campaign began. The law on contempt of court prevented the *Sunday Times* publishing vital information about the case. After taking the case to the Law Lords, they decided to go to the European Court of Human Rights. The Court found that the injunction on the *Sunday Times* not to publish was in breach of Article 10 of the European Convention of Human Rights, although the judgement was termed in a way to emphasize not so much 'the right of the press to publish' as 'the right of an individual to information which may affect his life, liberty and happiness'. (Evans, 1994: 83).

9 Reporters covering the Falklands War were told to omit the phrase 'horribly burned' (Harris, 1983: 60)

10 'Terrorism' is, of course, a contested term. In Spain ETA members are referred to as 'terrorists' and in the UK – to Spaniards' incredulity – the BBC refers to them as 'Basque separatists'. Terrorism involves violent and unpredictable acts against citizens who do not consider themselves engaged in war (see Carruthers, 2000: 163–6).

11 The most controversial examples were the interview with INLA representatives in 1979, after the assassination of Conservative Northern Ireland spokesman Airey Neave MP and the making of the BBC's 1985 documentary 'At the Edge of the Union' in the *Real Lives* series.

12 The filming of an IRA roadblock in the village of Carrickmore provoked government outrage.

13 Thames Television's 'Death on the Rock' in the *This Week* series investigated the killing of three unarmed IRA members in Gibraltar by the Special Air Service. It suggested that the government was operating a shoot-to-kill policy. See Bolton (1990) for an insider's account of this and the other controversies mentioned above.

14 See Kieran (1997) for a useful consideration of the issue of offence and also the application of the harm principle.

Sometimes, like Greta Garbo, we want to be alone; sometimes, like Mae West, we do not.

Lord Chancellor's Department and the Scottish Office, *Infringement of Privacy*, 1993.

We live in a society in which many people depend on publicity to make a living. Politicians, television 'celebrities', pop stars and sports personalities can't do without it. In the words of one British editor, Princess Diana would have 'withered on the vine' without the attentions of the press. But together with this cult of celebrity there is also a concern about invasions of privacy. In the 1980s and 1990s, it was the single biggest reason for criticism of British journalists' behaviour by politicians. Privacy is probably the greyest moral area for journalists and unwanted publicity perhaps one of the greatest causes of suffering to ordinary people. Public reaction to invasions of privacy reveals us at our most hypocritical: as coverage of the British Royal Family shows, we condemn the messengers while devouring the message.

Controversies about privacy have been important in shaping the self-regulatory environment in which the British press operates. The subject has also raised issues which, accentuated by developments in the Internet and broadcast media, are paradigmatic of a whole host of ethical concerns which also shade into legal questions. Where is the dividing line between the right to freedom of information and that of privacy? How can these rights be best protected in the age of the Internet? What are the limits editors and reporters should apply to their own reporting activities? When can they justify overstepping these limits? What are the attitudes and habits needed to make sure they get it right?

WHAT IS PRIVACY?

The notion of privacy has changed across time and cultures. If we think about it in its most straightforward sense as one's physical space, we need only compare a conversation between Italians and another between Finns to see how this can differ from culture to culture. What for one is normal, friendly behaviour, for the other is uncomfortable intimacy and invasion of personal space. Again, the presence of courtiers at Louis XIV's toilet and undressing in seventeenth century France is unimaginable at the twenty first century court of Elizabeth II. The exact limits of what we mean by privacy change.

The notion of privacy only arises in contraposition to the notion of the public. In the ancient world privacy was, as Hannah Arendt put it, 'the other, the dark and hidden side of the public realm, and while to be political meant to obtain the highest possibility of human existence, to have no private place of one's own (like a slave) meant to be no longer human' (1958: 64). To be purely private, however, was not to reach the fullness of human existence. The Greek term for a purely private person – *idiotes* – reflects their ambivalence about the private: not to be part of public life was also to be an ignorant, awkward person, an idiot. The Latin *privatus*, to be withdrawn from public life, is linked to *privare*, to bereave and deprive. In the Marxist view privacy ceases to exist altogether: the withering of the State establishes a utopian world where the private is public.

Despite the shifting boundaries and status of the private, the existence of a personal sphere over which we have control is a constant need and feature of human existence. The most momentous events in human life – birth, death, sexual intimacy – are normally shielded from view. In this sense, privacy is linked to the notion of secrecy, something which is *secretum* 'hidden, set apart', akin to the concept of the sacred. However, as Bok has pointed out, there is a crucial difference between secrecy and privacy. A secret is something kept intentionally hidden while privacy is the 'condition of being protected from unwanted access by others' (1982: 10). Secrecy can be a form of privacy but that which is private is not always secret. Privacy, rather, relates to concepts such as identity, autonomy and dignity. It is defined in the Oxford English Dictionary (1989) as 'The state or condition of being withdrawn from the society of others, or from public interest; seclusion.' And as 'The state or condition of being alone, undisturbed, or free from public attention, as a matter of choice or right; freedom from interference or intrusion.'

We can consider privacy to consist of the spaces around which we construct boundaries and to which we seek to control access; these boundaries can circumscribe thoughts, actions, property, objects, names and words. Privacy allows us to ensure that the experience of everyday life is not offered to the public gaze.

As Belsey points out (1992), privacy should not be understood in an entirely individualistic way; although always pertaining to the person (we wouldn't speak, for example, of a bank's privacy), it is also shared with others, with friends and family. Belsey describes three types of privacy (1992; 83):

1 Physical privacy: a body space in which we can function free from physical intrusions.
2 Mental or communicational privacy: the space which allows a person to be alone with thoughts and feelings; to record and communicate them to those they wish, free from eavesdropping or other forms of intrusion.
3 Informational privacy: the protection of personal information such as medical records, financial data etc.

Archard prefers a narrower understanding of privacy where 'privacy has to do with keeping personal information non-public or undisclosed. Personal information is that set of facts about oneself a person does not wish to see disclosed or made public' (1998: 83). An invasion of privacy can only occur when personal information is made public. Thus, if someone steals letters I've written to my dearest friend yet doesn't make the information public, there has been no violation of my privacy. Archard's account does not assume a right to privacy, only that we have a strong interest in preserving it for ourselves. However, the notion that because an unwanted intrusion into our privacy is 'unexploited' it is not a violation of my privacy, seems to underestimate the significance of privacy in human life. George Orwell's *1984* vividly shows how the knowledge that we are being constantly observed and exposed to the gaze of others erodes our ability to function as moral beings. This recognition, and that of the threat posed by totalitarian states, saw the incorporation of the right to privacy in the United Nations Declaration of Human Rights in 1948 and to the European Convention on Human Rights (see Box 7.1).

BOX 7.1 Rights to privacy

Article 12 of the Universal Declaration of Human Rights 1948

No one shall be subjected to arbitrary interference with his privacy, family, home or correspondence, nor to attacks upon his honour and reputation. Everyone has the right to the protection of the law against such interference or attacks.

Article 8 of the European Convention on Human Rights 1950

1 Everyone has the right to respect for his private and family life, his home and his correspondence.
2 There shall be no interference by a public authority with the exercise of this right except such as in accordance with law and is necessary in a democratic society in the interests of national security, public safety or the economic well-being of the country, for the prevention of disorder or crime, for the protection of health or morals, or for the protection of the rights and freedoms of others.

Privacy can be considered a good. It is, in the words of the Younger Report on Privacy (1972: 113), 'a basic need, essential to the development and maintenance of a free society and of a mature and stable personality.' However, its contours are imprecise and there are countervailing goods – freedom of information or the revelation of corruption – which might outweigh the value of preserving privacy.

We also live in curiously voyeuristic times where the value of privacy, discretion and the keeping of confidences is undermined by the exhibitionism exemplified by *Big Brother* and the *Jerry Springer Show*. We connive in the conversion of human life into spectacle. The three-dimensional complexity of human beings is flattened out into television or newspaper images, their intimate lives spread out before us, the victims complicit in their own destruction. Princess Diana's television 'confession' of adultery on 20 November 1995 in the BBC *Panorama* programme was watched by over 21 million people in Britain and millions more across the world. It was a haunting example of intimate self-betrayal and our prurient appetite for the private. When privacy is so easily surrendered, it becomes difficult to recognize its value. And yet without it, relationships would lose depth and substance and the spiritual and emotional intimacies which enrich our life would vanish.

PROTECTING PRIVACY

The understanding that privacy is a good has meant that a number of countries recognize a legal right to privacy. In the *Harvard Law Review* in 1890 two American scholars, Samuel Warren and Louis Brandeis, argued for a separate legal right to privacy. Their arguments paved the way for statutory protection of privacy across much of the United States. The situation is similar in Canada. France, Spain and Germany also have privacy legislation.

Debating privacy

In Britain the debate about protection of privacy has been a kind of weather-vane of wider social and political attitudes to the media. It has also been crucial, as I mentioned earlier, in influencing the self-regulatory framework in which the press operates.

Up until 1998, English law provided no general protection against the disclosure of personal information in the form of a right of privacy. This was famously shown in 1990 when the actor, Gordon Kaye, was 'interviewed' in a semi-conscious state by *Sunday Sport* reporters. He sought an injunction preventing publication but the Court of Appeal found that there was no right of privacy recognized by common law.[1] The possibility of framing such a right had been debated by the Younger Committee on Privacy in 1972.[2] They concluded that existing safeguards and the difficulties in defining privacy made such a law unnecessary (see Box 7.2). Nevertheless, in 1987 and 1988 attempts were made to introduce legislation through private members' bills by Conservative MPs, William Cash and John Browne, reflecting the growing public and political unease about tabloid practices. Indeed print media was the source of most concern, given that the broadcast media was and is strictly regulated by various statutory bodies.[3]

The growing concern also led to a committee of national newspaper editors drawing up the first ever formal (and voluntary) code of practice for the newspaper industry in 1989 and to the government's establishment of an Inquiry into Privacy and Related Matters. Chaired by David Calcutt QC, it was charged to look into the issue of press intrusion and the existence of satisfactory remedies to prevent abuse. In May 1990 the Calcutt Comittee published its report which, *inter alia*, recommended an improved system of self-regulation to replace the largely ineffectual Press Council. The Calcutt Report concluded that if the new body failed to provide adequate protection for privacy, the government should introduce statutory regulation of the press. Government minister, David Mellor, described the press as 'drinking in the Last Chance Saloon'.[4]

BOX 7.2 Legal remedies to protect aspects of privacy

- **Seclusion** can be protected by *torts of trespass to land and nuisance*. However, it would not be possible to take action against a person who stands in the public highway to take intimate photographs. The *1997 Harrassment Act* provides a civil and criminal offence against stalking and harrassment.
- **Personal information** The *law of breach of confidence* can prevent publication of information given in confidence. It was used by Princess Diana in 1993 after photographs of her exercising in a gym were published in the *Sunday Mirror*. It was also used by the Blair family in 2000 to prevent their nanny from publishing details about their family life in the *Daily Mail*. It differs from a privacy right because it depends upon the imposition of an obligation of confidence. This law might be used against the 'kiss and tell' kind of story beloved of some of the tabloids but it would be of no use against the publication of a photograph of a grieving relative at the site of an accident. The *1998 Data Protection Act* governs any computer or manually stored information about an individual so that strict conditions must be satisfied for its lawful use. Reporters are exempted from some of its provisions in certain conditions.
- **Private life.** Laws concerning *defamation*, *malicious falsehood* and *libel* permit an individual to protect their reputation and honour. The *1998 Human Rights Act* incorporated articles of the European Convention on Human Rights, including Article 8 protecting privacy.
- **The vulnerable.** Various laws admit anonymity for victims of sexual assault (*Sexual Offences (Amendment) Acts 1988 and 1992*). The *Rehabilitation of Offenders Act 1974* prevents revelation of a criminal past after a certain period of time has elapsed. The *Children Act 1989* prevents identification of children below the age of 18 in certain circumstances.

Privacy and self-regulation

The Press Complaints Commission (PCC) was established by the newspaper industry in 1991. All national editors signed up to a code of practice incorporating principles of ethical journalism (see Appendix 1); funding for the new body was provided by the industry itself. Two years later Sir David Calcutt issued his *Review of Press Self-Regulation*. The spate of controversial privacy cases and the palpable failings of the PCC had left Calcutt unimpressed.[5] He considered self-regulation to have failed and recommended the introduction of a statutory complaints tribunal and a new civil wrong or tort for the infringement of privacy, taking note of the widespread recognition that the protection provided by the law to tackle alleged breaches of privacy was both fragmented and incomplete.

Despite support from the National Heritage Select Committee, the Lord Chancellor's Department and the Scottish Office, the proposals were rejected by

John Major's government in its 1995 response, *Privacy and Media Intrusion*.[6] The press industry had fought a successful rearguard action in the intervening two years (Shannon, 2001).

Lord Wakeham was appointed as a tough new chairman of the PCC in 1995 and a Privacy Commissioner was appointed in 1994 with powers to initiate investigations and also to examine urgent complaints about breaches of privacy under the code. Newspaper editors were told that they were 'duty bound' to publish adjudications with due prominence and that disciplinary action could be taken against reporters who breached a revised code of practice. The PCC was re-constituted with a non-press majority. In 1997 the PCC extended its jurisdiction to publications on the Internet whose publishers already subscribe to the code of practice.

The light touch of self-regulation had triumphed over the heavy hand of legislation as the guiding principle for encouraging ethical press behaviour. It was soon to be sorely tested by an entirely unexpected event.

DEATH IN PARIS

When Tony Blair came to power in May 1997 he declared that he had no intention of introducing a law on privacy. His government did, however, plan to introduce legislation governing freedom of information and to incorporate the European Convention on Human Rights (ECHR), including rights to privacy and freedom of expression, into English law.

Three months later Princess Diana died when the car she was travelling in with her companion Dodi al-Fayed careered out of control as it sped away from a posse of pursuing paparazzi. The public reaction was overwhelming. The media was blamed for its relentless pursuit of the Princess and her brother, Earl Spencer, agreed. Some parts of the press, he said, 'have blood on their hands'. The irony of the public reaction was not lost on the satirical magazine, *Private Eye*: its front-page showed the headline 'MEDIA TO BLAME' emblazoned across a photograph of grieving crowds outside Buckingham Palace with three speech bubbles. The first said, 'The papers are a disgrace', followed by 'Yes. I couldn't get one anywhere' and finally, 'Borrow mine. It's got a picture of the car' (2 September, 1997).

A fierce debate broke out among editors about the need for a privacy law. *The Guardian*'s Alan Rusbridger argued in favour as long as a countervailing freedom of information act was introduced and the law on libel changed. Breaking ranks with the tabloid press, he wrote: 'I think it's a mistake for liberal journalists to get sucked into supporting a Murdoch tabloid agenda' (8 February, 1998). Media arguments against a legal right to privacy maintained that: a) those who want a privacy law are the rich and powerful; b) British society is already too secretive c) it would be impossible to frame a workable law.[7]

In fact, the arguments about a privacy law were overtaken by the incorporation of the ECHR into English law in 1998. The government reassured the media industry that the new legislation would not introduce a general law on privacy, including in the *Human Rights Act 1998* a clause specifically to protect freedom of expression.[8] Speaking during the passage of the Bill in Parliament, the then Home Secretary, Jack Straw, said:

> The Government have always made clear our support for effective self-regulation as administered by the Press Complaints Commission under its Code of Practice. We have also said we have no plans to introduce legislation creating a general law of privacy. . . . On self regulation, the new Clause provides an important safeguard by emphasizing the right to freedom of expression. Our intention is that that should underline the consequent need to preserve self-regulation. That effect is reinforced by highlighting in the amendment the significance of any relevant privacy code, which clearly includes the Code operated by the PCC. (Hansard, 2 July, 1998)

Once again the principle of self-regulation was reinforced, although the longer-term impact of the *Human Rights Act* is more difficult to predict. In its judgement in December 2000 concerning an order by film actors, Michael Douglas and Catherine Zeta-Jones, to restrain *Hello!* magazine from publishing photographs of their wedding, the Court of Appeal recognized a right of privacy in English law. Lord Justice Sedley declared (2001):

> What a concept of privacy does . . . is accord recognition to the fact that the law has to protect not only those people whose trust has been abused but those who simply find themselves subjected to an unwanted intrusion into their personal lives. The law . . . can recognize privacy itself as a legal principle drawn from the fundamental value of personal autonomy. (www.wood.ccta.go.uk/courtser/judgements/nsl)

However, subsequent judgements in early 2002 showed that judges were far from keen to establish a privacy law through the back-door. In March 2002 super-model, Naomi Campbell, won £3,500 in damages against the *Mirror* newspaper for breach of confidence after the paper revealed details of her treatment for drug addiction. Two weeks previously the Court of Appeal rejected the privacy claims of a footballer, Gary Flitcroft, who had sought to prevent the *Sunday People* from identifying him in a kiss-and-tell story. In the view of media lawyer, Dan Tench, both cases showed that 'the risk of an onerous new privacy law appears to be receding' (1 April, 2002). If Tench's assessment is correct, effective self-regulation will continue to be the principal guardian of privacy rights in Britain. This is why it was important that lessons be learnt about privacy from the circumstances surrounding Princess Diana's life and death. Her death focused special attention on the tabloid press. Their response was to support the PCC's proposals for more stringent requirements to protect privacy. In November 1997 substantial changes were agreed to the Code of Practice. The main changes were:

- The recognition that everyone is entitled to respect for privacy; stipulations prohibiting the taking of photographs on 'private property' were expanded to include 'private places', understood as areas where one has a reasonable expectation of privacy.

- To deal with the problem of harassment, pictures taken as a result of 'persistent pursuit' were banned and editors forbidden to publish material from freelances that did not meet the code's standards.
- More protection for children was stipulated, including the removal of the sixteen year age limit, protecting them from 'unnecessary' intrusion (see Box 7.3). A ban on payments was included, except in the child's interests, and a clause added protecting the children of those in the public eye.
- Sensitivity in publishing stories at times of grief and shock was stipulated.
- The public interest clause was strengthened to protect children so that an 'exceptional public interest' justification must be shown in reporting on children.
- A clause was added to the stipulations on accuracy to rule out the use of inaccurate, misleading or distorted photographs.

BOX 7.3   PCC Code Clause 6 Children

i   Young people should be free to complete their time at school without unnecessary intrusion.

ii   Journalists must not interview or photograph a child under the age of 16 on subjects involving the welfare of the child or any other child in the absence of or without the consent of a parent or other adult who is responsible for the children.

iii   Pupils must not be approached or photographed while at school without the permission of the school authorities.

iv   There must be no payment to minors for material involving the welfare of children nor payments to parents or guardians for material about their children or wards unless it is demonstrably in the child's interest.

v   Where material about the private life of a child is published, there must be justification for publication other than the fame, notoriety or position of his or her parents or guardian.

PCC Code Clause 7 Children in sex cases

1   The press must not, even where the law does not prohibit it, identify children under the age of 16 who are involved in cases concerning sexual offences, whether as victims or as witnesses.

2   In any press report of a case involving a sexual offence against a child
   i   The child must not be identified.
   ii   The adult may be identified.
   iii   The word 'incest' must not be used where a child victim might be identified.
   iv   Care must be taken that nothing in the report implies the relationship between the accused and the child.

These changes reflected the PCC's concern to protect the Princess's young sons, who would inevitably become the renewed target of tabloid interest.[9] However, the editor of the *Daily Telegraph*, Charles Moore, underlined the difficulties in making self-regulation work where there exists a 'philosophy of intrusion'. All the codes in the world would make little difference, if reporters and editors saw no harm in exposing private lives to public view. Even though they might admit privacy to be a good, other considerations would always weigh more heavily in the balance.

MAKING THE PRIVATE PUBLIC

What are the arguments or considerations offered to justify media intrusion into privacy? We should first distinguish between the way in which personal information is obtained and the publication of the information. As Archard says, 'To publish what should be private is one kind of possible wrong; to find out what is private by illicit means is another kind of wrong' (1998: 85). Thus, whether or not publication was right, the covert filming of Princess Diana's gym sessions, the stealing of the lawyer's letter detailing former Liberal Democrat leader, Paddy Ashdown's extramarital affair or the secret taping of Prince Charles' conversations with his lover, Camilla Parker-Bowles, raised questions about justifiable methods of information gathering. It is hard to see any overwhelming good which was served by any of the examples given.

What about justifications for making public that which is in the private domain? Belsey (1992) argues that any intrusion which places information in the public domain which should be there, is not an invasion of privacy. So that, for example, if a newspaper can successfully argue that a certain piece of information should be in the public domain, then to put it there does not intrude upon the person's privacy.

This doesn't seem to get us very far. Even if an editor can convincingly show that information about a politician's private life should be made public, we might agree yet still maintain that his or her privacy has been intruded upon but, in this case, for good reasons. In other words, the realm of the private or the intimate continues to subsist even when we find sound arguments for spotlighting elements of it.

What are these sound arguments? When can an editor justify revelations about private lives? One approach, taken by Belsey (1992) and Kieran (1998), is to argue that privacy attaches to people according to their position. Belsey distinguishes three groups of people who might find the light of publicity cast upon them:

1 politicians/power-wielders
2 celebrities/personalities
3 ordinary people unexpectedly thrust into the public eye.

For the first group, 'the protection of privacy is at best very limited' (Belsey, 1992: 89). All information can be considered fair game. There can be lapses of taste but not invasions of privacy. For this group Belsey argues that private life is relevant and sexual morals especially relevant, particularly if private behaviour exposes hypocrisy. For the second group, consent to revelation of private information is assumed while for the third, Belsey maintains that consent is necessary. Archard (1998) examines three reasons given for intruding on someone's privacy: i) they are a public figure; ii) there is a strong public interest; iii) the public is interested in knowing. I'll look at these arguments next.

PRIVATE LIVES AND PUBLIC FIGURES

It is a commonly expressed view that celebrity and/or public position mean you forfeit entirely or in part the right to privacy. It is hard to make out the argument that all rights to privacy should be lost. Why? Privacy is a necessary good for *all* human beings, however famous and powerful. A less extreme view considers that there is a trade-off between fame and power on the one hand and reduced privacy on the other. This view holds that there is a price to be paid by those who court publicity or wield power. What might the reasons be for this? They are of three kinds:

1 *Self-immolation* Those who seek publicity 'invade' their own privacy. By placing much of their private lives on the record, they cannot complain when the media delves deeper.
2 *Integrity* Those who have power must uphold a certain standard of behaviour. Thus, we are entitled to know if their private behaviour contradicts their public conduct on the grounds that private morals have a bearing on public ones: if you can lie to your wife, you can lie to your country. Furthermore, public servants should be responsible and honourable in discharging their public trust. In order for this to be seen to be so, they have to bear more searching scrutiny of their personal lives than the ordinary citizen.
3 *Hypocrisy* A person who is guilty of private vice and publicly expounds a contradictory set of values should be exposed as a hypocrite. This was the rationale for the press onslaught against Conservative MPs during the Major government. John Major's 'Back to Basics' campaign included a call to traditional values when a number of his MPs were being less than 'traditional' in their private behaviour.

Invading your own privacy

The *self-immolation* argument is often used by reporters and is accepted in part by reporters' own codes of practice. In 1995 the former wife of England rugby player, Will Carling, brought a complaint against *The Sun* for invasion of privacy, inaccuracy and harassment. The PCC declared that in its adjudication it had taken into account the extent to which individuals have already put their lives into the public domain and indeed it was on this basis, not public interest, that the paper had justified its story. In the PCC's view, 'persons who put matters involving their private life into the public domain may not be able to claim the protection of the code when articles are published without their consent, and which seek to comment on, contrast or clarify the impression given by the information provided by the persons concerned.' On these grounds, all of Julia Carling's complaints were rejected. However, the PCC further stated that the placing of certain matters about one's public life in the public domain did not then give reporters *carte blanche* to report on any private matter whatsoever (Report No. 32, 1995).

This justification of the invasion of privacy shows the malleable character of privacy and its reliance on our wish to conserve it. If we simply do not wish to be alone, reporters will make sure we're not. The risk is that those who live by the media will die by it. Politicians, celebrities and members of the Royal Family could well have looked to the example of the Queen Mother. Her last interview before her death in 2002 was in 1922 and yet the patent shunning of publicity did nothing to dent her popularity.

Integrity and hypocrisy

The question of *integrity* is considered key to the trust we invest in public figures. We expect them to uphold standards of behaviour which are consistent in public and private life. The PCC's code indicates that invasions of privacy are acceptable where what is revealed is relevant to performance in public life and it is on this basis that many invasions of politicians' private lives have been justified.

The Guardian's scrutiny of Jonathan Aitken, for example, was prompted by strong suspicions of serious misdemeanours and the disclosure of corrupt behaviour has usually been taken to justify intrusion into a politician's private life. But what about the thorny question of the relationship between private and public morality on a minor scale, particularly in relation to private sexual behaviour? Certainly shoddy private conduct causes unease and disappointment. But should reporters give it publicity? It is not at all clear that duplicitous private conduct translates into public life. To know of a politician's sexual misdemeanours may lower our esteem for them but we cannot deny that they may continue to be a good public servant.

Reporting of politicians' sexual lives usually serves no other purpose than general titillation. In autumn 1998, for example, there was a flurry of press interest in the subject of homosexual politicians. The stories began with reports concerning the Welsh Secretary, Ron Davis. After having being mugged, he rapidly resigned admitting to an error of judgement. This triggered rumours about his sexuality and the eventual news that he was gay. Agriculture Minister, Nick Brown, was subsequently 'outed' on the most spurious 'public interest' grounds, followed by the fortuitous revelation on the BBC's *Newsnight* that Peter Mandelson was gay.

In the cases of Brown and Mandelson there is no question that their privacy was invaded without justification. Brown's homosexuality was known to friends and intimates (although not, it seems, to his aged mother); it was neither secret nor hidden. He had simply not made his sexuality an issue but quite suddenly found it broadcast against his will to the nation. His sexuality was not a crime nor did it encourage others to crime. He himself had not given the impression in public that he was against homosexuality nor did he crusade for gay rights. So why publish the news about him?

Political editor of *The Sun*, Trevor Kavanagh, argued first that his sexuality might have a bearing on his public performance influencing, for example, his vote on the age of consent. And in all likelihood it did. Just as the fact that someone was beaten as a child might affect their view of corporal punishment. It would seem no more than common sense to accept that who we are and what we have experienced affects our public performance. But if we are not engaged in illegal activity, it is hard to see why the public has a *right* to know about these things.

Kavanagh's second argument was that publication helped start a discussion about the possibility of the existence of a 'gay mafia', a network of homosexual politicians who helped their own. It is the kind of dangerous allegation often made about minority groups – Jews, Catholics, Old Etonians – and is almost impossible to prove false. Without hard evidence there appeared to be no justification for a mainstream publication to make such a fuss about what were no more than rumours.

What about the view that invasion of privacy is necessary to uncloak *hypocrisy*? This is not set down in any code of conduct but is very often used as an argument for intrusive journalism (Midgely, 1998). We can first ask whether hypocrisy is defensible? Hypocrisy has been described as the compliment that vice pays virtue: the hypocrite wants to give the impression of virtuous behaviour, and therefore tacitly recognizes its value.

Hypocrisy can, then, have a useful social function even though it is in itself detestable. So how important is it to reveal that someone is a hypocrite? Like many matters, it is surely a matter of degree. Most of us would admit to weakness in certain areas of our lives. Most of us can point to inconsistencies in our behaviour. Very few people are utterly beyond reproach. This should not bar us from continuing to maintain views about what is right and wrong. The fact that I regularly dine out and contribute little to charity, doesn't mean that I can't decry starvation in the world. Of course, the greater the inconsistency between words and deeds, the more blameworthy we are. And there are levels of hypocrisy – campaigning for women's rights and treating your own wife with contempt, for example – which are particularly nauseating. Great hypocrisy shows deep fissures in character and on the grounds that a reliable and trustworthy character is necessary for someone in public life, it is possible to see a justification for invasions of privacy where gross hypocrisy is found.[10]

Private lives and public curiosity

In autumn 1998 the *Mirror* ran a couple of articles on one of the Royal Princes. The first concerned the story that Prince Harry had had his head shaved. The

Mirror published a mocked-up photograph of a skinhead Prince. The other story concerned a rugby accident suffered by Harry. Palace officials complained to the paper and to the PCC about the *Mirror*'s intrusion and asked the *Mirror* for an apology which it refused to give. For the *Mirror* the question was: 'Does the public have a right to be informed about the health of the third in line to the throne?' In fact, the story concerned a sprained wrist.

Given the PCC code's special protection for reporting on children, the *Mirror*'s public interest defence of the public's right to know about a skinhead haircut and a minor injury was far-fetched. In fact, the paper's defence was more along the lines that a haircut and an injury were in the public domain and therefore publishable. Because people could see the haircut and watch Harry play rugby they were no longer private. This understanding of private life would mean that privacy would effectively disappear. This was clearly a case of stories being interesting to the public but certainly not in the public interest.

Again, on April 5, 2000 the *Mirror*'s front-page showed a photograph of Camilla Parker-Bowles in bathing costume headlined 'Camilla as you have NEVER seen her'. Inside, more pictures showed the 'Bathing Belle' and one was captioned 'THE BOTTOM LINE: Riding has given her a firm rear while her long legs are cellulite-free.'

In March 2000 the Blairs obtained an injunction against the *Mail on Sunday* to stop publication of their former nanny's story of her life with them. Tony Blair issued the following statement (7 March):

> As Prime Minister I obviously accept there's a great deal of media interest in me and my family.
> But I'm not just the Prime Minister but also a father and a husband and Cherie and I are absolutely determined, no matter how unusual our own lives may be because of the nature of my job, that our children have as normal an upbringing as possible.
> In this we are asking for no more than any family is entitled to. We cannot allow a situation where the children are fearful that any and every aspect of their lives, past, present and future, is liable to become public.
> We do not seek injunctions lightly and we will do whatever it takes to protect the legitimate privacy of our family life and to protect our children from unwarranted intrusion in their lives.

The *Mail on Sunday*'s headline on 5 March, 2000 was unequivocal: 'GAGGED: BLAIRS BAN NANNY'S STORY'. Tony Blair and his wife successfully prevented publication of details of their family life on the grounds that she had broken a confidentiality agreement. *The Guardian* argued that 'politicians and their families deserve some privacy' and that a freedom of information defence for someone who has broken a confidentiality agreement is rather lame. Even *The Sun* declared in an editorial 'Nobody should have the spotlight shone on everything they do in their own home. This kitchen tittle-tattle had no public interest justification' (6 March, 2000).

None of these stories necessarily placed their subjects in a bad light. They were gossip and were published because they would interest the public. Can this count as a good enough reason for the media to invade privacy? Commercial success certainly makes it a tempting route. Archard also makes a case for the valuable social purposes served by gossip arguing that it unites a community, articulates shared moral values and demystifies the powerful (1998: 91–2). Gossip may indeed serve these purposes; it may be enjoyable. But it is likely that it also does harm.

This is most clearly seen in the reporting of the private lives of ordinary people. People who normally live far away from the limelight can suddenly find themselves catapulted mercilessly into the public glare. Despite the PCC's commitment to 'serve the people and the vulnerable,' the casual cruelty of headlines such as 'VICAR'S WIFE LEAVES HYM FOR HER' (*News of the World*, March 22, 1998), 'CHEATING HEAD KEEPS FIT WITH GYM MISTRESS' (*News of the World*, 28 September, 1997) or, about a reclusive lottery winner, 'RICHEST ANORAK IN BRITAIN' (*News of the World*, 24 May, 1998) are routine occurrences in the tabloid press.[11] The reporting of these stories and the public appetite for them says more, perhaps, about an adolescent kind of morality and our own culture's immaturity in sexual matters, than providing a rationale for the social significance of gossip. Here invading privacy because people are interested is the moral equivalent of stripping someone in public against their will.

Reporting that Camilla is cellulite-free is not a crime. But neither is it harmless for it chips away at a person's autonomy and freedom to be left alone.

PUBLIC INTEREST AND PUBLIC GOOD

The public interest, it has often been said, is not giving people what they are interested in.[12] The editor's view that reporters should give people what they want is not a serious argument. Psychopaths want to kill and sadists torture and if we live in a voyeuristic society where there is, as Libby Purves put it, 'an unwholesome taste for peering at distant people instead of having human relationships with close ones' (7 March, 2000), this is not a reason for pandering to that appetite.

Most reporters and editors accept that invasions of privacy have to have a sufficient justification which is not simply that of curiosity or prurience. This justification has been formulated in terms of the 'public interest', understood in the narrow sense of exposing crime, preventing risks to health and safety and ensuring people are not misled by individuals or institutions. The broadcast industry's formulation of 'public interest' is less precise but broadly covers the same ground.

Undoubtedly the notion of public interest serves a useful normative role: it is the yardstick by which editors, publishers and broadcasters determine the boundaries of ethical behaviour. However, it is also unclear and abstract. McQuail has written about its 'elasticity' (1993: 25).

The notion would repay closer scrutiny and perhaps recasting in the form of public or common good rather than that of 'interest' which smacks of economism. Invading privacy for the public good expresses the truth that justice sometimes requires a private good to be subordinated to a public one.[13] Publishing private correspondence is justified when that is the only way to prove widespread government corruption. Privacy is precious but if we use it to shield actions which undermine the common good, then the purpose of privacy itself – to allow the human being to flourish – is not served. But the reverse is also true. The careless invasion of privacy – publishing names and addresses or details which permit the jigsaw identification of child victims of sexual crimes (expressly forbidden by the PCC code; see Box 7.3 and Note 11) – simply undermines journalists' claims to be truly serving the people.

NOTES

1 Lord Justice Bingham expressed his outrage at 'the monstrous invasion of his [Kaye's] privacy' but was powerless to act for 'it alone, however gross, does not entitle him to relief under English law'. Kaye v. Robertson (1990), Appendix 1 to the *Calcutt Report* (1990).

2 Debates about a privacy law began in the early 1960s. The first Private Member's Bill on the subject was introduced by Lord Mancroft in 1961. See the consultative document published by the Lord Chancellor's Department and the Scottish Office (1993) for further background.

3 At the time of writing, the independent broadcast industry is regulated by the Independent Television Commission (ITC), the Broadcasting Standards Commission (BSC), the Office of Telecommunications (OFTEL), the Radio Authority and the Radiocommunications Agency. The BBC is regulated by the BBC's Charter administered by the Board of Governors. All these bodies have strict guidelines about invasions of privacy. The 1996 Broadcasting Act lays down the functions of the Broadcasting Complaints Commission (BSC). Most of these bodies will be superseded by 2003. The 2000 Communication White Paper proposed the introduction by 2003 of a unitary regulatory body, the Office of Communications (OFCOM), to replace the plethora of institutions which currently exists. OFCOM was established by the Office of Communications Act in March 2002 and its functions set out in the draft Communications Bill. Lord Currie of Marylebone and Dean of Sir John Cass Business School in London was appointed chairman of the new, 'light touch' regulator, which was expected to become fully operational in 2003.

4 The first Calcutt report (1990) also concluded that existing remedies for the protection of privacy were insufficient and that a new set of criminal law offences should be created.

5 The early 1990s were dominated by Royal and political scandal stories. The PCC was accused of being slow at dealing with complaints and insufficiently independent of the industry. It was (and is) funded by the press, its membership was decided by the press and more than half of its members were industry figures.

6 The Lord Chancellor's Department and the Scottish Office published a joint consultation paper in July 1993 entitled *Infringement of Privacy*. On 16 March 1993 the National Heritage Select Committee published its Fourth Report on the subject.

7 The claim about the insurmountable difficulty of framing a workable law was rejected by the Lord Chancellor's Department and the Scottish Office's joint consultation paper (1993). The claim smacks of special pleading, especially when it is considered that the US, France, Germany and Denmark have privacy laws. Indeed, the argument that privacy is too vague a concept, doesn't stop editors advocating the equally difficult concept of freedom of information. It is sometimes alleged that privacy legislation would stymie investigative reporting; France is usually the example given. Again, the evidence for this is slender. There have been no shortage of corruption stories uncovered by French

reporters and the fact that the French press does not publish details about politicians sexual lives may have more to do with cultural norms than legal constraints.

8 See Rasaiah (1998) for a lucid discussion of the newspaper industry's concerns about the impact on press freedom of the 1998 Human Rights Act and the 1998 Data Protection Act.

9 The press had agreed to respect Prince Williams' privacy when he began school at Eton. In a speech on 9 September 1997, Lord Wakeham congratulated the press on its behaviour and asked that they continue to respect the boys' privacy (see PCC *Annual Review* 1997).

10 It may also be argued that it is preferable that the press be overly critical rather than unduly deferential, even if they sometimes get it badly wrong. As the French nineteenth century statesman, Thiers said: 'It is terrible, but for my part, I would rather be governed by honest men who are treated as though they were thieves, than by thieves who are treated as though they were honest men'. Cited in Ogden Rollo (1918: 7).

11 It is notable that while every complaint by the Palace regarding an alleged invasion of privacy has been upheld, this is far from being the case for ordinary people. Lord Wakeham was keen to emphasize the PCC's commitment to protecting all citizens after the Blair case. In a published statement he said (*Times*, 7 March, 2000): 'It has always been my belief that the protection of vulnerable groups of people – such as hospital patients, victims of sexual assault and innocent relatives of people convicted of crime – is at the heart of newspaper self-regulation. On this subject our code (which is the toughest in Europe) has a great deal to say, with by far its most stringent terms relating to children. One provision relates to a mercifully small group – those involved in sex cases. This has been extremely successful in largely eradicating the problem of jigsaw identification, an admirable example of something a voluntary code can achieve that the law failed to do. These rules provide a level of protection for all children which could never be guaranteed by statute. And they are rules which work day in, day out to stop intrusive stories, unauthorized photographs and children being disturbed at school. And school is crucial: the way in which the press have respected the privacy of Prince William at Eton is just one very visible example of the way in which they treat all children – leaving them alone until they are old enough to take responsibility for themselves. (. . .). The code works well to protect all children – regardless of their parents' means or influence. A privacy law, requiring bottomless pockets to use, would undo all that, arguably providing protection only for the super-rich. Some papers might be tempted to do something they could never get away with now – intrude into the privacy of ordinary children, safe in the knowledge that they would never be pursued in the courts.'

12 This was clearly stated in the PCC's first report (1991) in its adjudication against the *News of the World*'s reporting of the private life of Claire Short MP. Her complaint that the paper had intruded into her private life without this being justified in the public interest was upheld and the PCC declared, 'The "public interest" is not whatever happens to interest the public.'

13 This is not a utilitarian argument but an argument about hierarchies of good.

The bloody massacre in Bangladesh quickly covered over the memory of the Russian invasion of Czechoslovakia, the assassination of Allende drowned out the groans of Bangladesh, the war in the Sinai Desert made people forget Allende, the Cambodian massacre made people forget Sinai and so on and so forth, until ultimately everyone lets everything be forgotten.

Milan Kundera, *The Book of Laughter and Forgetting*

We discovered that the camera was never a filter through which we were protected from the worst of what we witnessed. Quite the opposite. The images were burnt on our minds as well as our films.

Greg Marinovich, photographer

Reporting tragedies is necessarily intrusive. However, Dunblane was different. As one journalist said, it was the 'first tragedy . . . in which the usual black jokes which act as a kind of safety valve . . . were suspended' (Linklater cited in IPI (International Press Institute) report, 1996: 27). On 13 March 1996 a gunman had walked into the primary school in the Scottish town of Dunblane and shot dead sixteen small children and their teacher. He then shot himself.

On the first day, the reporters didn't approach the bereaved parents. On the second day they did, with the exception of Scotland's *Sun* which forbade its reporters from doing so. As the week wore on, standards slipped. A woman was rung at two in the morning by a reporter checking a lead in a rival paper; long-lens cameras were used to take photographs of grieving relatives; there were some angry scenes between locals and journalists. In the end, the broadcasters pulled out from coverage of the funerals. The BBC asked itself later whether it had been the right decision? 'Some of the American broadcasters were amazed that we could pull out before the most heart-rending pictures had even been put on tape, let alone broadcast' (Unsworth cited in IPI report, 1996: 20). A journalist for Independent Television News (ITN) said: 'The joint decision to leave Dunblane physically and not cover the funerals was without precedent. . . . A policy of withdrawing from news because the participants in a situation may be upset by our presence makes me very uneasy' (Thomson cited in IPI report, 1996: 23). It is not a criteria usually applied. British broadcast organizations have always shown Northern Ireland funerals, often against the wishes of the bereaved families.

ITN's Richard Tait drew three lessons from the Dunblane coverage: i) Assign experienced reporters to this kind of story; ii) The priority must be to inform; you can't create a make-believe world in which people don't cry; iii) Listen to the community you're working in (see IPI report, 1996: 33). Another ITN journalist drew a more sceptical conclusion. She said:

> Four days later, more than a hundred young people died in a fire in the Philippines. The news programmes here showed not only the inside of the burnt out disco, but relatives weeping outside the hospitals . . . no-one complained [there were 150 complaints about the ITN's shots of grieving Dunblane relatives]. It seems that showing grief on television is OK, so long as the grieving people live far away. (Burns cited in IPI report, 1996: 4)

Reporting suffering is fraught with difficulties. Journalists must deal with it daily: accidents, deaths, suicides, murders, war. They have to speak to bereaved parents, parents whose children have been murdered, died in an accident or a terrorist bomb. They also have to witness suffering: a child dying from starvation or, the carnage in the wake of the NATO attack on a civilian convoy. Reporters must speak and write about, film or photograph these events.

How should journalists report suffering? Is it true that 'watching and reading about suffering . . . has become a form of entertainment' (Moeller, 1999: 34)? Do the reporter's professional ideals of independence and detachment exclude the possibility of compassion in reporting? 'Everyone knows that good reporters are hard', says Randall, 'Cynical, cold, calculating and maybe even a little cruel. The sort of people who can look a corpse in the eye – and smile' (2000: 122). He tells a story about one man with such a reputation, Ben Hecht, reporter with the *Chicago Daily News*. One day he was sitting in court reporting on the trial of a man who had murdered his entire family. As the judge sentenced him to death, the man sprang forward and plunged a butcher's knife into the judge's heart. All the reporters including Hecht froze, except one man from the rival paper who carried on scribbling. Hecht recounted later what happened:

> None of us in the courtroom had the presence of mind to write a single word, paralysed as we were by the attack. Yet here was this guy from the *Inter-Ocean*, who had nerves of steel, who had never paused in doing his job. I just had to find out what he had written. Hecht ran after the copyboy, caught him by the arm, and grabbed the pages. On them, written over and over again in a shaky hand, were the words: 'The judge has been stabbed, the judge has been stabbed. . .' (cited in Randall, 2000: 122)

Being a good reporter is not being emptied of humanity.

SUFFERING, COMPASSION AND PITY

The experience of suffering and pain is intimate, personal. It is something that we cannot communicate. As Arendt says, 'great bodily pain, is at the same time the most private and least communicable of all [experience]' (1958: 50–1). Suffering is a further refinement of pain, known by beings who are aware of what they experience. Babies may cry in pain but their suffering is less than that experienced by adults. Knowledge, memory and anticipation of pain all contribute to the experience of suffering.

Our reaction to suffering is often to feel a kind of embarrassment: we want to comfort or turn away. To stand and stare, to expose the person who suffers to the public gaze, is refined cruelty. The Romans realized this: they reserved crucifixion as a form of execution for non-Romans; the exposure of the dying criminal to the gaze of others was considered particularly humiliating.

In the best of people suffering will prompt feelings of pity, mercy or compassion. The word 'pity' in English, has become associated with condescension. Someone who pities does not suffer. Compassion, on the other hand, is directed to specific suffering human beings. It is defined by the Oxford English Dictionary as 'the feeling or emotion, when a person is moved by the suffering or distress of another, and by the desire to relieve it; pity that inclines one to spare or to succour.' Aquinas uses the term *misericordia* (literally to have a 'merciful heart') to name the virtue which is the capacity for grief and sorrow at another's distress that moves us to supply what they need. It is not simply the feeling of sorrow. As MacIntyre explains, 'Sentiment, unguided by reason, becomes sentimentality and sentimentality is a sign of moral failure' (1999: 124).

The archetypal display of *misericordia*, mercy or compassion, is found in the New Testament story of the Good Samaritan which Jesus tells in response to the question 'And who is my neighbour?'[1] A man is attacked by robbers, and left wounded and bleeding on the road. Two other men – a priest and a Levite – pass him by. The man who stops, takes him to a nearby inn and pays for him to be treated is a Samaritan. It is as if a Palestinian today were to stop and help an Israeli Jew. This is the essence of the *virtue* of *misericordia* as opposed to a *feeling* of compassion. We are moved to act not because of any 'interest' or family link to the person who suffers but simply because he or she is a fellow human being.

Lack of compassion can be at the heart of some of the more unsavoury journalistic practices. 'Pack journalism', the 'ambush' interview of someone who has no experience of reporters, invasions of privacy and other dubious methods lend support to Conservative politician, Alan Clark's, observation that 'there is no such thing as mercy in the media' (1999: 286). But reporters and editors without a spark of mercy have forgotten why they are in the business in the first place. The thrill of the hunt has replaced the fundamental interest and curiosity about other human beings which is what makes journalism worth doing.

COVERAGE OF SUFFERING

How do journalists decide what material it is appropriate to show or publish? Newsrooms receive all kinds of gory footage. The picture of the calcinated Iraqi soldier on the road out of Kuwait City was one of the emblematic images of the Gulf War and one of the first to show that people had actually died. The *Observer* newspaper received the photograph and, unlike most of its competitors, decided to publish it (3 March, 1991). After much debate about its suitability for the front-page, it was eventually decided to put it on an inside page so as not to upset the readers' breakfast. The journalists responsible for this decision now believe they should have made the riskier decision of publishing it on the front-page (Trelford, 2000a).

The sequences of images of the two planes crashing into the World Trade Center in New York on 11 September 2001 will be seared into the memories of all those who saw them in the newspapers and on their screens. They were replayed over and over again. Not, however, on the American ABC network. Its president felt their effect was so depressing for the American people that they should not be repeatedly used in news reports.

The images of people throwing themselves off the doomed towers from hundreds of feet up sent 'a collective shudder' around *The Guardian* newsroom. But the paper's picture editor, Danny John, had no doubt that one of these images should be used. He explained, 'Some pictures we see cannot be published because of their truly horrific nature.' But in this case the person 'caught by the photographer in those few frames was not identifiable and, while it was inevitably upsetting to some readers, we believed it was not our job to sanitize or censor the awful circumstances in which these innocent victims found themselves' (17 September, 2001: G2).

In 1999 NATO mistakenly bombed a refugees' convoy leaving Kosovo. The regional paper in the area of Spain where I was staying ran a shocking front-page photograph showing a dismembered victim. It was an image which would never have been used in a British paper. When I asked a Spanish journalist what criteria would have been used to judge whether to publish the picture, he said the criterion was distance. As the dead were foreigners, the image was considered acceptable. It was the application of the principle cited by the American newsman that: 'One dead fireman in Brooklyn is worth five English bobbies, who are worth 50 Arabs, who are worth 500 Africans' (cited in Moeller, 1999: 22).

Coverage of suffering is clearly influenced by cultural factors. Death may be less of a taboo in Spain than in Britain.[2] However, the fact that such a shocking picture would not have been shown of a Spanish victim shows that some kind of moral sense is at work.[3] I'll examine below what considerations do and might apply in the different circumstances of war, disaster and domestic tragedy.

DEATH AND DISASTER

Natural and man-made disasters

Britain's greatest sporting tragedy was to show reporting of suffering at its worst. Ninety-five Liverpool football fans were crushed to death at the Sheffield Hillsborough stadium in April 1989, largely due to the inadequacies of crowd control measures. It was the FA Cup semi-final and the stadium was full of journalists and sports photographers. They recorded the tragedy as it unfolded before them, taking thousands of pictures, 'many of which showed such harrowing detail of death and suffering it was almost an impossible editorial decision to decide which could actually be printed' (Chippindale and Horrie, 1999: 332).

On the national tabloids, concern for the victims and their families was swept aside in the rush to get the pictures out and meet competitive pressures. Even though, for the first few days there was no way of knowing whether those shown crushed or lying on the pitch were alive or dead, the photographs were published anyway. The *Mirror*'s colour pictures showed in painful detail the faces of the dying (Chippindale and Horrie, 1999: 335). These images provoked a storm of protest in Liverpool but did nothing to dent newspaper sales. On the other hand, the *Sun*'s notorious headline 'THE TRUTH', detailing alleged appalling behaviour by Liverpool fans, brought down the wrath of Merseyside on Kelvin MacKenzie and a boycott of the paper.

The editor's rush to judgement, his one-sided portrait of the behaviour of Liverpool in which three front-page subheadings declared, 'Some fans picked the pockets of victims. Some fans urinated on the brave cops. Some fans beat up PC giving kiss of life' was the triumph of prejudice and sensationalism over good reporting. Chippindale and Horrie later concluded that 'there was no evidence of any kind to support them, and none was ever to be produced' (1999: 346).

The reporting of the Paddington train crash in which 30 people died in October 1999 showed how matters had improved. Newspaper reporters made a group decision to wait on the other side of the street from where the relatives of victims were staying.[4] Editors agonized over which pictures to publish: '. . . the *Guardian*'s front-page picture showed two women, their faces buried in their hands, near the crash site. Four other papers chose similar pictures for page one but *The Guardian*'s was closely cropped in order, says Rusbridger [*Guardian* editor], to minimize the chances of identification. It was used because it was considered symbolic of people's suffering' (Greenslade, 11 October, 1999).

As media commentator, Roy Greenslade, put it, 'it's fair to say that, during disasters, the media does see itself as performing a public service' (1999).[5] News organizations must gather and broadcast or publish information as quickly and accurately as possible, often in situations of great confusion and distress. To do so reporters have to deal with bereaved relatives. Despite criticism of ghoulish or vulpine journalists, this is a necessary, if delicate, part of a reporter's job. 'For every snub at a grief-stricken household', wrote Greenslade, 'there are five others who open their doors and offer tea, opening their hearts to the stranger with a notebook' (1999).

National tragedies resonate. Foreign tragedies don't necessarily. News of African famines can provoke a 'been there, done that' attitude. 'Formulaic coverage of similar types of crises,' writes Moeller, 'makes us feel that we really have seen this story before. We've seen the same pictures, heard about the same victims, heroes and villains, read the same morality play' (Moeller, 1999: 13). As in war reporting of far and distant lands, the challenge for the reporter is to engage the audience. Given the probable logistical difficulties of getting to where a foreign tragedy is unfolding, the mere fact that the reporter is there at all is a triumph. The next question is how to make the editors and the public care about the story. Associated Press's Tom Kent says it depends on how you write it: 'Have you ever picked up the *New Yorker*,' he asks 'and found a page and a half about how ball bearings are made, which you'd never read, but it's so well done you're reading it? That's what we have to do with foreign news' (cited in Moeller, 1999: 23).

In 1984 against all the odds, the BBC team of reporter Michael Buerk and cameraman Mohammed Amin got into Ethiopia. What they saw there were scenes of unimaginable suffering, thousands upon thousands of people dying of hunger with no hope of help. Their ten-minute report showed the reality of famine – the rows of corpses, the death of a three year old in her mother's arms, and Buerk's commentary:

> Dawn, and as the sun breaks though the piercing chill of night on the plain outside Korem it lights up a biblical famine, now, in the 20th century. This place, say workers here, is the closest thing to hell on earth. Thousands of wasted people are coming here for help. Many find only death. They flood in every day from villages hundreds of miles away, dulled by hunger, driven beyond the point of desperation. . . . 15,000 children here now – suffering, confused, lost. . . . Death is all around. A child or an adult dies every 20 minutes. Korem, an insignificant town, has become a place of grief. . . . (cited in Moeller, 1999: 111)

This report sparked a huge international response. Its measured tones and understated yet emotional response to the tragedy of the Ethiopian famine made Westerners care about Africans. 'The magnitude of the suffering had helped create the impact', observes Moeller, 'but it was the quality of the images that made the scenes so arresting'. For Americans unused to British news styles, the slower pace of Amin's camera-work allowed its audience to form strong impressions. 'It was as if each clip was an award-winning still photo,' said William Lord, executive producer of ABC's *World News Tonight*' (1999: 117).

Good reporting connects, and avoids cliché. This was what Amin and Buerk had managed. The challenge would be to repeat the achievement in covering future African famines, Asian floods or Latin American earthquakes. The 'compassion fatigue' of newsrooms and audiences is not easily combated. However, the BBC team showed that sober, accurate reporting is a *sine qua non* for journalism which can stir people's hearts.

War

War reporting has been the occasion of some of the finest journalistic work ever produced, and the worst.[6] As we saw in Chapter four, it tests to the limit the reporter's commitment to truth telling. Where one's own country is engaged in conflict, reporters often expect and are expected to contribute to the objective of winning the war.

Showing enemy casualties, especially where they contradict the narrative of a humanely prosecuted war, is discouraged. The BBC's heavily censored images of the civilian Iraqi casualties from NATO's bombing of the Al Amiriya shelter, earned it the sobriquet 'Baghdad Broadcasting Corporation' from sectors of the print media: *The Sun* newspaper described it as 'the enemy within' and the *Daily Telegraph* refused to publish any pictures of the incident to avoid giving succour to Saddam Hussein.[7] Carruthers concluded that 'elements of the British and American media – and their publics – are *less* willing for dissent to be aired, or potentially damaging images of suffering to be screened' (italics in original; 2000: 157). During the Gulf War reporters were forbidden from filming or photographing soldiers 'in agony or severe shock' or 'patients suffering from severe disfigurement' (Taylor, 1992: 35).Where wars are fought on our behalf by our soldiers, we prefer not to know the details of pain and death and, on the whole, the media prefers not to tell us.

What about wars and conflicts in distant lands? Here the rule appears to be that the more remote and distinct from us the people who suffer, the greater the willingness to show images of their suffering. We accept images of bloated corpses floating down rivers or bodies being loaded unceremoniously onto the back of lorries if it is Rwanda. Not if it is Canada. The reporting of the war in the former Yugoslavia showed some of the horrors of the conflict but for former BBC correspondent Martin Bell, not nearly enough:

> What we do not show is what happens at the other end – the killing, the maiming, the wounding, and the suffering, the irredeemable waste of young lives, which is what war is . . . [television] prettifies and sanitizes. Taken over the months and years of a conflict, it promotes the idea of warfare as a costfree enterprise, not even shocking anymore but almost an acceptable means of settling differences. (1998: 105)

More important, however, than what is shown is how and in what context it is given to us. As BBC reporter, Fergal Keane, wrote about coverage of the Hutu massacres of Tutsis in Rwanda in the 1990s:

> Much of the coverage of Rwanda in the early days neglected the part that power and money had played in the calculations of those who launched the genocide. Where television is concerned, African news is generally only big news where it involves lots of dead bodies. The higher the mound, the greater the possibility that the world will, however, send its camera teams and correspondents. (1996: 7)

What could we make of the horrific images without any sense of the humanity of the victims or the reality of their lives? Genocide in Rwanda, where 'in one hundred days up to one million people were hacked, shot, strangled, clubbed and burned to death' (Keane, 1996: 29), became part of a narrative of the 'dark continent', 'the horror, the horror' of the closing lines of Joseph Conrad's *Heart of Darkness*.[8]

Showing the suffering of war can be a kind of visual pornography and contempt for the humanity of those who suffer, if there is no moral engagement. But for reporters herein lies the dilemma. It is true that, 'The spectator of suffering cannot speak about what he has seen in objectivist terms. . . . It would be considered "indecent" or "inhuman" to give a purely factual description of a hanging say, or of victims of a famine' (Boltanski, 1999: 24–5). However, should the reporter become an advocate? This is what Bell seems to suggest.[9] But surely more powerful than advocacy is the power of the journalist to bear witness. Bearing witness with integrity and compassion will speak for itself, as did much of Martin Bell's own reporting of Bosnia.

DOMESTIC TRAGEDY

Most journalists will probably not report a war. Most will report on a suicide, crime or accident. They will be asked to get family details, a photograph of the victim, quotes from the victim's family. They will have to report court proceedings; children might be involved. On these occasions, more than any other, the reporter's sensitivity and good judgement will be called upon. Families might be unwilling to talk, information may be difficult to come by and a hard-pressed journalist might be tempted to apply inappropriate pressure to obtain what he or she needs. Or, where the story is particularly newsworthy – a celebrity suicide, a child's murder, a vicious rape – the temptation might be to include painful detail which can only immeasurably increase the suffering of the victim's family and feed our morbid curiosity. Some of these areas – crime reporting, for example – are hedged round with legal constraints on what may be published or broadcast. Reporters are, for instance, forbidden from identifying alleged offenders or witnesses at youth courts if they are under the age of 18.

The PCC's code covers some of these areas too (see Box 8.1). It has particularly stringent requirements to avoid identification of children in sex cases who appear as victims, witnesses or defendants (see Clause 7).[10] Similarly, it advises against identifying victims of sexual assault except where there is justification and it is legal to do so (see Clause 12). Clause 10 on reporting of crime requires the press to avoid identifying friends or relatives of alleged criminals without their consent and to pay particular regard to the vulnerability of children who are witnesses or victims of crime. However, Clauses 7 and 10 are subject to a public interest exemption. The broadcast industry has similar guidelines.

These guidelines have arisen out of mistaken and damaging practice. They show that, despite the rhetoric, editors and reporters accept the need for compassionate practice. The need for compassionate practice is also recognized in Clause 5 of the code dealing with intrusion into grief or shock. It calls for sympathy and discretion. This means not behaving like the reporter who, having already imposed on a grieving family whose child had choked to death on a Christmas tree decoration, was then told by his editor to phone back to check on its colour (Goodwin, 1995: 259). Or running a story about someone who is dying simply because he is a relative of a well-known politician. The *Mirror*'s story headlined 'Lilley's nephew dying of Aids' was censured by the PCC in 1995 for invasion of privacy (Report 29, 1995). It also means knowing how to behave sensibly in unexpected circumstances. The *Daily Record* reporter who went to a family's home whose daughter was missing and 'blurted out' the news that a body had been found 'could have spared the family's feelings simply by acting in accord with common sense when she realized they did not know that a body had been found' (Report 37, 1997: 23).

Most of the time reporters seem to get it right.[11] Columnist Magnus Linklater was asked to prepare a feature on the restoration of capital punishment. His research involved interviewing relatives of murder victims. He was surprised by the cordial reception he received. '. . . some of those I talked to even had fond memories of the traumatic period when their front gates had been besieged by the waiting press. One woman, whose sister had been brutally strangled, showed me a Christmas card she had kept from the *Daily Express* reporter who had covered the story' (cited in IPI report, 1996: 27).

BOX 8.1 PCC Code: protecting the vulnerable

Clause 5 Intrusion into grief or shock

In cases involving grief or shock, enquiries must be carried out and approaches made with sympathy and discretion. Publication must be handled sensitively at such times, but this should not be interpreted as restricting the right to report judicial proceedings.

Clause 10 Innocent relatives and friends

The press must avoid identifying relatives or friends of persons convicted or accused of crime without their consent.

PICTURE POWER

Pictures are immeasurably more powerful than words. One of the reasons James Bulger's murder was so etched into Britain's conscience was that we have the video footage of him being led away by his murderers. Pictures pose difficulties for those who take them and those who must decide whether to use them.

Taking pictures

What are suitable subjects for pictures? Why did so many viewers complain about images of grieving relatives at Dunblane? What makes us feel uneasy about focusing on pictures on the bereaved, the dying and the dead? The BBC *Style Guide* provides specific advice to its reporters and editors on the kind of images to be shown and to be avoided:

> We do not want to cause distress by dwelling unnecessarily on graphic detail, in words or pictures. In television, we do not linger needlessly on pain and suffering, keeping shots short and angles wide; we do not zoom in to shots of blood, but pull away in deference to the victim. We should be particularly mindful of the distress we will cause if we show identifiable pictures of dead or injured people before their relatives have been contacted. (1995: 12)

In a small American town, a photographer happened to be present at a tragic incident. His photograph captures the moment just after a tractor tyre exploded at a petrol station killing the station operator and his son (see Patterson, 1998). The father lies dead and so does his son, almost naked, his clothes blown off by the force of the blast. The photograph captures the moment when the wife and mother of the boy arrives and appears to look straight into the camera with a horrified, anguished expression. Was he right to take the picture? These are hard decisions to make. Often responses are instinctive and it is hard to criticize a photographer for reacting professionally to a dramatic incident. Perhaps the real question is whether the image should have been published, an issue to which I will return.

In 1993 freelance South African photographer, Kevin Carter, took a photograph of a Sudanese toddler too weak to continue the short distance that remained to a feeding centre; behind her was a watching vulture. It won him a Pulitzer prize. Two months' later he committed suicide. A friend and fellow photographer wrote later:

> Questions about Kevin's ethics and his humanity were beginning to be asked more frequently: the pressure on him was building. The strain was all the greater because Kevin had his own doubts about his actions during that hot day in Ayod, and wrestled with them almost every day.

> Kevin told Nancy Lee, the *Times'* picture editor, that he was sure the girl had made it to the feeding station. But Lee, like many others, felt uncomfortable; if Kevin was that close to the feeding station and the child was on the ground, why had he not gone there and got help? What do you do in cases like this? What is the obligation of any news professional in the face of tragedy in front of them?

> I don't know: I have a humanistic feeling about it and a journalistic feeling about it. If something terrible is about to happen and you can stop it, if you can do something to help once you've done your job, why wouldn't you? It bothered me as a person. He could have done it, it would have cost him nothing. She would have weighed something like 10lb. He could have picked her up and carried her there (. . .). (Marinovich, 20 August, 2000: S5)

This view would not be shared by all reporters, some of whom believe that their first duty is to observe and report the news, not to try and change it. In Chapter four I referred to the incident in which a Buddhist monk burnt himself to death on the streets of Saigon in what appeared to be a protest against the war in Vietnam. Two AP reporters took pictures of the whole event, images which were shown across the world. One later explained that he could perhaps have 'prevented the immolation by rushing at the monk and kicking the gasoline away if I'd had my wits about me. As a human being I wanted to; as a reporter I couldn't' (Arnett, 1994: 119). The AP man's response reveals the breakdown of moral sense. If it had been his son he would probably have rushed to save him. His inaction showed more about a lack of *misericordia* than the triumph of professionalism. Photojournalists interviewed in the United States had different views to Arnett. One said, 'You're a member of the human race first and a journalist second' and another, 'The picture is in the paper only one day and I have to live with myself every day' (Goodwin, 1995: 314).

Selecting pictures

As deputy editor of the *Daily Express* in the early 1960s, Bob Edwards, had to decide whether to use a picture or not:

> One evening Ted Pickering and I were on the backbench when the picture editor brought us dramatic, exclusive photographs of four maids leaping to their deaths from a burning hotel in Rome. In each case their nighties had lifted, revealing their naked bodies. . . . Neither of us had the stomach to ask the picture retoucher to paint in panties or extend the nighties. Without any discussion we turned the pictures down. Sure enough, it appeared suitably altered in the *Daily Mail* with the hypocritical claim that it was being published as a warning against fire. (1989: 100)

Publication of the picture of the son and father lying dead after the explosion of a tyre and the shocked wife staring into the camera was justified on similar grounds; namely, that it showed the danger of this kind of accident. It is a brutal image, snatched at the moment of most terrible grief. A woman who was filmed reacting hysterically to the news that her daughter had died in an aircrash later described her feeling that she had been 'visually raped' by the media. Publication or broadcast of these pictures seems hard to justify, especially when reporters are told not to interview those who are in shock.

Broadcast and photographic images of suffering can convert us into spectators, passive consumers of other people's tragedies at best, and vulture-like voyeurs at worst. However, it is also true that images of accidents, natural disasters, wars or crimes can be a call to action. The sinking of the Herald of Free Enterprise ferry in 1986 with the loss of 193 passengers brought about improved ferry safety. Handguns were banned as the result of Dunblane. Images which 'connect' us to those who suffer, make their suffering real, is what makes them acceptable.

'ONLY CONNECT'

Most people would agree that information about human suffering is acceptable; it depends how it is presented. Good news is not generally news. When the BBC's Martyn Lewis tried to promote this idea he was laughed out of court. When a political party tried to set up a paper on these lines, it was a failure. As American journalist Tom Palmer put it: 'Media moguls have long known that suffering, rather than good news, sells. People being killed is definitely a good, objective criteria for whether a story is important. And innocent people being killed is better' (cited in Moeller, 1999: 34).

Telling stories, informing about suffering tells us the truth about human life. We can't live in a make-believe world where no-one cries. Bad things happen. People suffer. We want to know about such things because in a certain way they can reassure us. They are the out-of-the-ordinary, they are strange, which is why they are reported. But what are the parameters for such news? Where do we find the measure for what might be appropriate or not?

Information about suffering is not *simply* about transmitting data; it is about creating an emotional link between you and the person who suffers to engender compassion. This was the secret of the Italian film *Life is Beautiful* (1998). It didn't show the usual visual cliché of piles of emaciated bodies to depict the Nazi atrocities against the Jews, but was a touching story about a Jewish Italian family caught up in a nightmare world.

The challenge for journalists is to capture the intimate, incomparable character of the person affected or the tragedy which has occurred. Of course the limits of time and space can make this impossible. A local paper might just be able to include news in brief stating '50 killed in Indian bus accident'. However, where it is possible to give time to a story, images or words which impose, steal intimacy or caricature, or rob the person of their dignity make the journalist appear a person without scruples. That is perhaps what is at the root of people's unease at images of torn bodies, grieving mothers or heaps of corpses. This is why famed photographer Donald McCullen was set upon by the Lebanese woman whose grief he had just photographed. Think of how we feel when a person starts to cry. The person loses control even of their appearance. We feel it is a violation of someone's intimacy to be there. We see vulnerability, defence-lessness. And it demands our utmost respect.

Similarly for reporters. They must be professional enough to deal with the story – it's no good if they dissolve into tears themselves. However, the story will be better told if the reporter is able to capture the personal dimension of the tragedy, if the context is a sense of the worth of the human being. Otherwise why should we give a damn that a hundred people have died in a bus accident in Burundi?

Compassionate reporting will mean that journalists and news executives would take into account a number of very practical issues. The following list provides a starting point:

- Not to be led by technology. If not hasty, ill-judged decisions can be made. A Spanish television news programme showed the blown-up gobbets of human flesh with the excuse that as the stories were coming in direct off the wires, there was no time to editorialize. However, as the BBC *Producer Guidelines* say:

  > It's inevitable that the images of a disaster are painful for those personally involved and perhaps for other spectators too. But we shouldn't lower our standards about what it is appropriate to show because of the volume of material we have available or because of the speed with which we receive, transmit and edit it.

- To minimize the inevitable intrusion by organizing pools. Not only the news itself has an ethical dimension but the means used to obtain it. Pools can be a good way of avoiding some of the intrusion of a pack of reporters covering an event. Journalists must be sensitive to their impact, particularly TV crews which are especially intrusive. Over three hundred journalists descended on the small town of Dunblane as well as numerous overseas reporters.

- To be sensitive about interviews. Journalists should be moderate in the way interviews are requested and in how they're done. They shouldn't interview or try to interview anyone in a state of shock. They shouldn't try to do an interview without the person's permission and they should always explain clearly the rules of the game. It may well be the first time that the person in question has done an interview.
- To be careful in publishing or broadcasting distressing material. Taking care, for example, in showing material about on-going situations – kidnappings, for instance – which could be painful for the family. Or about information on anniversaries by contacting those involved. Or announcing to the audience that painful or shocking images are going to be shown.
- Assign experienced staff to the story. For Dunblane, ITN assigned a senior editorial manager to view pictures as they came in to ensure policies and standards were observed. On the whole they were.
- Let the humanity of the reporter come through: tragedies can't be reported as though they were a village fete. For the reporter this means showing a sense of feeling without abandoning the story.

NOTES

1 Luke 10; 30–37.

2 When the Spanish parent company of *Hola!* brought out its English edition, *Hello!* it followed the same diet of celebrity features, deaths, marriages etc. It soon found, however, that the English audience found its coverage of funerals, with pictures of coffins and crying relatives, distasteful. Such coverage was subsequently reduced.

3 More respectful coverage of national tragedies has also been true in Britain, as we saw in the reporting of Dunblane. Bob Edwards, former editor of the *Daily Express*, relates how his paper published a photograph of a train crash victim in the early 1960s: 'Until then newspapers never published pictures of bodies in domestic disasters like this, though foreign plane crashes abroad were regarded as fair game' (1989: 102). Television had changed things.

4 Broadcast journalists failed to do this and, as is often the case, were far more intrusive than their print colleagues.

5 The broadcasters are quite clear about the public service they provide in reporting disasters. See BBC *Style Guide* and *Producers Guidelines*.

6 *See* Carey's *Faber Book of Reportage* (1996) for examples of some of the best and Knightly, *The First Casualty* (2000) for examples of the worst.

7 The BBC's Michael Buerk warned viewers that 'Many of the pictures coming from Baghdad of burned civilian bodies are considered too dreadful to show you' (cited in Taylor, 1992: 191). Subsequent audience research found that 57 per cent thought the BBC was right to show the sanitized images, while 23 per cent thought it was wrong for the story to have been covered at all (Morrison, 1992).

8 Christopher Hitchen has written in *Vanity Fair* that all reporting of Africa is a pastiche of Waugh's *Scoop* and Conrad's *Heart of Darkness*.

9 Bell argued that more explicit coverage of the horrors of Bosnia was necessary. He believed that this would help prompt a more vigorous western response to the conflict. In fact, as Carruthers suggests, 'Former Yugoslavia offers the best illustration of the absence of an automatic link between media images of suffering and decisive intervention to alleviate it' (2000: 213).

10 The PCC issued specific advice in 1993 on the use of photographs which might lead to identification of victims of sexual assault or of children under the age of 16 involved in any way (Report No. 21).

11 The number of complaints to the PCC on these issues is relatively small. In 1999 they constituted 5.8 per cent of the total number of complaints made to the PCC (*Annual Review*, 1999).

> What gives journalism its authenticity and its vitality is the tension between the
> subject's blind self-absorption and the journalist's scepticism. Journalists who
> swallow the subject's account whole and publish it are not journalists but
> publicists.
>
> Janet Malcolm, *The Journalist and the Murderer*, 1990.

In February 2001 Prince William was invited to a party held by the Press
Complaints Commission to celebrate its tenth anniversary. Newspaper editors
would be present. *The Times* journalist, Matthew Parris, warned the heir to the
British throne to stay away:

> A newspaper is not an entity capable of sustaining a friendship. It is unpro-
> fessional in a career-journalist to foster trust except in hopes of future
> indiscretion. There is only one useful rule to be followed by a person whose fate
> it is to be interesting to such people. Stay away from them. They will kill you.
> (3 February, 2001)

A journalist's work involves a constant tension between nurturing trust and
maintaining scepticism. This is nowhere clearer than in the relationship between
reporters and sources. Sources are essential for journalists; at the same time
sources have their own agendas to which they will inevitably seek to enlist a
willing reporter. But, as Parris points out, sources play a dangerous game when
they take a journalist into their confidence: unlike the relationship between other
occupational groups and their confidants, reporters seek to disclose information
they are given. Doctors, lawyers and priests should keep the secrets they are told;
journalists usually should not.

Disclosure is what reporting is about. And yet, there will be times when
sources will only divulge information on condition that their identity is kept
secret. A degree of trust is necessary; without it reporting becomes impossible
and rumour and propaganda replace news. Sources need to know that where
necessary their identity will be protected and reporters that what they are told
has a semblance of truth. This chapter will examine the *liaisons dangereuses* of
reporters and sources.

REPORTERS AND SOURCES

Stories often just happen. A man goes into a school in Japan and stabs eight
children to death, the Peruvians elect their first president of Indian descent,
Concorde goes up in flames. Stories can happen as part of the cycle of political,

economic or social life: weddings, elections, publication of inflation figures. These are 'diary' stories, programmable, mostly predictable. An election campaign is one long diary story, structured around the parties' morning press conferences and leaders' activities. Stories also happen out of the chaos of nature and human life: earthquakes, terrorist attacks, accidents or murder. These are unpredictable, non-diary stories that all media will cover. Then there are the off-diary stories which enterprising reporters dig out from all kinds of likely and unlikely places: official reports, specialist magazines and journals, an overheard conversation.

For all these stories, reporters need sources and these relationships can prove one of the most contentious areas of journalistic practice. An influential current of media analysis holds that the media is structurally biased towards powerful sources, who achieve the status of 'primary definers' from both a temporal and an ideological perspective. The organization of journalistic practice is here seen as promoting the views and interests of authoritative sources (Hall et al., 1978). This is undoubtedly true in part. News coverage maps power (see Gandy, 1982 and Deacon and Golding, 1994).

A more extreme view is that the reporter-source relationship is inherently corrupt, that 'the moral ambiguity of journalism lies not in its texts but in the relationships out of which they arise – relationships that are invariably and inescapably lopsided' (Malcolm, 1990: 162). Janet Malcolm explores this relationship in her account of the trial of a reporter sued by his subject – a man convicted of murder – for misrepresenting him and playing the part of a false friend for financial motives. Malcolm's view of the journalist–source relationship is emphatic and startling:

> Every journalist who is not too stupid or full of himself to notice what is going on knows that what he does is morally indefensible. He is a kind of confidence man, preying on people's vanity, ignorance, or loneliness, gaining their trust and betraying them without remorse. . . . Journalists justify their treachery in various ways according to their temperaments. The more pompous talk about freedom of speech and 'the public's right to know'; the least talented talk about Art; the seemliest murmur about earning a living. (1990: 3)

At one stroke reporting is dismissed as an ethical practice. This goes too far. Reporters are neither totally beholden to powerful interests nor are they always false friends.

The complexity in journalists' relationships to news sources is especially apparent in cases where conflict and misunderstanding arise between the journalist and the source. When suspicion dominates the relation between journalists and official sources – the prevailing mood between most reporters and politicians – or when official sources lose credibility during times of crisis and scandal, it becomes obvious that structural constraints cannot tell the whole story of journalists' relationships to sources (see, for example, Schlesinger and Tumber, 1994, Negrine, 1996, Jones, 1996 and Sanders, Bale and Canel, 1999). Sources may try to use journalists but journalists can all too easily 'use' sources.

TRUST AND CONFIDENTIALITY

Trust is the whole basis upon which the reporting edifice is founded: when we watch a news report about AIDS in Africa, listen to the football results on the radio or read that interest rates have been reduced, we rely on the testimony of others. Editors rely on the testimony of their reporters and reporters on that of their sources. For a news organization being trustworthy, building a reputation for accuracy, reliability and speed, is of supreme importance. News wholesalers, organizations like Reuters, Associated Press and the Press Association (PA), trade in trust. The announcement by PA that Princess Diana had died in 1997 turned what had been rumour into hard fact. Information produced by reporters must be trustworthy which means they must know how to sift the truth from the information provided by sources. If an editor cannot rely on the testimony produced by reporters, the whole edifice comes tumbling down.

This is precisely what occurred in the oft-told Janet Cooke case.[1] Cooke worked for *The Washington Post* and in 1980 produced a compelling series of reports about an eight-year old heroin addict called Jimmy. *Jimmy's World* won Cooke a Pulitzer Prize for feature writing. The story caused public consternation and the paper was criticized for failing to identify the child so that he could get help. When the *Post*'s editors pressed Cooke to provide such information, she couldn't. Jimmy did not exist. The prize was returned in 1981 and the *Post*'s ombudsman wrote that the paper's performance had been 'inexcusable', concluding that the 'editors abandoned their professional scepticism' (Green cited in Klaidman and Beauchamp, 1987: 174). Cooke was too easily able to appeal to the principle of confidentiality and the editors were too ready to accept anonymous sources without any corroboratory information. The case highlighted two major issues which I will consider next: first, what are the standards for judging the reliability of testimony and second, on what terms should information be confided?

Standards of trust

Not all human testimony and authority is reliable. Every day news desks are faced with the challenge of sorting the credible from the incredible. What are the conventions by which they should do this? One strategy is similar to the principle used in scholarly research known as 'triangulation'. This is where claims or accounts provided from one source can be contrasted with those provided by another. This principle can be seen at work in the account given by one of *The Guardian* reporters who investigated allegations by Mohammed al Fayed that Members of Parliament had taken cash for asking questions in the House of Commons:

> I remember going through with the lawyers three reasons why we might believe Fayed. . . . One was the Ritz hotel. There was nothing in the parliamentary register. You couldn't prove anything about the Ritz hotel. The only hint you had about the Ritz was from Tim Smith [an MP accused of taking cash for questions] when he landed Hamilton in it. So you had confirmation [Neil

Hamilton was the main target of the allegations]. Fayed had told us that and we had the bills signed by Hamilton and they were real. So one, he told us a fact that was true. The second thing was the documents he was able to produce showing there were meetings. And the other thing was turning up questions written on Greer's notepaper [Ian Greer was the lobbyist employed by Fayed] and Greer having Hamilton's notepaper to use. All that evidence was pretty good. The fourth thing was I couldn't see how self-incrimination was in Fayed's interest. He was actually giving us a story which said 'Harrods man bribed MPs.' (Hencke, 2001)

Hencke was able 'to triangulate' Fayed's claims and *The Guardian* went ahead and published them in October 1994. However, allegations against another government minister were never published because first, 'there was no *prima facie* document which had ever been produced; second, it was hearsay. . . . All that knocked it down and we couldn't stand it up properly' (Hencke, 2001). The standards of judgement to establish the reliability of information included:

- Corroboration of testimony by testimony from other sources
- Documentary evidence
- Examination of motives
- Suspicion of second-hand testimony

We can add to these:

- Getting the other side of the story. This is particularly important when a controversial claim is made or when someone is being attacked. Not giving those involved in a story time to respond is mean-spirited and risks serious mistakes being made. However, it is also open to the abuse that, in the name of even-handedness, equal credibility is given to different claims which are patently not invested with equivalent authority.

Knowing when to trust sources and when to trust a reporter's story demands discerning judgement and a cool head from journalist, editor and public. One way of building up a view of a story's credibility is to examine how key facts are sourced. Where anonymous or unnamed sources are too often used, alarm bells should ring; on some publications – the *New York Times*, for example – stories based on non-attributable sources are never used while others, such as the BBC, will only use stories for which at least two sources can be provided. There are occasions, however, when confidentiality may be justified and we will look at those now.

Conditions of confidentiality

Sisella Bok has rightly argued that terms such as 'confidentiality' or 'national security' or 'the public's right to know' have often been used 'as code words to create a sense of self-evident legitimacy which is not borne out by rigorous argument' (1982: 115). Keeping the identity of sources secret can be one such journalistic shibboleth. It is the only duty designated in the PCC's code as a 'moral obligation'. Clause 15 – Confidential Sources – states:

> Journalists have a moral obligation to protect confidential sources of information.

Why should this be so? And is it always the case? Certainly a promise to keep someone's identity secret should never be given lightly. Making a promise constrains our future freedom. If I promise to pick you up from work, I am not then free to go for a drink at the time I said I would collect you. However, we can envisage circumstances which would excuse us from this promise (my mother becoming ill, for example). We can also imagine types of promises which should never be given or accepted, such as a promise to assist in a murder. The goodness or not of fulfilling promises depends on the content of the promise and the attendant circumstances.

What about promises to protect source confidentiality? It can be argued that keeping confidences is useful to society and to individuals. The work of priests, doctors and lawyers depends on it. However, in the journalist and source relationship, as Philip Meyer puts it, 'What the sources . . . often fail to realize is that they are not the clients in the reporting process. The real client is the reader' (1991: 194). However, keeping promises of confidentiality – where there are not other more important considerations – can permit information to be put into the public domain which otherwise might not be. Those who provide information about wrong-doing from within their organization – so-called 'whistle-blowers' – are such an example. It is sensible, then, that reporting of information given in confidence should respect the arrangements entered into between the source and the journalist. The PCC underlined this principle in an editorial in which it stated that deliberately misleading a source by giving them false assurances of confidentiality and then publishing their comment 'on the record' would leave the reporter with a case to answer under the code (Report 24, 1994). As a matter of fair play, it recommends that reporters should distinguish between those accustomed to dealing with the media and those who are not, those who know the rules of the game and those who don't.

A pattern of consistent behaviour which builds a reputation for trustworthiness is valuable to anyone but particularly to someone interested in receiving information on controversial matters. *Guardian* journalist, David Hencke, explained how his work on the cash for questions scandal meant that others would come to him with sensitive information:

> My source came to me because he knew I wasn't part of the lobby network and I was independent. I would go away and look at it and I protected the source. I wasn't particularly in any camp. I was known for the cash for questions scandal. . . . That meant I was definitely privy to confidences. (2001)

Confidentiality has its uses. In Britain, however, a reporter's pledge to protect confidences is no protection where the law demands disclosure; reporters and editors have paid fines and risked prison rather than reveal a source.[2] This guarantees a reporter's reputation for trustworthiness but again questions have to be asked as to why a pledge of confidentiality was given in the first place, whether the person was right to accept it and in what circumstances one might break it. Certainly if a reporter promises to keep a source secret he or she should make sure that the source cannot be identified by any documentary evidence.[3] The failure of *The Guardian* to do this with a Ministry of Defence memorandum leaked by a civil servant, Sarah Tisdall, led to their source's imprisonment in 1983 for violation of the Official Secrets Act.[4]

The reporter should think very carefully about giving promises of confidentiality. The conditions and rationale should be clear and its use should be the exception rather than the rule, otherwise reporters make themselves vulnerable to charges of hypocrisy. Sisella Bok has expressed the dilemma well:

> The press and other news media rightly stand for openness in public discourse. But until they give equally firm support to openness in their own practices, their stance will be inconsistent and lend credence to charges of unfairness. It is now a stance that challenges every collective rationale for secrecy save the media's own. Yet the media serve commercial and partisan interests in addition to public ones; and media practices of secrecy, selective disclosure, and probing should not be exempt from scrutiny. (1982: 264)

Source conventions

Journalists have developed a vocabulary of their own to describe different terms of confidentiality. Something 'off the record' has typically been understood as not for public release or information for background purposes. Sources also sometimes use it to mean 'non-attributable' that is, information which can be used but not attributed to a named source. 'Non-attributable' information is often used in political reporting.

On many occasions it is a euphemism for purveying gossip and rumour. Briefing on 'lobby terms' – on a non-attributable basis – was the understanding upon which the Prime Minister's press secretary informed the lobby group of political reporters until October 1997 when Tony Blair's spokesman, Alastair Campbell, decided to go on the record first as 'the Prime Minister's official spokesman' and then, on 13 April 2000, as Alastair Campbell himself. Until then only those in the know realized that references to 'sources close to the Prime Minister' and later, 'Downing Street sources' were journalists' code for reports of the Press Secretary's twice weekly briefings to the 240 or so accredited lobby correspondents.

Briefing on lobby terms continues. Ministers' press secretaries and political advisers continue to use the anonymity of these briefings to undermine rival ministers and policies; reporters have been only too happy to find evidence of rifts and conflict between political heavyweights.[5]

The British culture of non-attributed information, particularly in political reporting, has risks. Reporters can be used to spread damaging gossip which, as the Babylonian Talmud vividly puts it, is 'like a three-pronged tongue' which destroys three people: 'the person who says it, the person who listens to it, and the person about whom it is told' (cited in Bok, 1982: 94). It was used to devastating effect in the final throes of the Major government where hardly a day passed without some report of a rift, conflict or sleaze scandal (Major, 2000: 550–2). Lobby correspondents can, in the words of *The Times* political commentator, Peter Riddell, act as 'tame lapdog, alert watchdog and fierce fighting dog' often on the same day.

The conventions of non-attribution can only work in a clubbable world – Westminister being the prime example – where reporters and sources are willing to observe the rules of the game. It is also undoubtedly useful, allowing more freedom of exchange than would be possible in a world where all information is attributable. However, unwillingness to go on the record often indicates less than honourable motives and a reporter more interested in reporting news than gossip should be suspicious of a culture where non-attributability is the norm.[6] Some newspapers, *The New York Times* for example, don't permit the 'pejorative blind quote'. Reporting of derogatory comments about a person or institution must be attributed to a named source. If the information is important and cannot be fully attributed, it should be paraphrased. Through these rules the *New York Times* seeks to avoid becoming a vehicle for vendettas, smears and innuendo and so maintain its credibility with the readership (Jenkins, 2 February, 2000).

One old established convention in the source–reporter relationship is that of the embargo on publication of information until an agreed date. This works entirely on the basis of a relationship of trust in which reporters are provided with information ahead of an event on condition that they respect the understanding that they will not publish or broadcast it before it officially 'happens'. The Queen's New Year's Honours List is an example of this kind of embargoed information, released to the media before Christmas to allow them to prepare features about the recipients of the awards. Embargoes are also used for information which could have security implications. *The Sun* ran a 'Sack Kate Adie' front-page story (10 October, 2001) after Downing Street accused the BBC reporter of breaking an embargo on information relating to Tony Blair's travel plans in the Middle East, an error committed by a number of news organizations in the early days of October 2001.

Whistle-blowing and leaks

Whistle-blowing is where information is covertly disclosed from within an organization to uncover some kind of abuse. Sometimes it occurs after the employee resigns as in the true story told by Michael Mann's film *The Insider* (2000). The film reveals how a former tobacco company executive supplied information to the media proving that the harmful effects of their products were known but hidden from policy makers and the public. Source confidentiality is key to the informant being prepared to offer information. This is also true of 'leaks' where there is unauthorized release of information. Leaking can be an instrument of government, often used to gain political advantage over opponents. It can also be a form of surreptitious whistle-blowing, as was the case in Clive Ponting's leaking of Defence documents showing that Parliament was being misled about the events surrounding the sinking of the Argentinian ship, the *Belgrano*, during the Falklands War (Ponting, 1985). The leaking of the Spanish secret service papers to the newspaper *El Mundo* to show that illegal activities had been sanctioned by the Socialist government was also an example of high-level whistle blowing.

Leaking is not, however, an ideal form of communication. It is unaccountable and has great potential for manipulation. It both feeds on secrecy and encourages its existence, something no journalist would want to encourage. As Bok explains, 'Without secrecy there would be no need to leak information. As government secrecy grows and comes to involve more people, the opportunities to leak from within expand; and with increased leaking, government intensify their efforts to shore up secrecy' (1982: 217).

TYPES OF SOURCES

Secret sources

An anonymous source was famously used by Bob Woodward and Carl Bernstein in their disclosure of the Watergate scandal. The identity of their key source, 'Deep Throat', is still unknown. The risks involved in using anonymous sources need little explanation and there are few occasions where their use could be justified. More common, as we have already seen, is the use of unnamed sources. When I interviewed *Sunday Times* journalist, Mark Skipworth, about the original cash for questions story, I asked him whether the original source had been Mohammed al Fayed. His response was testament to the principle of protecting confidentiality:

> He [*Sunday Times*' editor, Andrew Neil] was approached by a prominent businessman whose identity we've never divulged and never will. We had a gruelling session with the Privileges Committee. At that time, the Solicitor General, Sir Nicholas Lyell, gave us a really hard time on that very issue. We've never yet divulged the information. Neil was given a tip. At that time it was just an assertion and we were asked to look at it. (Skipworth, 1999)

The knowledge that reporters will respect source confidentiality ensures a steady flow of information about all kinds of matters from all kinds of people. 'My experience of newspaper informers, even those who were not paid', wrote former Fleet Street editor, Bob Edwards, 'is that they were inevitably tawdry' (1989: 48). This certainly appeared to be the case when the 'friend' and landlord of Antonia de Sancha tape-recorded for sale to a tabloid newspaper her adulterous meetings with Conservative minister, David Mellor. The editor of the newspaper who bought the recordings mused on the ethical implications of this:

> This ******* decides he's going to sell his friend down the river. Now there's a big debate there, isn't there? A big ethical debate of whether or not a newspaper should take a tip from someone who's quite plainly as awful as the person he was taping. Antonia de Sancha wasn't awful, she was just used. The

other answer is would you suppress it then? If you find out there's something bad happening but the information's been obtained by not the most legitimate means, would you suppress the information? Of course that's nonsense. How would the police ever function? (Hagerty, 2000)

A politician's adultery hardly seems a sufficiently grave enough matter to justify either the friend's actions or the *People*'s in publishing it.[7] It also raises two other major issues: the payment of sources and the use of documentary sources.

Chequebook journalism

In the first edition of *The Universal Journalist*, Randall's advice is 'Never pay money for stories' but admits that in 'some countries, like Britain and Japan, this practice is becoming a disease' (1996: 71). Four years later his view is less radical and he acknowledges that there are instances of 'cheating public figures exposed solely through a paid-for story' (2000: 51).

Paying sources – or 'chequebook journalism' – is, however, potentially corrupting. It encourages the embellishment of information and stifles the free flow of information. It becomes particularly problematic when these payments are made to sources who are witnesses to crime or have been convicted of crime.

Controversy about 'buy-ups' of witnesses occurred in the Moors murders case (1966), the trial of former Liberal leader, Jeremy Thorpe (1979) and during the Yorkshire Ripper case (1981). The issue flared up again during the trial of Frederick and Rosemary West in 1995 when nineteen witnesses or potential witnesses were offered payment by newspapers. In 1996 the PCC tightened up Clause 16 of their code to deal with the problems which had been highlighted by the Wests' murder case (see Box 9.1 and Annual Report 1996). This did not solve the problem. In 1999 the *News of the World* paid a £25,000 'conviction bonus' to the key witness in the child pornography case against former pop singer, Gary Glitter.

The chief problem raised by paying witnesses is the danger that witnesses 'promised or hoping for payment may exaggerate or distort evidence to make their stories more newsworthy, or omit to give part of their evidence in court to ensure that an exclusive angle remains marketable' (Epworth and Hanna, 1998: 5). It is also a practice that journalists themselves seem to find unethical. A survey of journalists conducted in late 1996 and early 1997 found that 70 per cent believed media payments to witnesses put justice at risk (Epworth and Hanna, 1998: 23).

Payment to convicted criminals raises the different issue of whether the media should appear to reward those who have committed crime. In May 2001 *The Sun* made payments to and hired a plane for the return to Britain from Brazil of convicted train robber, Ronald Biggs. In previous cases where the PCC had held that the material published had glorified crime, newspapers were censured. However, where publication had, for example, brought new material to light or served the public interest by highlighting possible miscarriages of justice, the PCC backed the newspaper concerned. In the Biggs case, the PCC considered that, in returning to justice a wanted criminal who had been at large for over three decades, the newspaper had acted in the public interest (Report 54, 2001).

BOX 9.1 Chequebook journalism

PCC code Clause 16 Payment for Articles

i Payment or offers of payment for stories or information must not be made directly or through agents to witnesses or potential witnesses in current criminal proceedings except where the material concerned ought to be published in the public interest and there is an overriding need to make or promise to make a payment for this to be done. Journalists must take every possible step to ensure that no financial dealings have influence on the evidence that those witnesses may give.
(An editor authorizing such a payment must be prepared to demonstrate that there is a legitimate public interest at stake involving matters that the public has a right to know. The payment or, where accepted, the offer of payment to any witness who is actually cited to give evidence should be disclosed to the prosecution and the defence and the witness should be advised of this).

ii Payment or offers of payment for stories, pictures or information, must not be made directly or through agents to convicted or confessed criminals or to their associates – who may include family, friends and colleagues – except where the material concerned ought to be published in the public interest and payment is necessary for this to be done.

Documentary sources and the Internet

Documentary sources – official reports, proceedings, company reports – have become increasingly accessible thanks to the enormous resources available on the Internet. Rigorously interrogated, they can be an excellent and untapped source of stories, as David Hencke discovered when he began to report neglected areas of Parliament business:

> I . . . discovered that the Public Accounts Committee wasn't well reported and that the National Audit Office was just reported by Arts specialists, when it did a report in its area. So I went for that in a big way because it fitted into my investigative role. (2001)

Documentary sources supplied by others – audio or video recordings or documents – need to be checked with particular care. When the editor of the *Sunday People* was approached by someone claiming to have taped the conversation of Conservative politician, David Mellor, Hagerty (2000) was cautious: 'We went to an audio tape screener to establish it was Mellor's voice and not an impersonator. It was definitely Mellor.'

Other publications were not so careful. In 1985 the *Sunday Times* published a series of documents purporting to be Hitler's diaries. Eleven years later *The Sun* published images from a video claiming to show Princess Diana cavorting with an unknown man. The video and diaries were elaborate fakes bought by papers who *wanted* the stories to be true. The opportunity for hoaxing is greatly magnified by the use of digital technology and the dissemination of false information through the Internet which makes caution all the more necessary. The Internet also allows a journalist anonymity in following up leads and conducting interviews. Some publications, the *Wall Street Journal* for example, have an informal policy instructing reporters to identify themselves as such when they are working in a professional capacity.

The Internet is itself a new and not entirely reliable source. In the view of the editors of the *Columbia Journalism Review*, it has speeded up the news process and given more scope for false reports so that 'there is less time to think, to ponder, to judge, to confirm, to reconsider'. The gossip site of Matt Drudge, who broke the Clinton–Lewinsky story, claims only a 50 per cent accuracy rate which led the *CJR* editors to conclude that 'Never was there greater need for gatekeepers with sound and unimpassioned editorial judgement who refuse to be stampeded in the pressure of competition' (March/April, 1998).[8]

Cuttings and archives

Cuttings and archival material are basic sources of information which need to be treated with care. Uncritical use of cuttings can lead to the perpetuation of fundamental errors. The PCC also warned against excessive reliance on cuttings to write-up stories. It cited one example where a magazine, unable to contact a woman who had been attacked by her husband, 'wrote up the story on the basis of newspaper reports, inventing dialogue to put the story into the magazine's style'. The result, said the PCC, was an article 'which contained serious inaccuracies and was to a degree fictitious' (Report 7, 1992). In the same editorial, the PCC warned against the practice of misleading the reader by representing a telephone interview as though a personal face-to-face interview had taken place. It concluded: 'Information derived from cuttings and brief telephone interviews should never masquerade as reports of in-depth face-to-face interviews.'

Interviews and quotations

Quoting sources can be a particular source of controversy. Making notes and recording conversations and interviews are commonsensical precautions for both reporter and source.

At times misunderstandings can arise from the journalistic practice of tidying up quotes. American journalist, Janet Malcolm, argues that:

> When a journalist undertakes to quote a subject he has interviewed on tape, he owes it to the subject, no less than to the reader, to translate his speech into prose. Only the most uncharitable (or inept) journalist will hold a subject to his

literal utterances and fail to perform the sort of editing and rewriting that, in life, our ear automatically and instantaneously performs. (1990: 155)

This is a controversial view which landed Malcolm herself in trouble when she was sued by one of her interviewees for allegedly making up quotes. The British journalist, Lynn Barber, takes the opposite view. 'How accurate should quotations be? In my view, *entirely* accurate, dud grammar and all.' (italics in the original; 1999: 202)

The answer probably lies, as in most virtuous behaviour, in finding a balanced approach which is neither excessively inventive nor overly literal and offers, without distortion, what the source said. Such an approach removes any question of sources vetting copy.

Being trustworthy is vital for reporters and news institutions. It is this quality which makes the BBC website one of the most visited on the Internet. It is hard to earn and easy to lose which is why those institutions that have the public's trust, place such a high premium on practices which maintain it. Acting critically and responsibly towards sources is a key area of trust-building practice which ensures that news does not become propaganda.

NOTES

1 The case has become a kind of morality tale for American journalists. See, for example, Eason (1988) and Day (1997).

2 Section 10 of the Contempt of Court Act 1981 says that a Court may require disclosure of a source of information in a publication where it is necessary 'in the interests of justice or national security or for the prevention of disorder and crime.'

3 In Britain there is no legal obligation upon journalists to keep documents or records made during the preparation of an article or programme unless and until they are the subject of a formal request from the police or the Courts. However, British law requires anyone who discovers information which could prevent a terrorist act in the United Kingdom or lead to the arrest of a terrorist wanted in the UK to reveal it at the earliest opportunity.

4 The BBC states in chapter 17 of its *Producers Guidelines* that: 'Promises of confidentiality given to a source or contributor must be honoured. The BBC's journalism will suffer if people who give us information on condition that they remain anonymous are subsequently identified'. Given the possible legal difficulties of source anonymity, the BBC recommends that journalists seek other ways of dealing with confidential sources which do not put the reporter at risk such as, for example, establishing 'a source's authenticity without ever becoming aware of his or her identity or information that would lead to it'. Thus 'no document, computer file or other record kept by the journalist or by the BBC should identify a source whose identity cannot ever be revealed. This includes notebooks and administrative paperwork of all sorts as well as video or audio tapes.'

5 During the first Blair government (1997–2001), the power centres of the Prime Minister and his Chancellor of the Exchequer, Gordon Brown, generated rumours of rifts, fuelled by over-eager lieutenants. Brown's press secretary, Charlie Whelan, was sacked in 1997 for such activities. Former minister, Peter Mandelson, was also blamed for using the lobby system to undermine fellow Labour politicians (see Routledge, 1999). The lobby culture was further undermined when Tony Blair began his open, Whitehouse-style press conferences in June 2002. Earlier that year it was announced that lobby briefings

would be opened up to non-lobby journalists, including correspondents from overseas publications.

6 There have been attempts to break down the 'lobby rules' culture. In 1986 *The Guardian* and *Independent* newspapers withdrew from the lobby briefings to show their disapproval of the system. However, they eventually returned when they found themselves outside the information loop. Veteran Labour parliamentarian, Tony Benn, refused to play the lobby game. He always carries a tape-recorder with him to record all his conversations with journalists. All Benn's words are 'on the record'.

7 The case was considered by the Press Complaints Commission. Hagerty claimed that the story was in the public interest because Mellor was too exhausted by his extra-marital activities to carry out properly his ministerial duties. The PCC failed to agree and no adjudication was made. Instead it declared that 'the Code was unclear in its definition of the public interest' (Shannon, 2001: 101).

8 The *Drudge Report* scooped *Newsweek*'s investigation of allegations that Monica Lewinsky had had an improper relationship with President Bill Clinton. The story was reported on the Drudge website on Monday, 19 January 1997. *Newsweek*'s next issue date was not until the following Saturday so the story was posted on its website on Wednesday, 21 January.

10 Conflicts of interest

Whose round is it? What are we havin'? Where's the pub? When's it open?
Why don't we have another one?

The 5 Ws of journalism (Ian Hislop and Nick Newman)

The Duke of Wellington's famous phrase, 'Publish and be damned' is sometimes taken to be a ringing endorsement of the principle of freedom of speech. In fact, it was an insult hurled at a corrupt reporter attempting to extort money from the Duke for suppression of a scurrilous story about him. 'Conflicts of interest' were the order of the day for reporters of earlier times. You paid your money and you got your favourable (or suppression of unfavourable) coverage. Newspapers emerged out of a world of contentious reports of battles, diplomatic relations and political machinations. They were usually wildly partisan and accepted payments from interested parties.[1] The whole notion of objectivity would have been risible to the reporters of Grub Street. As George Crabbe's eighteenth-century poem, 'The Newspaper', put it:

Some, champion for the rights that prop the crown;
Some, sturdy patriots sworn to pull them down;
Some, neutral powers, with secret forces fraught.
Wishing for war, but willing to be bought.

Newspapers came to satisfy that general curiosity about the world which Chesterton so vividly described at the beginning of the twentieth century:

A newspaper does not exist to give you information; it leaves that low work to an encyclopaedia. A newspaper exists to give you a panorama of this wonderful world; to force you to care for something else besides music; to prevent you being shut up inside your everlasting organs. When you are growing narrow with the worst narrowness, the narrowness of the artist, it cleans you out with a great besom of life. It washes you with politics. It purifies you with murders. (1906: 301–3)

The notion of a 'conflict of interest' could only arise in a setting where reporters were expected to tell the truth without fear or favour, their prime duty being to purvey news rather than promote views. In other words, the notion that a 'conflict of interest' is a moral problem entails a specific understanding of what journalism is.

The UK print industry's code does not mention the issue except in reference to financial journalism (see below). However, the broadcast industry's codes have extensive guidance about avoiding conflicts of interest and the British National Union of Journalists' Code of Conduct lays down the stern admonition that 'A journalist shall not accept bribes nor shall he/she allow other induce-ments to influence the performance of his/her professional duties'. It would be difficult to muster a defence of journalistic bribery. But what does it mean to say that a journalist should not allow their performance to be influenced by other inducements? Is this realistic?

INTENTIONS AND MOTIVES

Intentions and motives are key to evaluating actions as morally good or bad. If I set fire to a chair by accidentally dropping a match on it, this is a very different matter to setting fire to it with the intention of incinerating my younger brother. The accidental incineration of my younger brother is a tragedy; his intentional incineration is murder. I might kill my brother by accident or not manage to kill him when I meant to; I would be considered 'bad' (rather than just 'unlucky' or 'ill-fated'), if it were known that I'd intended to kill him even if I didn't achieve my aim. In other words, motives matter.

Understanding the moral weight of motives and intentions, can help clarify the discussion about conflicts of interests. When we watch a BBC news pro-gramme, most of us assume that its intention is to give us the news as accurately and fairly as possible. Its proclamation and tradition of respecting public service principles make this a reasonable expectation. However, if I were to discover that an, albeit accurate, news report had been made with the intention of undermining an opposition political leader, I might find my trust in the BBC's integrity undermined. I would be troubled to find the bastion of public service promoting hidden agendas. This concern would be compounded if I were to find that the programme producer was motivated by personal hatred of the poli-tician. However, if I were to read such a report in a government supporting newspaper, I'd be unlikely to be concerned. The publication's partisan views are declared and well-known; it makes no claims to impartiality. On the other hand, if I were later to discover that the writer of the piece had secretly received government money to do so, my confidence in the reporter's integrity would be shaken.

In part, the ethical issues about conflicts of interest arise from the set of expectations we have about certain practices. On the one hand, intentions and motives can be found to be at odds with those publicly declared. On the other, the very motives and intentions themselves can be considered dishonourable. Intentions and motives are tricky things to disentangle. We are not always entirely sure ourselves what our motive is for an action, let alone able to judge those of others. However, we can arrive at one clear conclusion: if the public's trust in what they see, hear and read is to be maintained, the motives and interests behind the news should be made as transparent as possible.

In the United States this principle has been taken further. Journalists' codes of conduct prohibit any activity which may be understood to establish an interest that conflicts with professional duties and undermines the reporter's credibility. Thus, many organizations forbid reporters from receiving anything but the most trivial gift (a pen or calendar, for example); others, such as the *Wall*

Street Journal, insist on paying their way for everything, including contributing to the rental costs for the government pressrooms they use in Washington; others, such as the *Washington Post*, do not allow their reporters to cover subjects on which they are known to have taken a partisan stance. The issue here is not that a reporter necessarily has been seduced into writing a favourable article about say, a holiday destination because of the all-expenses paid trip, but that it is the *perception* that favours may have been purchased which should be avoided. This strict interpretation of the possibility of conflicts of interests, imports a principle which has come to be applied in public life. In his resignation letter of December 1998 the British Labour politician, Peter Mandelson, wrote:

> I do not believe that I have done anything wrong or improper. . . . But we came to power promising to uphold the highest standards in public life. We have not just to do so, *but we must be seen to do so.*

His acceptance of an undeclared loan from a fellow minister whose business interests Mandelson's own ministry was investigating gave the appearance of a conflict of interest and he was forced to resign. Journalists are often the fiercest critics of politicians in these circumstances and they increasingly seem to be applying the same standards to themselves.

BRIBES, JUNKETS AND FREEBIES

In its strictest sense, bribery is the act or practice of giving or accepting money or some other payment with the object of corruptly influencing the judgement or action of another. Although commonplace in seventeenth and eighteenth century journalism, it is a practice which would seem to have all but disappeared from modern British journalism. A modest contemporary descendent is the 'freebie', that is any goods or service received for which no charge is made, and the 'junket', an all-expenses paid trip to promote a product. For many years these were considered to be perks of an often poorly paid job. While many reporters are still badly paid, media organizations have become increasingly squeamish about accepting them. *The Independent* newspaper, for example, pays for the holidays that its reporters review. Broadcast organizations have strict rules which even extend to relatives. In its *Producer Guidelines* the BBC, for example, states that 'Individuals must not accept personal benefits or benefits for family/close personal relations e.g. goods, discounts, services, cash, gratuities, or entertainment outside the normal scope of business hospitality, from organisations or people with whom they might have dealings with on the BBC's behalf' (2001).

However, the absolute prohibition on freebies is still not common practice throughout the UK print industry. Journalists accept free books, CDs, film tickets, car loans, foreign trips etc. Why is this considered wrong? The argument is that such practices can be subtly corrupting, undermining a reporter's detachment and objectivity, or at least giving the appearance that they might. On some American publications policies are very strict:

> Reporters shouldn't accept any gifts from the people they may have to write about – no bottles of Scotch, vacations, fountain pens or dinners. Reporters don't even want to have to be in a position of having to distinguish between a gift and a bribe. Return them all with a polite thank you. (Day, 1997: 186)

Some areas of journalism are more susceptible than others to the seduction of freebies and allied 'perks'. Any kind of reviewing, for example, where the reporter must sample a range of products and provide what can be a highly influential judgement upon them, makes the reporter's integrity vulnerable on two counts. First, he or she must obtain the goods. Rich media institutions can insulate their reporters from the possibly corrupting effect of freebies by buying them or by having them loaned. This is, for example, the approved practice at the BBC. However, a cash-strapped provincial newspaper may find that if they do not accept free goods and services they have nothing to review. Second, reporters are vulnerable to the determined efforts of PR professionals to win favour and publicity for their particular product. The writer and reviewer A.N. Wilson expresses his concern at this development in the book industry:

> . . . why do I have the sense that the big conglomerate publishers, with their publicity departments and their grinning 'publicity girls', have not-so-subtly transformed the untidy world of literary Grub Street into a branch of marketing? Why do I get the sense that many of the so-called literary editors in what was Fleet Street are foolish enough to allow themselves to be lunched, and in effect bought by publishers, rather than offering the reader balanced criticism of the wares on offer? (1999: 20)

The process by which certain books receive massive publicity is carefully choreographed with reviewers acting as willing accomplices:

> The booksellers and wholesalers are told in advance what the bestsellers are going to be. It is quite shocking to me to see how, more often than not, the literary editors go along with this commercially motivated farce, giving vast amounts of reviewing space, not to the genuinely interesting book, but to the book which has gained the largest advance. (1999: 32)

Wilson's description of the book trade could equally well apply to travel writing, wine reviewing, motoring columns, music criticism and reviews of all kinds of consumer goods. The danger in such practices lies in the potential erosion of what should be the reporter's basic loyalty to the reader, listener or viewer.

In general, the trend seems to be towards a more transparent, less venal journalistic world. Expenses-paid trips are today far less common than they used to be and reporters are now even charged for accompanying political leaders on their election battle buses. Even reporters' expenses – 'exes' – are not what they used to be. The *Daily Mirror*'s fabled 'bank in the sky,' its accounts department situated at the top of the now demolished building just off Fleet Street, no longer exists. Even expenses, however, were regulated by an informal code of ethics so that:

A reporter specializing in religious matters was sacked . . . after sending all his Christmas cards, including one to the editor, via the *Sunday Express* post room. (Anonymous, 1999: 108)

As wages have improved in the national media, and media institutions have changed from personal fiefdoms to money-making machines in huge corporate empires, freebies, junkets and extravagant expenses seem to be going the same way as the print unions.

FINANCIAL JOURNALISM

On 5 May, 2000 the Press Complaints Commission issued a hard-hitting judgement condemning the actions of *The Mirror* 'City Slicker' columnists, Anil Bhoyrul and James Hipwell, and the negligence of the paper's editor, Piers Morgan. The 'City Slickers' column first appeared in *The Mirror* in May 1998. At first the column was not taken seriously, but with time its influence became considerable. As Bhoyrul put it, 'We had created a monster that was out of control. Every time I tipped a share the price shot up between 30 per cent and 100 per cent the next morning. Suddenly, *The Mirror* was engulfed in the Slickers craze – and it was getting scary. Its Top Ten Tips for 1999 produced a return of 142 per cent in terms of performance over the year' (Report 50, 2000).

Both reporters began to purchase shares which were featured in the column. They would identify a share that would become the next day's 'tip of the day'; then purchase a number of those shares, publish the 'tip of the day' and sell the shares on the day of the tip. After an internal investigation both journalists were summarily dismissed in February 2000 for gross misconduct. The PCC also censured the *Mirror* editor who bought shares that had been tipped by the 'City Slicker' columnists. Morgan justified his behaviour on the grounds that he was doing no more than the paper was suggesting its readers did. However, he was found to be in breach of Clause 14 of the code which deals with financial journalism (see Box 10.1). Its aim is to ensure that readers receive disinterested advice and information and that journalists and those connected with them do not profit as a result of the publication of financial information. The editor was also censured for his failure to take firm action against the reporters beyond giving them a verbal warning. It was pointed out that 'editors must ensure that the code is observed rigorously by their staff and others who contribute to their newspapers'. The PCC concluded that 'the editor's conduct in this case . . . had . . . fallen short of the high professional standards demanded by the Code' (Report 50, 2000).[2]

The *Mirror* incident was the one of the most serious to come to light since press self-regulation was introduced by the creation of the Press Council in July 1963. It provides a paradigm case of a conflict of interest in a way that freebies do not. A reporter whose financial predictions determined how much she or her editor might earn could not be trusted to tell the truth in an instance in which truthful information might adversely affect earnings. And it would no longer be

---

BOX 10.1   Financial journalism

PCC code Clause 14

i   Even where the law does not prohibit it, journalists must not use for their own profit financial information they receive in advance of its general publication, nor should they pass such information to others.

ii   They must not write about shares or securities in whose performance they know that they or their close families have a significant financial interest, without disclosing the interest to the editor or the financial editor.

iii   They must not buy or sell, either directly or through nominees or agents, shares or securities about which they have written recently or about which they intend to write in the near future.

---

possible to rely upon the truthfulness of a reporter whose motives had been so seriously traduced.

PUFFERY AND SUPPRESSION

Advertising has been seen as a source of possible conflict of interest on two counts. First, external advertising pressure to influence editorial content is cited as an area of ethical difficulty for journalists. Second, internal pressures from a media company's own marketing and publicity departments are said to attempt to drive journalistic content in certain directions. An example of the first was the threat and eventual withdrawal of advertising from the *Sunday Times* by the Distillers Company, angry at the paper's campaign against it on behalf of the thalidomide victims (Evans, 1994). An example of the second is the apparent 'puffery' in which the *Sun* and the *Sunday Times* engaged to promote the launch of Sky television, a sister company to the two as part of News International.

Evidence for these practices tends to be anecdotal. The first Royal Commission on the Press (1947–49) examined the issue of advertising influence on the press and found that individual attempts were infrequent and unsuccessful. But it would be surprising if corporate self-interest did not dictate certain editorial content. Rupert Murdoch is said to have pulled the BBC from his Star satellite service when it upset Chinese leaders. Former *Observer* editor, Donald Trelford, endured pressure from the publisher, Tiny Rowland, to suppress critical stories of Mugabe's rule in Zimbabwe where Rowland's Lonrho empire had extensive business interests. To his credit he resisted. He was not so successful in resisting his proprietor's interest in campaigning against his great rival, Mohammed al Fayed.

Broadcasters have stringent requirements to avoid the promotion of commercial products and services which also apply to their linked Internet sites (ITC

Programme Code, section 8, 2001).[3] The yardstick is that 'no impression be created of external commercial influence on the editorial process'. The BBC applies a similar rationale:

> The BBC's audience must be able to trust the integrity of BBC programmes and services. . . . There must be public confidence that editorial decisions are made only for robust editorial reasons. (*Producer Guidelines*, chapter 10)

Advertising and marketing departments have often been seen as the Great Satan by reporters, besmirching their journalistic purity in the search for filthy lucre. On American newspapers there is a tradition of maintaining a wall of separation between editors and business departments. As Meyer has pointed out, these attitudes are not always entirely sensible. 'An editor who understands the newspaper's financial situation is in a stronger position to fight for the resources needed to produce the kind of newspaper that readers deserve' (1991, 45).

In the main, the issues raised by advertising pressures are clear-cut, if not always easy to resolve. A greyer area is the extent to which a reporter's personal views can pose conflicts of interest.

PERSONAL VIEWS

The BBC's approach is rigorous:

> Associations with campaigning bodies can present great difficulties. Presenters and senior staff involved in news, topical and consumer programmes should not normally associate themselves with a campaigning body, particularly if it backs one viewpoint in controversial areas of policy. Conflicts of interest can also arise for any programme staff in this area. The Head of Department must give advance approval of any public association with a campaigning body. Non-political voluntary public office will often be acceptable even for editorial people in news programmes. This includes school governorships and being a magistrate. Programme people should be careful of involving themselves in controversial matters of public policy related to organizations like the Council for the Protection of Rural England or the National Trust. The outside activities of programme-makers must not improperly influence BBC programmes or services. (*Producers Guidelines*, chapter 10)

A survey carried out of American journalists found that most would not object to someone from a farming background writing about agricultural issues or someone with a law degree being assigned to court coverage. However, they strongly objected to an atheist writing about religious affairs or a trade unionist being asked to write about big business (Meyer, 1991: 72). The general principle seemed to be that it would be unfairly prejudicial to ask someone known to be antagonistic to sources or an issue to cover a story. Thus, someone who is a member of the Beaufort Hunt might not be best placed to write about hunt saboteurs. On this principle, when a *Washington Post* reporter joined a pro-abortion rally she was instructed by senior editors to take no further part in reporting the debate (Day, 1997: 184).

However, it does seem a little ridiculous to assume that all reporters must have a man from Mars stance of total detachment. Simply by virtue of being involved in the local community – as a school governor, shopper at the local grocery shop, dog walker in the local park, worshipper at the local church – may involve a reporter in what might be considered a conflict of interest: I might be asked, for example, to cover a story about the threatened local shop which I happen to use or the problems at the school my children attend. The easiest way to resolve these possible conflicts of interest in reporting a story is disclosure. As Meyer says, 'For every situation, there is one action, perhaps not taken often enough, that can mitigate a conflict problem on both the personal and the public levels, and that is to disclose it' (1991; 75). The BBC requires that:

> All programme teams should declare in advance in writing any significant personal, financial or professional connections they or close members of their family have with the subject matter of a programme. (*Producer Guidelines*, chapter 10)

Others go further. Keeble cites those who call for a 'new transparency' among journalists, calling upon them 'to declare their financial interests' much as public officials must now do (2001: 42). This would certainly help clear up malpractice in financial journalism. But how can reporting for the right reasons be promoted outside this specialist area? In other words, how can the notion be encouraged that reporting is about an 'honest search for the truth . . . an open-minded attempt to find out what really happened, accompanied by a willingness to print that truth, however uncomfortable it may be to our own, or the paper's, cherished beliefs' (Randall, 2000: 134–35)? Someone who is already corrupt – who writes favourable reviews in return for weekly crates of wine, for example – would not, in Aristotle's words 'listen to an argument to dissuade him, or understand it if he did' (*Nichomachean Ethics*, 1179b25). If a reporter is in the business *only* for money, fame, power, the thrill of the chase and being first, then why not accept those crates of wine? Without ideals about what journalism is for, all the registers in the world won't ensure that reporters act for the right reasons.

NOTES

1 *The Times* was one of the first British newspapers to refuse to accept government subsidies. Until then, however, such payments were the norm (see Koss, 1981 and 1984).
2 The PCC's investigation underlined the difficulties inherent in the editor's job: 'Morgan accepted that, as editor, he has executive responsibility for everything which appears in *The Mirror* and for the conduct of the journalists on the newspaper. Whilst normally he would have read about 75 per cent of the newspaper before it goes to press he is heavily reliant on senior production executives and lawyers to draw to his attention anything which worries them' (Report 50, 2000). However, the PCC was clear that the editor must take responsibility for serious and repeated breaches of the Code and for the content of the newspaper he or she edits.
3 The ITC also has a Code of Programme Sponsorship dealing with these issues.

11 The bottom line

> I should like it to be a fixed thing that the name of the proprietor as well as the editor should be printed upon every paper. If the paper is owned by share-holders, let there be a list of shareholders. If . . . it is owned by one man, let that one man's name be printed on the paper, if possible in large red letters. Then, if there are any obvious interests being served, we shall know that they are being served.
> 'The Faults of the Press', *The Illustrated London News*, G.K. Chesterton, 1907

When newspaper proprietor Lord Thomson was awarded the first independent television licence in 1954, he declared that it was a like being given a licence to print money. Media institutions are big business. In Britain the creative industries employ around one and a half million people. Most journalists are employed by companies who must compete directly in the market-place. Even those employed by the great British public service institution, the BBC, are not immune from market demands. Many of these companies make a great deal of money. For the last twenty years or so of the twentieth century the *Sunday Times* and *The Sun* have been cash cows for the Murdoch empire. Others – mostly in the regional and provincial sector – have struggled. The *Independent*, when it was part of the then Mirror Group, was known by *Mirror* workers as the 'Dependent' because of its incessant financial difficulties.

The economic realities of the media business can be one of the greatest obstacles to ethical journalism. Profits, audience share, advertising revenue and the bottom line drive the journalism. Information is itself a commodity. Sociologist Manuel Castells (1996–8) argues that information (communication of knowledge) has always been crucial in society but that we have now entered the informational age where information generation, processing and transmission have become the fundamental sources of production and power. He considers this to be as major a historical event as the Industrial Revolution. The progress of Reuters from nineteenth-century news wire operation to twenty-first century leader in financial information services expresses the central role information plays in the world economy, triggering transactions of trillions of dollars at the click of a mouse.

Journalists, editors and producers are accused of 'dumbing down' to shore up numbers of readers and viewers. Newspapers and television channels become enslaved to corporate finance. Fierce competition leads to corner cutting. The goods journalism should provide (the truth, for example) would seem to be incompatible with the demands of the market. In Stephenson's words, 'Consumerism rules!' (1998: 23). Where everything has a price, can anything have value? In this Karl Marx was right: 'The market in and of itself is beyond any religious, political, national and linguistic barrier. Its universal language is price and its community money' (Marx, cited in Grimaldi, 2000: 201). Rampant capitalism dissolves all value and as French philosopher, Nicolas Grimaldi, has expressed it: 'All value is absolute, but every price is relative. All value is imperative, but every price is negotiable. Where everything has a price, nothing any longer has value' (2000: 216). The question for journalists is whether the market and ethical practice can be reconciled?

CHASING THE MARKET

Newspapers and later television and radio channels have always needed a market for their services. The original wholesalers of news, the first international news wire services such as Reuters and Associated Press, served the business community; the origin of these services was the need of merchants for news about commodity prices, disasters, storms and ship movements. The shift to an advertising rather than subscriber business model, where advertisers 'bought' consumers, brought the market into the centre of the frame and heavy pressure to bear on content. Content became the 'bait' to catch readers and viewers for advertisers and audience figures the key to evaluating success.

This market media model is not, however, the only option. Adopted almost wholesale in the United States and other parts of the world, in Europe a public service model was preferred for what was at first the precious and scarce resource of the airwaves. Public service broadcasting was one of the most splendid inventions of the twentieth-century. The notion that an institution should function for the public good and at public expense was first enshrined in the BBC's 1926 Royal Charter. The public service remit was extended to the rest of the UK broadcast industry and is included in the twenty-first century communications legislation proposed by the Labour government.

Despite all the reports of its demise, public service broadcasting continues. In the words of media historians, Curran and Seaton: 'The BBC, despite the most determined onslaught it has ever faced, is still here. There are no advertisements in its programmes. Its market share, if threatened, is still large'. And it is still 'making an astonishingly wide range of programmes that people want to watch. Indeed, in the mid–1990s, conventional "old-style" public service programmes in the sense of television which reflects and moulds public taste, which innovates and educates, pleases and irritates, are still, so far, vigorously alive, at least in some parts of a radically transformed broadcasting landscape' (2000: 219).

But for how long? Maintaining a public service ethos in the new, highly competitive commercial and technological environment of the twenty-first century will be a huge challenge in thinking about change in order to stay the same. Critics who fear that the profit motive will sweep all before it usually point to three areas in which they believe that the market undermines the very possibility of ethical journalism:

1 the establishment of might is right and the marginalization of society's weaker voices
2 the integrity of the product (trends towards 'dumbing down', the misuse of the publisher–journalist relationship and advertiser pressure);
3 the integrity of the reporter (moves towards multi-skilling and cost-cutting).

Andrew Belsey warns that 'ethical journalism is under pressure, as is ethics in almost any walk of life, because we live in a world dominated by economic considerations and an economy driven by market forces' (1998: 13).

CONCENTRATING OWNERSHIP

The merger of Time Warner and America On-Line in 2000 created the biggest media company in the world worth $327 billion. It was followed in June 2000 by the merger of Seagram, Vivendi and French pay-TV channel, to create the world's second biggest media empire valued at $100 billion. Corporate consolidation of the information industries continues apace as our media outlets are increasingly owned by the same five or six media giants: AOL Time Warner, Microsoft/MSNBC/MSN, Disney/ABC, Viacom/CBS/MTV.

These global convergence trends were echoed at a national level in Britain by Granada's purchase of the Meridian, Anglia and Harlech Television TV franchises on 1 July, 2000. As controls on cross-media ownership in Britain are relaxed, the trends are towards further consolidation of the print industry and cross media partnerships.

Does any of this matter? The UK's first Royal Commission on the Press (1949) expected to find that 'the press as a whole gives an opportunity for all important points of view to be effectively presented in terms of the varying standards of taste, political opinion, and education among the principal groups of the population' (cited in Curran and Seaton, 2000: 288). This view reflects the classical liberal understanding of the market-place as being the guarantor of freedom through competition: freedom of enterprise and freedom to publish will provide a free and diverse press.

However, liberal theory breaks down on the grounds that, as we saw in Chapter six, putative freedom of expression is in fact a disguised kind of property right: you can express what you like as long as you have the money to do so. What emerges in an unbridled free market is media which represents the interests of the dominant groups. Weak groups or voices are marginalized or silenced. This was the situation of the Peruvian national press in the 1960s and 1970s. The major newspaper groups all belonged to larger business empires which controlled the commanding heights of the Peruvian economy. A large proportion of the population had no voice. The Peruvian predicament showed in stark form the pure application of market logic. The consequences of this logic were recognized by Britain's third Royal Commission on the Press (1977) which baldly stated, 'Anyone is free to start a daily national newspaper, but few can afford even to contemplate the prospect' (cited in Curran and Seaton, 2000: 288).

So how can plurality and diversity – necessary values in liberal democracies – be encouraged? According to Curran and Seaton, one possible option is to 'go down the American road of reworking traditional liberal theory around the concepts of social responsibility, internal pluralism and journalistic professionalism' (2000: 293). Alternatively, there is the Scandinavian model which attempts to repair the market through social market policies such as subsidies, grants and tax concessions. In Britain, at least, these approaches have been considered appropriate for the broadcast but not the print industry, despite some faltering efforts at reform.[1] More acceptable has been the view that limits should be placed on media concentration. The Conservative government's 1995 White Paper on *Media Ownership* put the case for this well:

> A free and diverse media are an indispensable part of the democratic process. They provide the multiplicity of voices and opinions that informs the public, influences opinion and, engenders political debate. They promote the culture of dissent which any healthy democracy must have. In so doing, they contribute to the cultural fabric of the nation and help define our sense of identity and purpose. If one voice becomes too powerful, this process is placed in jeopardy and democracy is damaged. Special media ownership rules . . . are needed therefore to provide the safeguards necessary to maintain diversity and plurality (1995a: 3).

Since that was written, however, media concentration in Britain and the rest of Europe has accelerated. These are developments which have worrying implications for the integrity of the product and those who work in media industries.

THE PRODUCT'S INTEGRITY

'Dumbing down?'

The great cry of the 1990s was that news had 'dumbed down' in its search for audiences. The *Oxford English Dictionary* defines the process as 'to simplify or reduce the intellectual content of (especially published or broadcast material) in order to make it appealing or intelligible to a larger number of people'. The fear is that the logic of the bottom line drives down standards.

> The small number of corporate owners are not competitive in a sense that could conceivably be expected to produce an improved product; but their financial rivalry will undoubtedly impose pressure to produce a cheaper one. That means an almost inevitable lowering of standards, since it is cheaper to buy an internationalized soap opera than to make your own drama. (Curran and Seaton, 2000: 313)

Programmes like the BBC's *Castaway* (2000) and Channel 4's *Big Brother* (2000, 2001 and 2002), the proliferation of talk and quiz shows (*Vanessa* and *The Weakest Link* on the BBC, *Trisha* and the *Jerry Springer Show* on commercial channels), the move of ITN's *News at Ten* in 1998 and the sidelining of the BBC's flagship current affairs programme, *Panorama*, have all variously been taken as signs that television had succumbed to the process of 'dumbing down,' which critics claimed had already occurred in Britain's quality newspapers.

The BBC is accused of a 'long descent into giggling inadequacy . . . a babyfood diet of superficial information which the most narcoleptic couch potato could absorb without difficulty' (Stevens, 1998: 32). And, as McLachlan and Golding put it (2000: 76):

> The re-vamping of television news by both major British networks in the last couple of years, culminating in 1999 in a national angst over the removal of the anchor-point 'News at Ten' bulletin on the national commercial network to make way for uninterrupted films, is seen as further evidence of the abandonment of a commitment to serve the needs of informed citizenship by news media wholly corrupted by the dominant forces of commercial competition.

The essence of the criticism seemed to be that editors and programme makers have allowed commercial criteria to be the decisive shaping force of programming and of programme and newspaper content. But the charge is difficult to substantiate.

Research into the alleged tabloidization of television programming is ambivalent as to whether news and current affairs programmes now follow a lighter, triter agenda (Barnett and Gaber, 1993; Barnett and Seymour, 1999); newspaper research is equally inconclusive. McLachlan and Golding's pilot study of tabloidization in the UK press between 1952 and 1997 painted an equivocal picture of the alleged shift to tabloidization in print media. They found that tabloids, for example, are 'covering more political or serious news than they were forty-five years ago' (2000: 86). Indeed, the notions of 'tabloidization' or 'dumbing down' require further precision and refinement to be of real heuristic value (Uribe, 2001).

Certainly decisions about news programming and the inclusion of more soft news in newspapers like *The Times* obey commercial dictates. But the Internet and 24 hour news channels such as CNN, Sky News, Middle East Broadcasting and BBC World means there is more news available now than there has ever been. And despite concern that scandal and celebrity news has replaced the serious news agenda, as political scientist Pippa Norris explains (2000: 312):

> . . . many post-industrial societies have seen diversification in the channels, levels and formats of political communication that have broadened the scope of news and the audience for news, at both highbrow and popular levels. Newspaper sales have not declined in post-industrial societies; the proportion of regular readers of European newspapers has doubled in the past three decades, and the social profile for readers has broadened. . . . The amount of news shown on public-service TV in OECD countries has tripled over the past thirty years, not contracted. Three-quarters of all Europeans watch TV news every day, up from half three decades earlier.

Even if the Internet has far more sites devoted to pornography than to politics, and *The Times* publishes a picture of Madonna and her new husband on its front-page, we cannot conclude that the profit motive has swept all before it and that *The Times* and the Internet are dumbed-down media. The multichannel, multimedia environment of the twenty-first century is more like a prosperous hypermarket whose shelves overflow with an abundance of goods from vintage wine to cheap, own-brand detergent. The real issue is who has access to the goods? In some Arab countries illiteracy rates for women are as high as 60 per cent (UNESCO, 1996). In 1998 there were 53 Internet hosts per 1,000 people in Canada compared to 0.03 Internet hosts per 1,000 people in Zambia (UN, 1999). Even in the UK in 2000 only 25 per cent of British homes had Internet access, rising to 40 per cent if those having access from work are included. The struggle to break down information apartheid will be one of the great challenges of the century.

Owners and editors

Much that has been written about the owner/editor relationship appears to accept the journalistic folklore that publishers should never interfere and that business and news functions should be separate. This theory has rarely, if ever, been true in practice. Editors who fail to get at least two of the three apples on the fruit machine lined up – circulation, editorial budget and advertising revenue – do not last. 'Editors who look after their budgets tend to last longer, so long as they also sell the paper,' wrote one former Fleet Street editor (Edwards, 1989: 41). Even the Scott Trust, owner of *The Guardian* and from 1993 of the *Observer*, acted with un-Guardian-like ruthlessness to restore the fortunes of the ailing *Observer*, quickly removing editors who failed to make a dent on the newspaper's sales figures.

For media analyst, Colin Sparks, owners' priorities are simply stated, 'the press exist to make money, just as any other business does. To the extent that they discharge any of their public functions, they do so in order to succeed as businesses' (1999: 46). Journalist, David Randall is unequivocal. He believes that, 'Owners' priorities have probably imposed more limitations on how journalism is practised than any other factor in the last 20 years' (2000: 17). Journalists' memoirs are full of stories of proprietorial interference (see Edwards, 1989; Evans, 1994 and Neil, 1996). The paradigm case is, of course, Rupert Murdoch. His own experience in Australian newspapers meant that he had a better understanding than most of how the news business worked. And, according to journalist Henry Porter (1999: 45):

> Murdoch reads the market better than anyone and what he understood a long time before most was the way that demographic developments in Britain, combined with a certain intellectual passivity, now required practically all newspapers to compete in the mid-market and therefore for mid-market material – show-business coverage, interviews, scandal, human interest stories, sports, health and fitness, and book chat.

What ethical issues are raised by the owner/editor relationship? There are two major issues: first, where the publisher attempts to influence content for corporate aims, and second, where working conditions and editorial standards are driven down by wider business considerations. Asking the editor to give special attention to an issue, or not to give any attention to it at all, for wider corporate reasons, does happen. One of the best-known examples, referred to in the previous chapter, was former *Observer* editor, Donald Trelford's, reporting of alleged massacres in Matabeleland in Zimbabwe against his publisher's wishes.

A few years later Trelford was faced with the opposite problem: pressure from the owner to pursue an issue for private and business reasons. Tiny Rowland was determined to expose the seamier side of Mohammed al Fayed's business activities after the latter's victory in the battle to buy Harrods store. The *Observer* newspaper became the vehicle for this ambition. Stories were published in the newspaper's business section, culminating in a special mid-week issue entitled 'The Phoney Pharaoh' which leaked the government report exposing Fayed's deceitful business dealings. As Trelford later admitted: 'the public perception . . . that the *Observer* had served the commercial interests of its proprietor was undoubtedly damaging to a publication whose main asset (in some ways its only one) had always been its reputation for plain dealing' (2000b: iii).

On the one hand, in dealing with owners – and any other special interest group for that matter – 'the editor must have it in him to defy the proprietor, the spin doctors, the pleas from Number 10, all legal advice and public opinion to publish a story that causes an almighty and nearly everlasting stink' (Porter, 1999: 47). On the other, editors have to resist pressures to have their storylines dictated to them.

Proprietorial pressure is usually less visible, as Andrew Neil explained in his account of his editorship of Murdoch's *Sunday Times*:

> There is a common myth among those who think Rupert Murdoch has too much power and influence that he controls every aspect of his newspapers on three continents, dictating an editorial before breakfast, writing headlines over lunch and deciding which politician to discredit over dinner. He has been known to do all three. But he does not generally work like that: his control is far more subtle. For a start he picks as his editors people . . . who are generally on the same wavelength as him. (1996: 164)

American journalist Philip Meyer's 1980s' analysis of a survey of American publishers and reporters threw up some interesting results. It fixed a typology of publishers as 'politicians', those who intervene for good and ill; 'fixers', those who intervene purely to seek their own interests; 'statesmen', who intervene helpfully and 'absentees', who do not intervene at all. His findings defied journalistic folklore. They showed newsrooms with absentee publishers were among the least happy. The happiest newsroom was one 'whose publisher takes an active role in producing and enhancing the editorial product – the statesman' (1991: 109). He concluded that a newsroom which has sensible mechanisms for resolving ethical dilemmas is one where there is mutual respect between editor and publisher and high staff morale. He found that nothing destroys morale as much as knowing that 'the place is being run without regard to moral values' and where decision-making is free from the application of rules (1991: 113).

Meyer's analysis highlights a central fact about the news business. It is not sensible to think that ethics is for journalists and grubby money-making for publishers. A cooperative model where on the one hand, publishers recognize that a high-quality editorial environment is necessary to attract and keep both audience and advertisers and, on the other, journalists realize that profit is not a dirty word and can provide the environment in which ethical practice is possible. In Meyer's words, 'The key goal is to put the entire weight and majesty of the newspaper behind its ethical decisions and not to dilute those decisions by partitioning them off to different segments' (1991: 115). Usually it will be the editor or producer who acts as the guardian of editorial integrity. Very occasionally it might even be the publisher.[2] Ideally, they will work together to create a top quality product.

Advertiser pressure

I glanced at the issue of advertiser influence in the previous chapter. Where media is financed to a great extent by advertising, and this is the case for much media in Britain except the BBC and the tabloids which rely on circulation sales, the potential exists for advertising to exert pressure on content. Advertisers pay for a certain kind of editorial environment. Even if *The Guardian* were to increase dramatically its readership by printing pictures of Page 3 girls, the loss of advertising revenue would not make it worthwhile for the paper to boost circulation in this way. Similarly, airline companies have been known to pull advertising around programmes about plane accidents. Advertisers seek audiences and ultimately consumers for their products. They are hardly likely to advertise in environments that are hostile to their products.

The difficulty arises when journalists begin to make decisions about coverage swayed by its probable effect on advertisers. For instance, American researchers found that women magazines which received substantial advertising revenue from tobacco companies were unlikely to run critical articles about the impact of tobacco on health. In Britain the evidence for advertising pressure is largely anecdotal. However, if reporters are to retain credibility, and in part advertisers pay for a credible environment, then most of the time they and their editors will have to resist advertiser pressure, be it from their own advertising department or from outside advertisers.

THE REPORTER'S INTEGRITY

In 1999 a survey by the British Film Institute showed that 70 per cent of television programme makers believed that the 'quality of broadcasting is falling' and that ethical standards and levels of accuracy had declined significantly during the decade. Most television producers attributed the worsening standards to cost-cutting (Quinn, 24 May, 1999). The conflict between good practice and turning a profit is one of the toughest of all. A reporter, like any other worker, is vulnerable to the temptations of cutting corners and management too comes under pressure to find ways of cutting costs through spurious multi-skilling which, as media scholar Michael Bromley has argued 'contains the potential for the final fragmentation of journalism, en-skilling some as "entrepreneurial editors" but de-skilling others to the status of machine hands and extensions of the computer' (1997: 350).

Reporters have evolved from Fourth Estate to 'mouse monkey', in the words of one BBC reporter I interviewed in the summer of the new millennium. Scandalously low starting salaries for most reporters, lack of union protection and fierce competition for jobs provide a harsh working environment for many young journalists where ethics can seem remote and irrelevant. In his research on the role of the British National Union of Journalists (NUJ) in raising concerns about ethics, Harcup rightly states that 'journalistic ethics cannot be divorced from everyday economic realities such as understaffing, job insecurity, casualised labour, bullying and unconstrained management prerogative' (2002: 112).

Several years ago I attended a seminar in which a Spanish journalist outlined ways of improving newsroom organization to increase job satisfaction and product quality. One participant responded by comparing this to rearranging the deck chairs on the *Titanic*. While we continue to accept a system largely driven by commercial imperatives, he considered any change to the superstructure cosmetic and futile.

So what approach should be adopted by a reporter working within a patently flawed system? Ethics is concerned with what depends upon our actions and choices. It implies that individual actions and choices can shape human practices and modify the conditions of our actions. The steady work of the United Nations War Crimes Tribunal in bringing Serbian leader, Slobodan Milosevic, to court in 2001 may make a difference. But the possibility of ethical practice does not exist in a vacuum. None of us starts from zero. We all start from somewhere, bounded by the limitations of history, family, genetic and cultural inheritance. At each given moment, we are faced with *our* reality and for most reporters this involves working within an imperfect system.

The German moral philosopher, Robert Spaemann (1995), has outlined three attitudes one can adopt to deal with the imperfect reality in which we find ourselves ineluctably immersed. The first is the attitude of the fanatic: fanatics believe they are possessors of all meaning and righteousness, that it befalls them to transform the world, to rid it of all injustice or to destroy it in the attempt. It is the attitude of a Robespierre or Pol Pot. A second possible attitude is that of the cynic who believes that the world is entirely bereft of meaning. Cynics sneer at the very notion of ethics. Life is about the survival of the fittest and anyone who believes otherwise is a sentimental fool. Lip-service is often paid to this attitude on tabloid newspapers. A third attitude is serenity. It was expressed by the SAS officer briefing British soldiers who had heard discouraging news of losses:

> I don't know why everybody's looking so sorry for themselves. Nobody sent us down here with any divine right to score all the goals. This is the way it is in wars – you win some, you lose some. It's the Argentines' day today – tomorrow it could be ours again. (Cited in Hastings, 2000: 316–17).

Serenity implies an acceptance of the limitations one finds. It does not, however, imply passive resignation and refusal to act to improve what can be improved, and much can.

'ETHICAL EFFICIENCY'

Business can be ethical. One of the great lessons of the last twenty years or so is that if organizations pursue profits to the exclusion of all else, they will end up losing customers and their best workers. The doctrine of corporate responsibility has been woven into the business strategies of many companies indeed their share value depends on it.[3] Work satisfaction is considered key to good company performance. All organizations inevitably have values because they are made up of people – and generations of people – whose values have been enshrined or are projected either explicitly or implicitly in an organization's culture.

The dichotomy posed by Belsey (1998) of 'industrial' versus 'ethical' journalism is overly pessimistic. However, he is right to underline the particular difficulties of embedding ethical practice in media organizations. They are fast-moving, with little time to examine or acknowledge mistakes. An instinctive aversion to reflection can harden into an arrogant rejection of criticism, a 'brittleness' (Meyer, 1991) and the development of journalistic cultures which are inimical to honest practice. Randall speaks of this on certain newspapers where

> Reporters competing to get their stories published anticipate executive values and are prepared (or feel obliged) to adopt practices which are at odds with their private values. This professional schizophrenia is at its most chronic where the prevailing culture is known to favour stories that are composed of vivid blacks or whites and not the messy greys and ambiguous mid-tones of reality. (2000: 17)

How can ethical industrial journalism be encouraged? Often it seems that the industry has seen ethics as a public relations problem upon which action need only be taken when problems arise. Ethical dilemmas inevitably arise for media owners and workers. In a brittle, highly competitive, secretive environment, the challenge is to resolve them in a manner which allows the organization and its workers to function as well as they can.

'Ethical efficiency' – having mechanisms which allow core moral values to flourish – works for the good of all. In the following chapters we will look at ways in which it might be achieved.

NOTES

1 The first Royal Commission on the Press (1949) was established to 'inquire into the control, management and ownership of the newspaper and periodical press and the news agencies'. It and the second (1962) and third (1977) Royal Commissions on the Press variously recommended ownership and concentration control, improvements in journal-

ism education and increased professionalism through the establishment of a Press Council on the lines of the General Medical Council. However, most of the proposals were ignored or were not properly put into effect. See Curran and Seaton (2000).

2 Murdoch has acted in this role, reprimanding his then *News of the World* editor, Piers Morgan, and forcing him to publish an apology for photographs of Countess Spencer in the grounds of a private clinic.

3 This is the rationale behind publications such as *Ethical Performance*, which is subscribed to by many big City companies. A large proportion of share value is in invisibles which include brand image and company values. In 2002 the scandals surrounding the US corporate giants Enron and Worldcom, demonstrated how unethical practices can have disastrous business consequences.

A colleague was asked by students interested in taking an undergraduate journalism degree whether they would study ethics? His response was that it was not
an essential part of the degree. If you are learning how to design a car in
mechanical engineering, he told them, you do not go and learn about being a
traffic warden.

He had a point. The practice of journalism – reporting, telling a compelling
story, building up a good contact list, accuracy – does not involve considering
whether Kant's account of the categorical imperative is a more satisfactory guide
to ethical behaviour than Bentham's felicific calculus. Reporters are not required
to be moral philosophers. Similarly, codes of conduct have less of an impact on a
reporter's daily decision-making than a journalist's own code of personal
conduct. Most journalists know that it is usually wrong to pay criminals for a
story. The more difficult question is when, if ever, is it right to do so? Most
reporters would accept that interviewing a child without their parent's or
guardian's permission is wrong. But what exceptional public interest might
override this? What does it mean to treat those experiencing shock or grief with
sympathy and discretion? If codes are simply lists of the do's and don'ts accepted
by most reporters, of what use are they? Do they help in promoting ethical
behaviour or are they simply window-dressing by an industry anxious to avoid
legislation?

PROMOTING ETHICAL BEHAVIOUR

Journalists' work is strongly related to telling the truth about things. Remove the
link to truth and journalism is dead. As long as it prints things which are true,
even the most sensational, outrageous tabloid paper may still claim to be a
newspaper, however tenuous we believe its grip on the truth may be. As we have
seen, the pressures on journalists not to be truthful are very great. They can be
summarized into three categories: the desire for glory – the esteem of one's peers
– the ambition for power and the desire for money. So far we have discussed
different kinds of moral dilemmas which arise from these conflicting desires. In
this final section, I will examine ways in which ethical behaviour can be
promoted.

Legislation

The formulation of laws is the first, most obvious way in which the boundaries of
behaviour and practice can be established. In Britain there are over 250 laws
affecting information disclosure including laws covering libel, defamation,

contempt of court, blasphemy, reporting of minors, terrorism and security matters. The 1990 and 1996 Broadcasting Acts set out restrictions on cross-media ownership and provide for regulatory bodies for the broadcasting industry. The Human Rights Act (1998) has provisions protecting privacy and freedom of information.

It is a well-known truism that the law is not necessarily equivalent to the just or good. However, if we agree that a body of law is just and good, is it the best way to promote ethical practice? Certainly it can set a framework for acceptable practice but it is likely that 'the legal route to media quality will not be sufficient. Neither legal rights for journalists, nor legal restrictions on the media, will in themselves produce good journalism' (Belsey and Chadwick, 1995: 465).

An alternative approach to the provision of the blunt instrument of a specific law is to establish bodies legally empowered to regulate the media. This statutory response to regulation has been preferred by successive British governments for the broadcast industry. Statutes – legislative provisions, made by the legislature, and expressed in a formal document – have established a number of broadcast bodies with legal powers to enforce rulings and maintain standards of quality and programming required by British and European law:

- Broadcasting Standards Commission for the whole broadcast industry (www.bsc.org.uk). The BSC administers codes on privacy and fairness as required by the 1996 Broadcasting Act. The BSC succeeded the Broadcasting Standards Council and the Broadcasting Complaints Commission. It regulates television, radio, cable, satellite, digital and text services. Its adjudications are published monthly and it can order them to be aired by the offending programme.
- BBC Governors for the BBC (www.bbc.co.uk/info/bbc). Under the BBC charter – due for renewal in 2006 – they are appointed by the government and in turn appoint the director-general and senior management. The twelve governors are responsible for monitoring performance and maintaining standards as set out in the *Producers' Guidelines*. Disciplinary action can be taken against those who breach the guidelines.
- Independent Television Commission for independent television (www.itc.org.uk). The ITC licences and regulates all commercially funded broadcast media transmitting from the UK. It replaced the Independent Broadcasting Authority in 1990. It has formidable powers including the ability to rescind a licence from a company guilty of serious breaches of its licence; it may levy fines of up to three per cent of a company's annual revenue; order programming changes; order corrections and apologies.
- Radio Authority for all independent radio services (www.radioauthority.org.uk). The RA has similar powers to the ITC. It is chiefly involved in standards issues related to the holding of a licence. It leaves privacy and fairness issues to the BSC.

Each of these bodies administers codes of practice. All of them must report annually to the Culture Minister.

Discussions about the new communication legislation, which will be enacted in 2003, recognized that the convergence of broadcast, Internet and telecommunication technologies and the overlapping functions of some of the existing regulatory bodies, called for a new approach to communication regulation. A new unified regulator – OFCOM – was created for the commercial sector (see p. 91). The BBC has sought to maintain its own regulatory framework. 'One of the strongest arguments for keeping the BBC out of an industry regulator such as OFCOM', according to academic Steven Barnett (2001), is that 'its funding and remit is set by Parliament, to whom it should be directly accountable. The culture select committee is the most public and effective parliamentary forum in which to pursue that accountability'. Whatever happens, even though Britain's regulatory landscape is set to change once more, statutory controls will stay in place for the broadcast media.

Codes of practice

As we have seen, statutory regulation makes use of codes of practice to encourage ethical conduct. Codes are usually, however, associated with an approach based on self-regulation such as the kind favoured for the UK print industry. The Code of Practice adopted by the Press Complaints Commission (PCC) for the newspaper industry is the most influential but not the only journalism code in Britain. The National Union of Journalists, the journalists' trade union, established the first code of practice in 1936. The Newspaper Publishers Association, the industry's trade association, has a code and most newspapers have stylebooks which give detailed, specific guidance on matters from style and spelling to guidance on conflicts of interest and source confidentiality. As Harris (1992) has pointed out, UK codes of practice are primarily concerned with news and reporting; they do not, for example, specifically cover areas such as advice columns.

The United States is the home of journalists' codes of practice and they were first established at the beginning of the twentieth century. In part they were an attempt to professionalize journalism in a similar way to medicine and the law. The International Federation of Journalists' code speaks, for example, of seeking to establish a standard of *professional* conduct for reporters. In Chapter one we saw that the profession/trade debate in Britain is far from resolved. Labour politician and journalist, Roy Hattersley (1999), is typical of many who believe journalism is a trade on the grounds that all journalists write to order and are not – and should not be – licensed. Many professional associations require registration of their members and serious breaches of behaviour can lead to members being struck off. The potential for state control and abuse of a licence regime for the journalists who must challenge state power is obvious.

If codes are not about the search for professional status – and the responsibilities this implies – what are they for? In Belsey and Chadwick's words, 'Adherence to a code . . . shows a collective public commitment to acknowledged ethical principles and standards' (1995: 467). In doing this they can serve a number of functions:

1 *Protection.* Codes can provide protection for a number of constituencies (Harris, 1992). First, they benefit readers or viewers by upholding standards of accuracy, fairness and impartiality. Second, they protect sources by maintaining the principle of confidentiality. Third, they can protect those in the news through provisions concerning harassment, privacy, use of discriminatory language and intrusion into those suffering grief or shock. Codes can also benefit journalists by protecting them from pressures to behave unethically. Finally, codes can protect particularly vulnerable members of society, children, those who are mentally ill and members of minority groups.[1]

2 *Education.* By setting out core values and principles, codes can provide an educational function for reporters and contribute to the creation of climates of acceptable behaviour.

3 *Public relations.* By articulating occupational ideals and atoning for past sins by forbidding practices which have come to be publicly unacceptable,[2] codes can provide a useful public relations function.

4 *Damage limitation.* Codes can function as an exercise in damage limitation, warding off threats of more onerous obligations.

However, there is also some scepticism among journalists and academics alike about whether codes alone can be effective. As media analyst, Chris Frost, puts it, 'No industry has failed to notice that codes of practice can add an aura of respectability and fairness without necessarily forcing any real need for responsibility' (2000: 101).

If codes are not obligatory and there are limited powers to enforce them, what protection can they really provide and how they can they effectively contribute to ethical practice?

Enforcement: self-regulation and statutory control

Much of the discussion about self-regulation centres on the argument that it can achieve more than the law. The former PCC chairman, Lord Wakeham, was unsurprisingly one of the chief apologists for this position and it is instructive to examine in more detail arguments he set out in a speech to lawyers in 1998.[3] His principled opposition to legal restrictions on the media is based on the view that 'freedom of the press is . . . a very important part of a democracy. And freedom to my mind is indivisible. Privacy laws or other forms of statutory control must, by their very nature, impinge on that freedom – with democracy the loser.' The notion that freedom of the press is 'indivisible' is, as we saw in Chapter six, open to criticism on a number of counts, not least because a newspaper's freedom to print details of your sex life impinges on your freedom to be left alone. Wakeham's support for self-regulation is also based on his scepticism that 'you can ever force people through law or statute to behave in a responsible fashion. Broadcasters are controlled by statutory authorities: they still get things wrong, and from time to time flout the jurisdiction of those seeking to control them.' However, one could equally argue that statutory control is not just about seeking to ensure that broadcasters act responsibly but is also about ensuring that they do not behave badly; furthermore, a few examples of irresponsible behaviour hardly amounts to failure, as Wakeham would also surely argue in the case of the PCC. He concludes his 'principled' arguments with the statement of his belief that 'responsibility and good conduct stem from many sources other than the force of statute: from peer pressure; from example; from the moral authority of voluntary rules – freely agreed to and framed by those who are to be bound by them.' Few would disagree with most of this statement; the question is, however, whether those who have framed the rules do, in fact, abide by them? Wakeham is on stronger ground when he examines the practicalities of self-regulation:

> Self-regulation does produce effective self restraint. It does work in the vast majority of disputes between individuals and newspapers – nine in ten of which we can resolve. It is free and easy and quick. It does produce responsibility without impingement on freedom. It will be a practical and flexible method of regulation in the new world of the Internet and the communications revolution we are now witnessing. And it is on the basis of that I am content to argue that – while it may not be perfect – self-regulation can deliver more for ordinary people than a formal legal system of press restraint ever could.

In countries which rely more heavily on statutory mechanisms to regulate media practice, journalists are certainly not immune from criticism. France, for example, has comprehensive statutory controls dating from 1881 but these seem to have done little to halt fierce criticism of its press (Texier, 1998). The debate about self-regulation or statutory controls in many ways seems sterile. The question should be how can good journalism be encouraged? What is the best way of promoting a vigorous and responsible media?

KEEPING THE CRITICS AT BAY

In Britain much of the impetus for more robust self-regulation, and the threat of worse, came from the periodic concerns raised by press invasions of privacy: the two issues have been inextricably entwined in the history of self-regulation in the UK (see Chapter seven). A General Council of the Press was first mooted by the first Royal Commission on the Press in 1949 and the first British General Council of the Press met in July 1953.[4] In 1963 it became the Press Council, to be replaced in January 1991 by the Press Complaints Commission.

The PCC adopted the Code of Conduct formulated by national newspaper editors in 1989. A number of years later Peter Cole, former editor of *The Sunday Correspondent* and Professor of Journalism at the University of Sheffield, pinpointed the self-interest at the heart of the editors' relationship with the PCC:

> There is to a certain extent a sort of tacit conspiracy between the editors and the PCC. The PCC knows it is only there because things had come to such a pass before. The creation of the PCC was a strategic avoidance by the newspaper industry of privacy legislation at the point it came into being. It is in the interests of both parties to be seen to be taking it seriously. (cited in Wells, 2000)

The Press Complaints Commission began work in January 1991, very much a creation of editors and publishers anxious to stave off threatened privacy legislation in the wake of irresponsible behaviour by sections of the press. However, as we saw in Chapter seven, the newspaper industry did not succeed in persuading Sir David Calcutt that the PCC's attempt to provide mechanisms for self-regulation for the print industry had been effective. In January 1993 he recommended that it be replaced by a statutory Press Complaints Tribunal with powers to investigate complaints, levy fines and order the industry to pay compensation or publish appropriately placed retractions or apologies.

In the meantime, the PCC and the industry fought to avoid the introduction of statutory regulation. The industry body set up to fund the PCC, the Press Standards Board of Finance (Pressbof), proposed a series of measures to reform the PCC and strengthen self-regulation. These included creating a lay majority on the Commission, giving it final power of approval to make changes to the code and increased publicity about its work. The retirement of the PCC's first chairman, Lord MacGregor, in December 1994 and his replacement by the vigorous and politically astute Lord Wakeham signalled the industry's recognition that it must raise its game.

In the Britain of the late 1980s and early 1990s no politician or member of the Royal Family (with the possible exception of the Queen and the Queen Mother) was safe from the attentions of the ferociously competitive tabloid press. Between 1989 and 1997 readers were regaled with sleazy tales of their ruling elites. When the *Sunday Times* serialized in 1992 Andrew Morton's account of the private torments of Princess Diana, the PCC chairman spoke of it being 'an odious exhibition of journalists dabbling their fingers in the stuff of other people's souls' (MacGregor, 1992 cited in Shannon, 2001: 89). Little did he know that the Princess had conspired in the writing of the book. Invasions of the privacy of lesser mortals, the stock-in-trade of the *News of the World*, received less attention.

In July 1995 the government published its response to Calcutt and the all-party National Heritage Committee *Report on Privacy and Media Intrusion*, which had recommended privacy legislation. The Major government took the view that 'industry regulation is to be much preferred' (1995b: 5), a view shared by subsequent Labour governments, and the threat of statutory control was lifted.

THE PRESS COMPLAINTS COMMISSION AND ITS EVOLVING CODE OF PRACTICE

The PCC has sixteen members. Seven are senior editors from the national, regional and periodical press. The remaining nine include the chairman and a selection of the great and the good (in 2001 a bishop, senior civil servants, quango executives and politicians). A senior academic, Robert Pinker, acts as the Privacy Commissioner and after Lord Wakeham's resignation became acting chairman of the PCC until Wakeham's successor, Sir Christopher Meyer, senior civil servant and diplomat, could take up his appointment. All commissioners are appointed by an independent Appointments Commission made up of the chairmen of the PCC and Pressbof and three others nominated by the PCC chairman from outside the newspaper industry. There is also a Code Committee of fifteen members composed entirely of editors.

The PCC acts as a complaint service for the public, who do not waive their legal rights by making a complaint. Third-party complaints are only dealt with if the affected party agrees or there is an exceptional public interest issue at stake. If a complaint is upheld, the publication is 'obliged' to publish the adjudication giving it 'due prominence'. The 'obligation' only has moral force as the PCC has no power to sanction any publication which refuses to publish its judgements. However, the fact that all the British press has signed up to the code and that it is increasingly written into the job contracts of reporters and editors means that in practice no publication has refused to comply with the PCC. Usually the PCC seeks to reconcile complainaints and the publication concerned. An average of 30 per cent of the 2,000 to 3,000 complaints made each year are solved by action taken by the publication. The great majority of complaints (around 65 per cent) concern matters of accuracy. The PCC only adjudicates between two to three per cent of the complaints made to it each year (Annual Reports 1991–2000).

The PCC and the code have increasingly become a standard-setter for good practice. The PCC provides advice to editors before publication on particularly contentious stories and has issued more detailed guidance on specific matters. After censuring *Mirror* journalists for breaching the code's guidance on financial journalism, for example, the PCC issued more general advice on good practice in which they recommended application of the 'Private Eye' test, that is 'if it would embarrass a journalist to read about his or her actions in "Private Eye", and at the same time undermine the integrity of the newspaper, then don't do it' (Report 53, 2001).

The code has changed considerably since it was first adopted by the PCC in 1991. Since then there have been approximately 30 changes to the code, which must be agreed by the Code Committee and ratified by the Commission. Changes have been made to tighten up provisions on privacy, harassment, reporting of minors in sex cases and the rights of children to privacy. The most extensive re-writing of the code took place after the death of Princess Diana and a substantially altered code came into effect in January 1998 (see Chapter seven). Many changes have been made in response to events and to new legislation. However, the Code Committee appears to have been less responsive to proposals for change from the public. In 2000, for example, eleven representations were made from 'members of the public and others' for changes to the code. None was accepted (Annual Review, 2000). The PCC makes no apology for this. 'The Code is, crucially, the industry's own Code,' wrote the then chairman of the Code Committee, David English. The fact that 'the Code is drafted by industry practitioners for the industry' is what ensures, 'the unswerving commitment of all sectors of the newspaper and magazine publishing sector to self-regulation' (Annual Report, 1995: 11).

Some critics are not so sure. *The Times* journalist, Libby Purves, reflecting on the *News of the World*'s coverage of a supermodel's struggle with alcoholism, was critical of the PCC's lack of teeth:

. . . if you are just a TV face whose wife has left home, or the parent of a murder victim who just happens to have a spent conviction for shoplifting, or a student prince who has been jilted by the local vamp, or a once-famous actor who has fallen on hard times and taken to the bottle, then it is not fair to turn you into mass entertainment. It is a form of assault. But it happens, every week, PCC or no PCC. Even when complaints are upheld the newspapers remain rich and unbothered. And most of the victims of casual press cruelty lack the resources to fight back in the courts. (6 February, 2001)

Another *Times* journalist, Matthew Parris, commenting on Prince William's attendance at the PCC's tenth anniversary party in February 2001, wrote, 'There's surely no suggestion that partying at this one will reinforce the PCC's resolve to guard the young Prince's privacy. Lack of resolve has never been the problem. The problem is lack of weaponry. In the end the Commission can do little more than splutter when newspapers intrude.'

For this reason, critics have argued that publishers should either agree to binding self-regulation, as in Sweden, with a press council empowered to require the publication of apologies, corrections and replies and, exceptionally, to impose fines. Failing this, a number of commentators argue for these powers to be underwritten by statute without imposing the kind of prior restraint that Calcutt proposed (see, for example, Curran and Seaton, 2000: 369).

There would appear to be a number of crucial challenges for the PCC. The first and most significant is the issue of sanctions. Without any power whatsoever to impose sanctions, the PCC – and those whom it seeks to protect – is entirely dependent on the goodwill of editors and publishers, and a forceful PCC chairman. When individuals step down and the going gets tough, there is no guarantee that the Commission will continue to be able to depend on compliant publishers.

Changing technology is the second great challenge. In its 1997 Annual Report the Commission declared that it had extended its jurisdiction to publications signed up to the code which appear on the Internet. But what about those publications on the Net which have not signed up to the code? How will ethical practice be encouraged across all Internet publications, taking into account the additional difficulties posed by cross-national jurisdictions? And what about the use of material distributed on the Internet? Plagiarism is not currently dealt with by the code but it surely will need to be in the future. New technology also raises questions about overlapping media jurisdictions. As media converge, regulatory bodies will need to work together more closely to provide integrated services.[5]

GLOBAL SELF-REGULATION AND CODES OF PRACTICE

In many other parts of the world the print industry has been subjected to a lighter legislative touch than its broadcast counterpart. Press councils have proliferated since Sweden established the first at the beginning of the last century. They can be found across all continents and all kinds of media systems and have been promoted as a way of regulating the press with varying degrees of success.

In 1992 the World Association of Press Councils (WAPC) was formed. The PCC was a founding member. However, it withdrew in March 2000, opposed to the WAPC's plans to establish a global code of ethics with a cross-border complaints authority to police it. It claimed that this 'could only be misused by authoritarian Governments seeking to control a free press' (Annual Review, 2000). To undermine the WAPC, the PCC was a founder member in 1999 of the Alliance of Independent Press Councils of Europe (AIPCE), described by the PCC as a 'loose-knit grouping of independent, self-regulatory Press Councils in Europe opposed to any form of global Code' (Annual Review, 2000).

If we look beyond the UK, what kind of consensus do we find about codes of practice? A survey of journalists in 21 countries found little consensus about professional roles, ethical norms and journalistic values (Weaver, 1998). In 1998 a conference held by journalists covering conflict sought to formulate common norms of conduct. A number of journalists argued that there are no special norms for covering conflict and that reporters should simply stick to the basic values of journalism. But it was clear that there was disagreement about what the basic norms of journalism are. In the words of one journalist, 'journalists are in the business of news, not truth' and news is what you can honestly find out that day.

Notwithstanding the difficulties of establishing universal norms, a number of organizations have established international codes of practice including the International Federation of Journalists. They express the view that there is good and bad journalism 'Whatever the audience. Whatever the culture. Whatever the language. Whatever the circumstances' (Randall, 2000: xviii). With some caveats, this is a view I will defend in the final chapter of this book.

GENERATING ETHICAL DEBATE

Understanding ethics as 'adherence to professional codes has limited and distorted the conceptions of media morality' because it encourages conformity to media organization routines, it leads to a professional arrogance which leaves little role for the 'layperson' and it casts media performance in 'amoral, functionalistic, instrumental, utilitarian terms' (White, 1995: 443–4). The opposite criticism is made by philosopher, Adrian Page, who says codes ignore consequences and that the 'emphasis on codes of practice carries with it an implication that all that can be done is to regulate how journalists gather information, not its effects. This is really a Kantian ethical position where the intention is more important than the eventual outcome and a good action is one performed with good intentions' (1998: 131).

Both these criticisms contain some truth. It is also true that codes in and of themselves are little more than lists of virtues to be applied and vices to be avoided, of scant use when making demanding decisions in difficult circumstances. Such decisions will often be less a function of deliberation and more of character. Codes can also do little to promote ethical thinking and action based on more substantial and sounder bases than the bare minimum contained in a code's clauses. The PCC's adjudication on the *Sun*'s payments to train robber, Ronnie Biggs, in May 2001, shows the limitations of codes of practice.

> Some people – including, possibly, readers of the newspaper – may well have found the exercize of the newspaper, and the prospect of Biggs returning to Britain ostensibly in the view of many to receive free medical treatment, offensive. However, it is not the Commission's job either to make purely moral judgements or to question the motives of Biggs himself . . . (Report 54, 2001)

Codes of practice can, however, be seen as holding up expectations concerning the character of a good journalist. However, they require a body with the capacity to apply them. Britain's broadcast industry already has this. The Press Complaints Commission is a start. Despite criticisms about its lack of teeth, it has begun a debate. By publishing its adjudications and guidance on controversial matters, the PCC is building up a corpus of jurisprudence which the print industry will find difficult to ignore. The generation of talk about ethics and journalism is one of the most valuable parts of the Commission's work and has already contributed to improved practice in a number of areas. Combined with other approaches – education, readers' editors and ombudsmen – the PCC and its code of practice may yet show how codes can be made to work.

NOTES

1 The slogan on the 2000 PCC Annual Review is 'Working together to raise standards, to protect the vulnerable and to serve the public'. Honourable sentiments, but one wonders who is working together? Certainly ordinary people have no part in any area of PCC decision-making. Reviewing PCC adjudications over the past ten years of its existence, it is notable that all formal complaints by the Royal Family about invasions of privacy have been upheld – hardly a vulnerable group – while the same level of protection does not seem to have been provided for other groups. On the credit side, the PCC has given detailed guidance on appropriate coverage of vulnerable groups.
2 The changes to the PCC code's provisions on harassment and privacy after Princess Diana's death in September 1997 come to mind.
3 Lord Wakeham resigned as PCC chairman in the spring of 2002. His association with the disgraced American utilities company, Enron, had made his position untenable. At the time of writing it has just been announced that Sir Christopher Meyer, formerly Press Secretary to John Major and currently the British Ambassador in Washington DC, will take over as PCC Chairman at the end of the year (2002).
4 A more detailed history of self-regulation of the British print industry can be found in Frost (2000). Shannon (2001) provides a definitive history of the PCC's first ten years.
5 In January 2000 Internet service providers set up the Internet Watch Foundation, an industry funded organization established to provide self-regulation for UK based servers.

Should journalists be accountable? Writing in 1999 *The Times* columnist, Simon Jenkins, in a piece entitled 'Don't blame the harlots' stated: 'The press may be without responsiblilty – who ever pretended otherwise? – but its power is a function only of what is granted by others' (5 February). He has a point. But to deny the media's responsibility does no one any favours, least of all journalists themselves. Without mechanisms to encourage accountability, reporters themselves could become prey to the pressures of unscrupulous owners and editors to behave in ways they'd rather not. In this chapter I'll examine how responsible journalism can be encouraged.

THE LIMITS OF THE LETTER OF THE LAW

Laws and codes serve useful purposes. Laws provide the outward boundaries of acceptable behaviour and codes hold up a set of expectations about good practice and the possibility that this will translate into the industry's own good custom and practice. It is, however, the underlying argument of this book that all the laws and codes in the world will not guarantee that we will act well: even to interpret and apply laws and codes properly, a modicum of virtue and practical wisdom are necessary.

Codes and laws have two further difficulties; first, they cannot cover every eventuality and it is precisely the hard cases that escape them. Second, external regulations can encourage a compliance with the letter of the law – the publication of an apology, for example – which is vitiated by accompanying actions. What are we to say, for instance, about Channel 4's action in agreeing to broadcast the apology demanded of it by the broadcasting regulators for screening *Brass Eye*'s satirical look at paedophilia without sufficient warning, and at the same time stating their belief that the ruling was 'confusing and contradictory'? Channel 4's director of programming, Tim Gardam, declared: 'We unequivocally stand by the programme and believe that we scrupulously followed the regulatory codes. What is disappointing and confusing about the ITC ruling is that it contradicts previous decisions where they supported programmes of a similar nature' (Channel 4, 6 September, 2001).[1]

Leaving aside the rights and wrongs of this particular issue, the example highlights the fact that complying with norms and acting well don't necessarily go together. Here Channel 4 obeyed the rule but at the same time, made it clear that it believed the ITC's ruling to be wrong and inconsistent: that way lie confusion and the undermining of the moral authority of regulatory bodies.

So if codes and laws don't have all the answers in what other ways may reporters, broadcasters and publishers be encouraged to act well? We will now consider the closely related notions of 'responsibility' and 'accountability'. Often criticisms of the media are made in the form that they have 'power without responsibility'.[2] Media organizations and journalists are considered 'irresponsible' and 'unaccountable.' What does this mean? Why should journalists be responsible? And to whom?

RESPONSIBLE AND ACCOUNTABLE

'Responsibility' is defined by the *Oxford English Dictionary* (1989) as the action or state of being responsible. The word 'responsible' itself has five definitions, the first two of which are obsolete. The three which concern us here define it as being, 'answerable, accountable (*to* another *for* something); liable to be called to account' and 'morally accountable for one's actions; capable of rational conduct'. Second, in an American usage, 'responsible' is being 'answerable to a charge'. And third, the term is defined as 'capable of fulfilling an obligation or trust; reliable, trustworthy; of good credit and repute'. The notion of accountability is closely allied to that of responsibility and is defined as 'liable to be called to account, or to answer for responsibilities and conduct; answerable, responsible' (*OED*, 1989).

Two things might strike us about these definitions. First, they are predicable only of moral agents. We could not call a baby to account and hold it responsible for continuous dribbling. In other words, we can only be responsible for what we voluntarily do as rational beings. Second, the definitions imply that being responsible means both taking ownership of conduct and actions and being prepared and able to answer for them.

Few journalists would quibble with the notion that they are 'responsible' for their actions in the first sense, that they can be held to carry personal blame or credit for an action or decision. But they have often been reluctant to consider that they might also be held answerable for their conduct. Journalists, especially in the print industry, have been notoriously slow to acknowledge mistakes and especially unwilling to be held up to scrutiny by people from outside the industry. However, if we understand the notion of 'responsibility' correctly, it must imply the ability to *explain* one's conduct. Being responsible is taking charge of behaviour and giving reasons for actions.[3] If moral choices cannot be explained, if we cannot give reasons for what we do, we might be considered intellectually or morally deficient. If an editor doesn't know why he or she showed an image of the mutilated corpse of a terrorist outrage, we would doubt the soundness of their intellectual let alone moral faculties. Here too we can see the sense of the Socratic notion that doing what is right is also about *knowing* what to do. The good person is good because he or she is also wise; acting badly is partly about being foolish. In other words, it is not enough to have good intentions: as a doctor, I may sincerely want to cure someone but if I inject them with ten times the required dosage of a life-saving drug I simply succeed in killing them.[4] A good person does good and to do good is also to know, to have learnt, to have practical wisdom.

All of us should, then, be able to give reasons for the choices we make. But to whom should reporters, editors, broadcasters and publishers have to give explanations? We might agree with the principle that responsibility implies the ability to explain, and with the view advanced by American philosopher, John Rawls, that moral principles and choices must be tested by publicity and be capable of public statement and defence (1971: 133). However, how and to whom should journalists be accountable?

SOCIAL RESPONSIBILITY

One way of answering this question is found in the *First Report of the Committee on Standards in Public Life* established by John Major's government to remove sleaze. The Nolan report set down seven principles of public life 'for the benefit of all who serve the public in any way' (1995: 14), and included the principle of accountability according to which those in public life are 'accountable for their decisions and actions to the public and must submit themselves to whatever scrutiny is appropriate to their office' (1995: 14). Here *personal* responsibility and accountability are at issue but the moot question is whether those in the media can be considered to hold positions of public trust. Apart from senior figures in parts of the broadcasting establishment (heads of the regulatory bodies; the chairperson, governors and director-general of the BBC), most people in the media can hardly be considered to be 'in public life' even though they might be considered to 'serve the public'.

Another way of answering this question is to frame it in terms of the media's 'social responsibility' or, particularly in the British broadcasting context, of 'public service'. The language of social responsibility was used by an independent commission established in the United States after the Second World War under the chairmanship of the head of the University of Chicago, Robert M. Hutchins. The Commission was charged to examine the state of the American media and it concluded that the media:

> . . . must be accountable to society for meeting the public need and for maintaining the rights of citizens and the almost forgotten rights of speakers who have no press. It must know that its faults and errors have ceased to be private vagaries and have become public dangers. . . . Freedom of the press for the coming period can only continue as an accountable freedom. Its moral right will be conditioned on its acceptance of this accountability. (1947: 18–19)

This view of the media's responsibility was predicated on the unique protection given to the American media by the First Amendment's commitment to the upholding of the freedom of expression. This argument was used to maintain that the media's privileged position under the American Constitution entailed a 'social responsibility' to serve democracy and provide the social goods of news and information for the public.

In the 1980s and 1990s, concern among many journalists and academics that the American media was failing to discharge this public trust, led to the creation of public or civic journalism as an attempt by local journalists and editors to reconnect to their publics by structuring news to cover their concerns.

By 1995 almost two hundred civic journalism projects had been established across the US, with widely divergent views as to the success and/or desirability of such initiatives (Jaehnig, 1998: 108).

In Britain discussion of the 'social responsibility' of the media has moved along two tracks: on the one hand, the history of the broadcast industry has been shaped by the notion that broadcasters must fulfill a 'public service' which has been classically defined in the BBC's mission to 'inform, educate and entertain.'[5] The challenge, however, is how to re-define and deliver this public service in the swiftly changing communications environment of the twenty-first century. The 2000 draft of legislation for 2003, *A New Future for Communications*, provided some notion of the scale of the changes taking place:

> By the end of 2000, well over a quarter of UK households will have digital television. . . . The number of television channels in the UK has risen from three, 20 years ago, to over 250 today. British viewers could choose from 300 hours of television in a week in December 1980. Today they could choose from over 40,000 hours. (2000: 7)

At the same time, it reaffirmed the government's commitment to maintaining public service broadcasting by providing a three-tier structure 'with the basic tier supporting standards across all services and with further tiers applicable to public service broadcasters' (2000: 51), stipulating core requirements to provide 'a strong regional focus including regional production and commissioning, a diverse, high quality schedule including news and current affairs and original production, educational programmes, children's programmes, religious programmes and coverage of arts, science and international issues' (2000: 54).

Broadcasting's unruly print cousins have always fought off any attempt by the State to lay down their obligations. In the twentieth century three government appointed Royal Commissions examined prevailing political anxieties about the power of the press. The first two Commissions in 1947–49 and 1961–62 explored the relationships between the State, ownership and freedom of expression; the third Commission (1974–77) examined the 'broader issue of the way the press related to its public', opening up, in one academic's view, 'the notion of accountability, beyond the realm of the traditional press-versus-the-State relationship, to one that drew accountability to the wider public into sharper focus' (O'Malley, 1998: 90). However, these State-inspired efforts to encourage press accountability have never met with much success, in part because of the lack of a countervailing First Amendment culture.

Social responsibility and justice

Underlying the talk of 'social responsibility' and 'public service', is the notion of justice. Justice is the virtue which implies the right ordering of our relationships to others.[6] If we are just, we learn to relativize our own interests and desires so that where my actions affect others, we recognize that it is not enough to justify them on the basis that they satisfy *my* interests. It is unjust to kill my neighbour simply because he annoys me; denying people the essential goods for their well-being, let alone their existence, is unjust because they are deprived of the possibility of living full human lives.[7]

The administration of justice is necessary in a world of scarce or unevenly distributed goods, of which news and information are one example, and most would accept that the State should have some role in ensuring that the weakest members of society can obtain both social and material goods. Regulation should be about promoting environments in which common or public goods are not the preserve of the few. In his *Commentary on the Book of the Powerful*, Aquinas states that: 'The corruption of justice has two causes: the false prudence of the wise man and the violence of the powerful.' Where governments don't act to protect the weak and media organizations do not recognize their social responsibilities, they do indeed corrupt justice.

At the same time, promoting a journalistic ethos in which both personal and social responsibility are considered a part of professional self-identity may achieve much that codes and laws cannot. A striking example of this came two days after the terrible events of 11 September 2001. Media speculation about those responsible centred on Islamic fundamentalists and the risk that anti-Muslim feeling could be whipped up, became very real. The *Sun* published a two-page editorial with the banner headline 'ISLAM IS NOT EVIL RELIGION'. It declared, 'If the terrorists were Islamic fanatics then the world must not make the mistake of condemning all Muslims. . . . The men who hijacked packed passenger planes and flew them into the World Trade Center and the Pentagon were evil. But the religion they practise is one of peace and discipline.' It continued: 'The Muslims in Britain ARE British. They may have a different culture to most of us but they love this country and they respect democracy' (13 September, 2001). This was responsible journalism.

IRRESPONSIBLE JOURNALISM

If we consider the harm done by irresponsible journalism, we can be in no doubt as to the importance of promoting responsible, accountable journalism. Irresponsible journalism is often a matter of straightforward ineptitude and much casual cruelty is inflicted by plain, professional incompetence. But it is also sometimes a failure of imagination and intelligence in thinking about the wider consequences of clichéd, stereotypical or superficial journalism.

Inaccuracy

The Press Complaints Commission receives more complaints about accuracy than any other issue. Getting a name right may seem relatively trivial to a young reporter but if it is the name of your murdered sister you will care terribly. Inaccuracy undermines trust in journalism. If reporters can't get basic facts right why should we believe anything they write or say?

Ignorance

Reporters can't be expert in everything but there are some areas where news organizations fail their public where, for example, important issues are covered by reporters who are just plain ignorant and don't recognize they are. Reporting about scientific and medical issues has often suffered from ill-informed coverage. Keeble cites the Reuters' style book's guidance on reporting medical cures: 'If a story making dramatic claims for a cure for AIDS or cancer does not come from a reputable named source, it must be checked with recognized medical experts before being issued (or spiked). If such a story is issued it should include whatever balancing or interpretative material is available from such authorities' (2001: 94).

Reporters' own ignorance fuels wider public lack of knowledge and understanding, for people depend on the media to inform them. About 73 per cent of the UK population watches television news every day and 16 per cent several times a week, figures much higher than the European average (Eurobarometer, 2000). 50 per cent of the British say they read a newspaper every day, 16 per cent several times a week and 15 per cent once or twice a week, discriminating between the media in the trust they place in them. In Britain 67 per cent trust television and radio news while only 15 per cent trust the newspapers. However, on the issue of the European Union about 36 per cent turn to television for information, 37 per cent to newspapers and 13 per cent to media generally. Examining coverage of the European Union by the British press, researchers concluded that it was inadequate, failing to show the contribution that the EU makes to the well-being of the British and among the reasons they found were 'low professional journalistic standards' and, in some cases, 'lack of specialized knowledge' (Anderson and Weymouth, 1999: 183)

Stereotyping

Member states of the European Union have suffered more than their fair share of stereotyped coverage, framed most frequently by the narrative of the Second World War. The *Sunday Mirror*'s facile 'BLITZED' headline (2 September, 2001) after the England football team's victory against Germany was all too predictable and recalled the ill-judged coverage of European Cup coverage in 1996 by its sister newspaper, the *Mirror*.[8]

Stereotyping, reducing people or groups to abstractions or clichés, is lazy, bad journalism. Reporting women solely in terms of their appearance; using insulting, pejorative terms for minority groups distinguished from us by their religion, ethnicity or sexuality; covering disabled people as though they were their disability or mentally ill people as 'nutters': such stereotyping fuels prejudice and worse. Fergal Keane's chilling account in *Season of Blood* (1996) of the media's role in the genocide in Rwanda demonstrates where it can lead. Newspapers and radio constantly spewed their hate propaganda against the minority Tutsi people, exhorting the Hutus to rise up against the invasion of 'cockroaches' and kill them.

We might agree that journalists should be responsible and therefore accountable. We might also agree that the media bears some kind of social responsibility for what it does without being precise about the details of this responsibility nor how best to achieve it. The next question is how to promote accountability and to decide to whom journalists should be accountable. According to Hamelink: 'Responsibility refers to professional attitudes towards colleagues, sources and clients. It also refers to the assumption of accountability for media products' (1995: 499).

Accountable to colleagues

One of the most effective ways of encouraging responsible behaviour is peer pressure. Acceptance by journalists themselves of minimum standards and naming and shaming of media and reporters who fail to meet them can be a very effective way of ensuring accountability. We saw in Chapter twelve how the print industry's Code of Practice provides some degree of both peer (and proprietorial) pressure. There are several other ways this can be achieved.

Media sections/programmes. The huge growth in the communications industry as well as the media's increasing fascination with itself has spawned a new specialist Media/Communications area. Programmes such as Radio 4's 'The Message' and newspaper sections such as the *Media Guardian* provide invaluable fora where journalists can debate the activities of their colleagues.

Media publications. The *Columbia Journalism Review* was founded in 1961 by members of the Journalism School of Columbia University with a remit to 'assess the performance of journalism in all its forms, to call attention to its shortcomings and strengths, and to help define – or redefine – standards of honest responsible service' (published on masthead). It has become a forum used by academics and journalists for debating key issues in journalism. The *British Journalism Review* has attempted to replicate the *CJR*'s role but has yet to establish a similar status to its American counterpart.

Accountable to sources

Should reporters be accountable to sources? Codes suggest that there is a duty to preserve confidentiality when it is requested. On the whole, however, journalists are wary about allowing sources any measure of control over their work because they believe it invites censorship. On the question of copy approval, in Randall's view: 'Showing someone what will inevitably be described as "the draft" of a story encourages the idea that it is being given to them for approval and, hence, possible alteration' (2000: 50). It is, he says, the reporter's job to produce accurate copy. More precisely, then, we can say that reporters have a duty of accuracy which implies that sources will be fairly treated. However, where a source or subject of a story has good grounds for believing they have been unfairly treated, it seems only sensible practice to allow a right of reply. One heartening sign on a number of newspapers is the increasing willingness to publish corrections.

Accountable to the public

If the public is the 'client', in what way should journalists be accountable to it? Certainly no figure is more invoked by reporters and editors to justify their actions than 'the public': journalists speak of the 'public's right to know', of 'giving the public what they want' but this can be little more than rhetoric if there are no mechanisms by which the public can have a voice.

Ombudsmen. One approach is the ombudsman. In Sweden the title is given to a government official charged with representing the public in its dealing with bureaucracy. Also known as readers' representatives, media ombudsmen can take up complaints on behalf of the public, monitor the media for accuracy and fairness and act as in-house critics. In the United States ombudsmen have become more media critic than readers' representative, writing regular columns on media controversies and by 1993 only about 30 out of over 1,600 daily newspapers had ombudsmen (Day, 1997: 45). In the UK *The Guardian* appointed an ombudsman to deal with readers' complaints, run a 'Corrections and Clarifications' column and comment on controversial media matters. The *Observer*, the *Independent on Sunday* and the *Mirror* have also appointed ombudsmen.

Press councils. Independent bodies established to monitor and evaluate the media's performance have had a variable record in promoting accountability. In the United States they have been an abject failure due largely to the lack of industry support. Industry support has been a key factor, as we saw in Chapter twelve, in ensuring that the British Press Complaints Commission has had a certain measure of success in ensuring some degree of public accountability for the press.

Readers' letters, phone calls and feedback programmes. These can be of some use in gauging public views but they are often limited to self-selecting groups and can be affected by the phenomenon identified by the German scholar, Elizabeth Noelle-Neumann, as the 'spiral of silence' (1984). This is where those who perceive that they are at odds with the apparent majority view keep silent, thus creating a spiral effect reinforcing the dominance of a view which may in fact be held by a minority.

Higher Education. The Hutchins Commission criticized the American journalism schools of the 1940s as being training establishments without commitment to raising standards or providing an evaluation of the media's performance. This is not the case today. The United States has over 400 journalism schools, some of which have become influential centres of journalism education and research, contributing to a debate with the industry on the principles and practice of journalism.

The widespread introduction of journalism into the university is very recent in Britain. It was confined until the 1990s to two vocational postgraduate programmes and its expansion has been confused with the development of media studies, a multidisciplinary area with roots in English studies, sociology, psychology and political science, and heavily skewed to a critical approach to journalism. A number of universities have now established journalism programmes and it is to be hoped that as there is more engagement between these institutions and the industry, the opportunities for constructive reflection and debate will increase.

American journalist and academic Philip Meyer, has proposed that they might be able to play a role in promoting the taking of an 'ethical audit' of news organizations. He suggests that the lynchpin could be the measurement of accuracy in news coverage (1991: 189–96). One way of doing this is to take a random sample of news stories, attach a questionnaire and send them to sources named in the stories. A distinction would have to be made between objective errors (misspellings of names, wrong addresses, ages and dates) and subjective ones (distortion, omission, emphasis). Meyer fully admits that 'the ethical problems of journalism go beyond anything that can be measured by such a simple evaluation'. However, he pragmatically points out that 'improvement must begin somewhere, and if it cannot begin at that simple and fundamental level, perhaps news people should face the possibility that it cannot be achieved at all. Fairness, balance, objectivity, and the defence of unusual methods are all empty without the basic capacity to gather and report the facts' (1991: 200).

Accountable to ourselves

Ultimately those who work in the media are accountable to themselves. We all have a moral compass which we ignore at our peril. Doing something which our conscience tells us is wrong is damaging, not only in its impact on others but also on ourselves. Accountability to ourselves is, in the end, more important than anything else. Excusing what we do because it's what the public wants is no excuse at all. As Britain's chief rabbi has said: 'The shapers of culture carry a moral responsibility. If a politician, in a racially charged neighbourhood, were to deliver a racist message, it would be no excuse for him to say that this is what his audience wanted to hear. To the contrary, the fact that they want to hear it is the very reason he should not say it' (Sacks: 2001).

Like the audience, those who work in the media also have an ultimate sanction. As David Randall says, 'we do not have to be mere creatures of the papers we work for: we have a choice. Just as readers can stop buying, so journalists can change jobs. We can decide that there are some things we will not do and leave the job. . . . If more of us did that, and made clear our reasons for doing so, journalism would be better for it' (2000: 133).

Of course, following your conscience doesn't mean you'll get it right, particularly if you're inexperienced in what you do. This is why many who have thought deeply about ethics have recommended seeking the advice of a good friend. The Roman writer Seneca (c.55BC–c.AD39) was clear on this:

> There is no real doubt that it is good for one to have appointed a guardian over oneself, and to have someone you may look up to, someone whom you may regard as a witness of your thoughts. It is, indeed, nobler by far to live as you would live under the eyes of some good person always at your side; but nevertheless I am content if you only act, in whatever you do, as you would act if anyone at all were looking on; because solitude prompts us to all kinds of evil. (cited in Bok 1980: 94)

But what if I don't want to be a good human being? What if I only want to make lots of money and I don't care who I damage on the way? Why shouldn't I act just to satisfy my own desires and interests? Aren't we, in fact, simply doing this anyway when we say we're acting ethically? I'll look at these difficult questions in the final chapter.

NOTES

1 Channel 4's chief executive, Michael Jackson, was even more robust in his comment on the regulator's decision: 'Despite the ITC ruling, Channel 4 is unwavering in its support for Chris Morris and *Brass Eye*' (6 September, 2001). The ITC censured the broadcaster for causing 'exceptional and gratuitous offence' to viewers by not giving a strong enough warning before the show was screened. The *Brass Eye* special was shown on 26 July, 2001 and to date is the most complained about show in British television history. Channel 4 received 2,000 calls, with an additional 1,000 viewers logging complaints with the ITC. The programme was also strongly criticized by children's charities and MPs. See Teather (7 September, 2001).

2 This oft-cited phrase was used by Stanley Baldwin with reference to the activities of the great press barons of the early twentieth century, Lords Rothermere and Northcliffe.

3 Some commentators, following Max Weber's distinction between an ethic of conviction and ethic of responsibility, have called for the adoption of the latter in journalism. Jake Lynch of *Reporting the World*, a group dedicated to promoting balance, fairness and responsibility in the coverage of international affairs, believes the ethic of responsibility to be particularly crucial in the reporting of conflict. He explores how journalists can all too easily become part of the story and that in reporting 'each individual journalist carries, at any moment, an unknowable share of responsibility for what happens next' (2002: 12).

4 Here I refer to knowledge which someone could and should have acquired. As a scientist friend of mine remarked, future generations may well look back on doctors' use of chemotherapy as a primitive practice akin to using leeches. However, given the current state of medical knowledge doctors cannot be criticized for using it.

5 In 1994 the Broadcasting Research Unit came up with eight basic principles for public service broadcasting:

1. geographic universality
2. universality of appeal. Broadcasters should show *EastEnders* and opera
3. universality of payment

4. programming distanced from vested interests and particularly from the government of the day
5. broadcasters should recognize special relationship to sense of national identity and community
6. minorities should receive special provision
7. should encourage competition in good programming rather than just in audience figures
8. public guidelines for broadcasters should liberate rather than restrict.

6 In his commentary on Aristotle's *Nichomachean Ethics* Aquinas stated that '*Justitia consistit in communicatione*' (8, 9, no. 1658). This could be translated as 'Justice consists in communication.'

7 St Thomas Aquinas maintained that a minimum of well-being is necessary for virtue.

8 The media is often accused of sensationalism, 'tabloidization' or 'dumbing down' in its coverage. As we saw in Chapter eleven, these terms have not been as clearly conceptualized as they might be which is why I have preferred not to deal with the subject here. Personality, sex and sleaze have appeared to replace coverage of weightier subjects in certain media and, it is alleged, with negative effects for democracy (see Franklin 1994; Fallows, 1996) but this subject requires more investigation (see Norris, 2000).

Every form of moral life . . . depends on education.

Michael Oakeshott

The terrorist attacks on New York and Washington on Tuesday 11 September, 2001 horrified the world. Three passenger-filled planes were used to crash into the World Trade Center and the Pentagon; another plane, headed for a target in Washington, came down outside Pittsburgh, thwarted by the action of passengers. Thousands of people were murdered on a particularly horrifying day in the blood-soaked history of terrorism. The following day the ten British national newspapers sold 15 million copies, 2.5 million more than usual. In many areas it was impossible to buy a broadsheet paper after midday.

Analysing the newspapers' performance a week later, *The Guardian* media commentator wrote: 'Journalism was properly fulfilling its task, telling us what it is like to live and to die on the day New York caught fire' (Greenslade, 17 September, 2001). In the same piece *The Times*' editor, Peter Stothard, said; 'Journalists are often criticized but they can take great satisfaction at telling this story so well and so sensitively'.

GOOD JOURNALISM AND JOURNALISTS

The Guardian's analysis of the reporting of that terrible September day included the views of most national editors. The consensus was that reporters and editors had done their job well by producing accurate, comprehensive, in-depth, fast and sensitive coverage. On these criteria the standard of reporting had been good if not excellent. Do these criteria help us to establish a baseline for determining good journalism from an ethical standpoint?

Professionalism

I think they do. Virtuous journalism is also virtuoso journalism. We saw in earlier chapters that being good is also about knowing *how* to be good. As Meyer suggested, achieving competent journalism – reporting which is accurate, for example – is a necessary first step to it being ethical (1991). If you cannot rely on what you read or what you see, how can the reporting be, in any meaningful sense, 'good'? Ethically good journalism begins with competent reporting.

Professional goals

What is journalism for? This is perhaps the area where there will be the greatest difference of opinion. There are a number of different journalistic traditions:

local and national reporting; tabloid and broadsheet journalism; western and developmental journalism; objective and peace journalism. Reporters from these traditions might variously reply that journalism is for fostering national development; scrutinizing the powerful; contributing to peace; revealing the virtues and vices of the rich and famous and giving the people what they want. Is good journalism also about successfully achieving the goals of the particular tradition in which we might work?

If we think back to some of the issues we have discussed in previous chapters, the answer to this has to be no. There are some journalistic traditions which straightforwardly encourage bad journalism because they countenance lying, distortion, voyeurism, the promotion of prejudice and hatred. For journalism to be good, it must have good aims. These could include:

- The provision of information
- The scrutiny of the powerful
- Providing a voice for all sectors of society
- The revelation of injustice

Aquinas makes a number of useful distinctions which help in understanding how to judge the goodness of actions.[1] First, we should look at the kind of action it is: on the whole, saving life is better than destroying it; providing information is better than not. Second, the goal of the action should be taken into account. If I publish information in order to inspire hatred of a minority group, then my action is in no way good. A third source of goodness, says Aquinas, is in relation to my judgement of whether what I do is right or wrong. If I do something which I believe to be wrong, in those circumstances it is wrong to do it. It is a source of badness in my action in the sense that I am doing something which I consider wrong. As Philippa Foot says, 'acting as one thinks one should not is a very radical form of badness in the will. How could a human being be acting well in doing what he or she saw as evil?' (2001: 74). So, if I'm asked to do something which I sincerely and clearly believe to be bad, then I simply shouldn't do it. Of course, I might be mistaken. I might have what Aquinas calls an 'erring conscience', an important matter to which I shall return shortly.

Character

Professionalism – understood as accurate, sensitive, comprehensive and fast coverage – and the kind of professional goals which aim to do good for the right reasons, don't just happen. Reporting of the terrorist attacks on the United States required immense hard work; determination; news sense; fascination with every aspect of the story (curiosity); attention to detail; a sense of urgency; imagination and sensitivity. It also required a consciousness that the media was performing a public service for all British citizens. Without these qualities – virtues – coverage could have been mawkish, careless, xenophobic or prurient.

That it largely was not is a tribute to the responsibility and good judgement of editors and reporters.[2] If these kinds of qualities are habitually exercised, then they are indeed virtues and help produce high-class journalism.

Character is also key to good journalism. According to the journalist, David Randall, almost any intelligent person can, with sufficient effort, be a *competent* reporter. To be a *good* reporter, 'you must have real talent and flair for either research, or writing, or both. And you should have the right kind of character; for if there is one thing that separates outstanding reporters from the ordinary, it is this' (2000: 8).

As we've seen throughout this book, doing the right thing is a function of who we are. It's no coincidence that an editor makes a good decision about which pictures to broadcast after a major train accident, if he or she has proved to be decisive and responsible in ordinary situations. Most of the time reporters and editors aren't faced with enormously complex moral choices; when they are it will be their habitual behaviour – whether they're brave, foolish, sensitive or uncaring – which will mark the decisions they make. In Oakeshott's words:

> . . . the moral life is a *habit of affection and behaviour*; not a habit of reflective *thought*, but a habit of *affection* and *conduct*. The current situations of a normal life are met, not by consciously applying to ourselves a rule of behaviour, nor by conduct recognized as the expression of a moral ideal, but by acting in accordance with a certain habit of behaviour. The moral life in this form does not spring from the consciousness of possible alternative ways of behaving and a choice, determined by an opinion, a rule or an ideal, from among these alternatives; conduct is as nearly as possible without reflection. And consequently, most of the current situations of life do not appear as occasions calling for judgement, or as problems requiring solutions; there is no weighing up of alternatives or reflection on consequences, no uncertainty, no battle of scruples. There is, on the occasion, nothing more than the unreflective following of a tradition of conduct in which we have been brought up. (italics in original; 1991: 468)

This view is reflected in the comment of an American reporter asked about his views on ethics and journalism. He said: 'The few unethical journalists I've known are really flawed people. It's not that they don't follow any codes – they're not interested in codes. They were poorly brought up and did dishonest things' (cited in Goodwin, 1995: 15–16). This might seem to be a counsel of despair. It needn't be. Laws and codes can be effective in creating climates of opinion and control mechanisms to ensure that flawed characters become *professionally* unacceptable. Good character can also be encouraged by a number of measures which I'll discuss at the end of this chapter. Finally, there is always the flickering flame of conscience.

Conscience

I mentioned the matter of conscience earlier and also alluded to it in the previous chapter. What is conscience? It can be thought of as the capacity and sense all human beings have of knowing what is right and wrong. When we act well we are at peace and when we act badly there is a nagging sense of unease or even dreadful remorse.

This sounds straightforward but of course it isn't in the least. Where someone's conscience tells them it is right to be a suicide bomber or to pay workers starvation wages, then we may wonder whether conscience counts for much. These are situations where we can speak of 'erring consciences' and in these circumstances the people concerned can never act well.

However, the situation where we are entirely certain that a certain course of action, which appears to go against the grain of good conduct, is right is thankfully rare. Usually in difficult circumstances, we will be uncertain as to the right course of action. Should an editor of a local newspaper publish a story and picture of a convicted paedophile who has been hanging around a school, a dilemma faced by the deputy editor of the *Nottingham Evening Post* (cited in Keeble, 2001: 144–5)? Should a journalist betray a source to help convict a terrorist? What should a good journalist do?

According to BBC journalist, John Simpson: 'All you can do is make sure your conscience is as clear as a profession full of compromise and uncertainty will allow it to be' (2000: 325). And the only way to do this is though sincere reflection and the seeking of advice from those wiser and more experienced than we are. In the words of the managing editor of *Time* magazine, Walter Isaacson: 'In the end, you're going to be judged on whether you got it right, not just on whether you got it first' (cited in the *Columbia Journalism Review*, March–April 1998). Conscience is, then, also related to practical wisdom or prudence. Even those with 'flawed' characters will have notions of right and wrong. The key is to find ways of showing them that being a good journalist is also a kind of enlightened self-interest.

TWENTY-FIRST CENTURY ETHICAL CHALLENGES

A remarkable feature in debates about ethics is that even after 2,500 years, the issues raised by the Greek philosophers continue to speak to us. It is also true, however, that we seem to be living in times of particular ethical complexity. Two issues which might be considered to pose special challenges to the practice of good journalism in the twenty-first century are: first, the questions raised by the development of cyberspace and second, the seeming absence of universal values which would seem to undermine the very possibility of understanding what good journalism might be.

Cyberspace challenges

Does the changing communication environment, the development of the Internet and other digitally-based technology, provide radically new ethical challenges for journalists? My answer is ambivalent. On the one hand, it is wrong to assume that we are driven by a kind of technological determinism, which tacitly assumes that technology is a free-standing force driving us on to an ineluctable destiny. The view that technology determines behaviour and social change, neglects the extent to which technology emerges out of human priorities, interests and ethical imperatives (Winston, 1998). New technology generates new complexity but it is hard to see that the ethical questions posed are qualitatively different to those already faced by journalists.

Like all new technology, digital technology makes life both easier and more complicated for the reporter.[3] The *Media in Cyberspace* study of American print journalists by Middleberg and Ross shows how Internet use has become part of 'the fabric and core of what journalism and communications are all about' (Merina, 2000). In 2000 the report found that three-quarters of those who responded to the survey went online at least once a day. In 1999 it was just 48 per cent and in 1994, when the study began, it was 16 per cent. More than half the newspaper and magazine journalists involved in the survey also said they communicated with readers via e-mail. And almost two-thirds of print journalists surveyed used the Internet to read publications online. The study showed that journalists are using the Internet 'for everything from story ideas and pitches to article research and reference needs.'

However, the study also identified areas of ethical concern, particularly related to:

- Copyright and the related issue of plagiarism.
- Sources and the problem of credibility.

Many websites lack credibility but in a worrying finding, 17 per cent of the respondents said they would report information found on the Internet, even if they could not confirm it elsewhere. The report's authors stated that: 'Many of our respondents also admit to publishing Internet rumors, often with little or no substantiation, and to using online sources whose credibility has not been adequately established.' It was also found that many journalists were reluctant to give credit to other publications' work when using their material from the Net.

A third area of increased ethical complexity is that of freedom and the kind of content to be found on the Internet. According to many commentators, 'the elusive and free-flowing ways of the Internet present far more of a challenge to authoritarian regimes than they do to open, democratic societies' (Hachten, 1998: 172). This may be so, as the examples of the use of the Internet to challenge regimes in Serbia and China demonstrate.

However, there is a dark side to the Web. The establishment of the Internet Watch Foundation in 1996 by Internet Service Providers (ISPs) was in direct response to the growth of child pornography available online. The foundation introduced a hotline allowing it to alert ISPs and national and international police authorities to the presence of possibly illegal material on their servers. And of course pornography is not the only cause for concern. The orchestrators of global terrorism and crime can use the Net to move money around, exchange information and plan operations. The new technology of freedom, which has allowed an enormous growth in online or e-journalism jobs and a huge expansion of possibilities for reporters, runs the risk of subverting the very world that brought it into existence. These are real ethical worries which journalists – the guardians of freedom of expression – will also encounter.

Personal ethics and universal values

In the Preface to his boldly titled book *The Universal Journalist*, the former assistant editor of the *Observer* sets out his credo:

> If you write and read enough stories, in the end you realize that there are only two types of journalism: good and bad. The bad is practised by those who rush faster to judgement than they do to find out, indulge themselves rather than the reader, write between the lines rather than on them, write in the dead terms of the formula, stereotype and cliché, regard accuracy as a bonus and exaggeration as a tool and prefer vagueness to precision, comment to information and cynicism to ideals. The good is intelligent, entertaining, reliably informative, properly set in context, honest in intent and effect, expressed in fresh language and serves no cause but the discernible truth. Whatever the audience. Whatever the culture. Whatever the language. Whatever the circumstances. Such journalism could be printed in any publication, because it is, in every sense of the word, universal. (Randall, 2000: viii)

We might not agree with each and every one of Randall's specifications of good or bad journalism but can we accept its underlying thesis? Can we agree that there are universal values which allow us to speak of good and bad journalism in global terms? In other words can we even speak of 'ethics and journalism' or should it be 'British ethics and journalism', 'western ethics and journalism' or 'Chinese ethics and journalism'?

Those who propose ethical relativism, who contend that ethical judgements are culturally determined and always relative to time and place, would certainly dismiss the notion of any kind of universal standard as a myth. There are also those, of which I am one, who believe that our very survival depends on discovering at least some globally shared values.

In fact, much modern and postmodern thinking about ethics does not abandon the aspiration to universality. The German philosopher, Jürgen Habermas, advocates discourse ethics, espousing a universalistic outlook that rests on the assumption that humans are able to negotiate universally binding norms and are rational, emancipated human beings. Although feminists offer a critique of universalistic models of ethical thinking which ignore the 'difference' of women, this view is advanced as applying to all women and is used to promote a universal ethics of care. British sociologist, Nick Stevenson's discussion of these ethical projects refers us to the work of Zygmunt Bauman who has written of the possibility of a 'morality without ethics' (1999: 30). He advocates a postmodern ethics in which it is recognized that it is the individual who must be moral by taking ownership of their actions because: 'Being a moral person means that I *am* my brother's keeper' (Bauman, 1993: 51). Stevenson (1999: 32) is concerned that this view places too much emphasis on the individual, 'the worst kind of moralism,' which does not connect to the community. Warnock, however, gives a simple, perhaps obvious answer:

As they [children] more and more clearly see the implications of being human, they will want, as Aristotle might have put it, to be good specimens of humanity. In ethical terms they will want to be good. Without this underlying private want, they cannot be relied on to try for the ethically best in the public sphere. The morality that lies behind all efforts to improve things in the world at large, to defend human rights, to pass generally acceptable laws, to seek peace and justice, is essentially that of private standard-setting and of private ideals to be pursued. (2001: 180)

This account perhaps pays insufficient attention to the fact that we are fashioned by the communities we live in. Our concepts, experiences, feelings and the language we speak, are shaped by our living in society. Indeed, good behaviour can only be learned in interaction with others. And this brings us full circle. For of course, the community is in part constituted by the media itself. The British chief rabbi, Jonathan Sacks, has explained how this works:

At the heart of any culture is the process by which we bring successive generations into a narrative, the story of which we are a part. There is, of course, not one story but many, but storytelling is the place where identity is found, it is the vehicle of continuity. (Sachs, 2001)

Historically this was the role of the elders, the priests, the bards and the poets. Now it is the role of the media. And the role of story-telling is immensely important for the values of a community:

Stories tell us who we are, where we came from and what we might aspire to be. A culture is defined by its narratives. If they make strenuous demands on the mind and spirit, then a culture has the most precious legacy of all. That is why the great dramatists, poets and novelists have an influence deeper and more enduring than politicians or military leaders. If the great stories are lost, forgotten or ignored, then a culture has begun its decline. (Sacks, 2001)

The story-tellers matter as do the stories they tell. They can celebrate diversity and the stranger in our midst or denounce and despise difference. The attitude expressed in Constantine Cavafy's poem, 'Waiting for the Barbarians', is all too easy:

And now, what will become of us without the barbarians/Those people were a kind of solution.

The British Defence Secretary's comment on Radio 4's *World at One* news that: 'Unfortunately the Taleban don't seem susceptible to reasonable argument' expresses the frustration when shared values seem impossible to find (Hoon: 17 September, 2001). But this can open the door to cynicism and cynicism is just the flip-side of fanaticism. Being cynical destroys the possibility of conversation about the very existence of standards. And fanatics don't converse.

To return to my question: can we agree that there are universal standards regarding what is good and bad journalism? We cannot ignore that journalism is a culturally established practice which has developed in the particular historical circumstances of each country: Chinese journalism *is* very different to American journalism; British broadsheets are very different to their scholarly German counterparts. Do any of these traditions represent good or better journalism; bad or worse journalism? Of course, we might want to argue that this is indeed the case. And this returns us to the issue of agreeing what journalism is for. However, even if we can't all agree on this, I think we are still able to find values that all good journalism should share, the chief of which is the commitment to truthfulness.

ENCOURAGING GOOD JOURNALISTS

Accountability and responsibility, examined in the previous chapter, encourage good journalism. But how is it possible to encourage good journalists? Certain qualities can be taught, and reporters can be trained in the technical skills necessary for their job. But how do reporters become curious, enthusiastic, determined, wise? I offer some suggestions here.

Preparing for the job

Education for journalism can play a role. Traditionally, and rightly, journalism programmes have concentrated on training in core skills and knowledge and the cultivation of the right kind of attitudes. Any specific thinking about ethics has been largely confined to the study of industry codes. Increasingly, journalism courses also pay attention to ethics as a separate subject. This is a welcome development but it's probably not the way journalistic virtues will be encouraged. In some ways too it can encourage the impression that ethics is remote from practice, from 'real life.' Three strategies might help to avoid this and contribute to the cultivation of the journalistic virtues.

Stories and role models.   Some reporters attain legendary status among their peers and in the history books, not always for the best reasons. Writing about the United States, Goodwin acknowledges that there are many good role models in newsrooms, but 'there are also plenty of bad models, and the folklore of this country teaches unethical as well as ethical practices' (1995: 353). This is true. However, it is also true that there is much to be celebrated in the history of journalism and yet this is a neglected area of journalism education.

History's stories can inspire and educate: William Howard Russell's chronicles of the Crimea; Martha Gelhorn's reporting of the Second World War; the excesses of William Randolph Hearst's *New York Journal* in its reporting of the Spanish–American war; Michael Buerk's accounts of famine in Ethiopia. Journalism history can provide the stories and the role models – for good and bad – which transmit the values of good journalism.

Case Studies.   One of the most effective ways of thinking through ethical dilemmas – our motives, desires, attitudes and responses to them – is to be faced, as far as is possible, with the precise problems faced by working journalists. Material from the statutory and self-regulatory bodies can now provide the raw material for case studies which can help journalism educators do exactly that.

Integrating ethics. Randall's observation that 'ethics are not some optional extra but are integral to every aspect of the job' (2000, 134) is one that we should be able to apply to a journalism programme. Too often 'ethics' can appear bolted on as a set of unrealistic, unrealizable ideals, when in fact being a good reporter is about being a good reporter. Programmes which underline this in all areas of the curriculum, which emphasize that ethical practice is precisely that, good practice, will be more effective in getting across this message.

On the job

Journalists have very little time for reflection. If they do reflect, it's usually after a decision has been made. However, two potent sources of moral wisdom are at hand: colleagues and experience.

Peer example. Example is one of the most compelling ways in which we learn. In Oakeshott's words:

> We acquire habits of conduct, not by constructing a way of living upon rules or precepts learned by heart and subsequently practised, but by living with people who habitually behave in a certain manner: we acquire habits of conduct in the same way as we acquire our native language. (1991: 468).

Reporters learn in the newsroom and if cynicism is the prevailing ethical mood, it's hard for people to be fired up by what they do. Fortunately, cynicism is often no more than a mask adopted by many reporters to disguise the real passion and enthusiasm they have for their work. Journalists who care about truth, who are determined and seek precision, are the best media ethics teachers around.

Experience. One of Aristotle's great insights is that 'moral knowledge, unlike mathematical knowledge, cannot be acquired merely by attending lectures, and is not characteristically to be found in people too young to have much experience of life' (Hursthouse, 1999: 58). Textbook knowledge is of little use in deciding hard cases and sometimes the best we can do is look back on our own experiences and look to the advice of those wiser and more experienced than we are. The experience of getting things right and getting things wrong is a source of moral wisdom which good journalists are happy to share with others.

WHY BE GOOD?

This is the key question which I raised in Chapter three. Why is it worth trying to be a good journalist in the first place? Why be good at all? The question has exercised philosophers from Plato to the present day. In Plato's dialogue *The Republic*, Thrasymachus argues that morality is simply the interest of the powerful. Nietzsche re-formulated this view, seeking to undermine the foundations of morality and advocating the pursuit of excellence understood as the individual will to power.

Virtue ethics offers a different response. It says that by being good, by acting well we act rationally. In seeking to be loyal, hard-working, straightforward, truthful and courageous, human beings flourish as human beings. And if this is the case, we have reasons to be a good person.[4] As Philippa Foot puts it:

> If the sceptic does not succeed in refuting us here, but still goes on saying that he has not been shown that there is reason for acting as a good person would act, it is no longer clear what he is asking for. To ask for a reason for acting rationally is to ask for a reason where reasons must *a priori* have come to an end. And if he goes on saying 'But why *should* I?', we may query the meaning of this 'should'. (italics in original; 2001: 65)

If we hold up a standard of excellence in journalism related to the notions of professional competence and professional goals, it becomes possible to state reasons why being truthful and courageous, treating others with respect, keeping promises, caring about injustice, taking advice, not rushing to judgement and yet being decisive *are* qualities which journalists should cultivate. You simply can't be a good journalist without them.

In all likelihood the bad person or journalist doesn't *want* to act well. We've probably all had the experience of not doing something we should (making a phone call) – and rejecting the justification for it – because we simply don't *want* to do it. A reporter whose overwhelming desire is to make money won't *want* to see the reasons why being truthful is integral to good journalism and in these circumstances such a person cannot be convinced of why he or she should be good.

Being happy

And there is yet another, more profound reason why it is worth trying to be good at what at we do and through what we do. Put simply, it will make us happy. In the Aristotelian view, happiness is about the fulfillment of the person, *eudaimonia*. Scruton has said that 'much of our moral confusion comes from the fact that we no longer know what happiness is or how to obtain it' (1998). To be happy we have to approve of ourselves, find qualities in ourselves that we find in others and admire. Otherwise we feel truly wretched. So it's not enough to be nice to be happy. We must be good and to be good we need virtues.

It might be argued that being virtuous may at times require us to sacrifice happiness. The fire-fighters who rushed to save the lives of others in the World Trade Center knew that they were certainly risking their own lives and their happiness as fathers, sons and lovers. Those who survived said they were only doing their job. But it was a job which called upon them to be heroically virtuous. How can virtue which can end in death be compatible with happiness? The answer lies in thinking about what kind of happiness we would have if we turned our back on others. We might find a sort of happiness but one run through with regret. In this way, as Foot writes, it is possible to understand that someone who sacrifices their life for the sake of justice 'would not have said that he was sacrificing his happiness, but rather that a happy life had turned out not to be possible for him' (2001: 97). Such extreme circumstances are thankfully rare in the lives of most people.

NOTES

1 See Aquinas, *Summa Theologiae*, First Part of the Second Part, Question XIX. There has been a temptation among some modern British philosophers to dismiss Aquinas as a mediaeval theologian with little to contribute to contemporary debates. This is changing. Philippa Foot described Aquinas' discussion of conscience and particularly an 'erring conscience' as 'a wonderful piece of moral philosophy' (2001: 73) and the area of sources of badness in action, which Aquinas deals with in great detail, as a subject 'seldom well treated in modern moral philosophy' (2001: 74).

2 This is not to say that all subsequent coverage continued to meet the high standards of the first day. In particular, journalists became perhaps a little intoxicated by the 'frame' of war in the days which followed.

3 There seems to be a kind of hidden law at work when any new technology is introduced: we satisfy certain needs and desires but at the same time generate new ones. Better transport and labour-saving devices save us time, but we do less exercize and need to invent new machines (treadmills and fixed bicycles, for example) to keep fit.

4 Of course, these are deep philosophical waters. For readers who wish to explore them further I refer them once again to the work of Hursthouse and Foot where they will find attempts to show the rationality of morality from a virtue ethics perspective. The work of Bernard Williams expresses a sceptical view about the possibility of such a project.

The Press Complaints Commission is charged with enforcing the following Code of Practice which was framed by the newspaper and periodical industry and ratified by the Press Complaints Commission, 1st December 1999.

All members of the press have a duty to maintain the highest professional and ethical standards. This code sets the benchmark for those standards. It both protects the rights of the individual and upholds the public's right to know. The Code is the cornerstone of the system of self-regulation to which the industry has made a binding commitment. Editors and publishers must ensure that the Code is observed rigorously not only by their staff but also by anyone who contributes to their publications.

It is essential to the workings of an agreed code that it be honoured not only to the letter but in the full spirit. The Code should not be interpreted so narrowly as to compromise its commitment to respect the rights of the individual, nor so broadly that it prevents publication in the public interest.

It is the responsibility of editors to co-operate with the PCC as swiftly as possible in the resolution of complaints. Any publication which is criticised by the PCC under one of the following clauses must print the adjudication which follows in full and with due prominence.

1   Accuracy

    i)   Newspapers and periodicals should take care not to publish inaccurate, misleading or distorted material including pictures.

    ii)   Whenever it is recognised that a significant inaccuracy, misleading statement or distorted report has been published, it should be corrected promptly and with due prominence.

    iii) An apology must be published whenever appropriate.

    iv) Newspapers, whilst free to be partisan, must distinguish clearly between comment, conjecture and fact

    v)   A newspaper or periodical must report fairly and accurately the outcome of an action for defamation to which it has been a party.

2   Opportunity to reply

A fair opportunity for reply to inaccuracies must be given to individuals or organisations when reasonably called for.

3   *Privacy

i)   Everyone is entitled to respect for his or her private and family life, home, health and correspondence. A publication will be expected to justify intrusions into any individual's private life without consent.

ii)   The use of long lens photography to take pictures of people in private places without their consent is unacceptable.

Note – Private places are public or private property where there is a reasonable expectation of privacy.

4   *Harassment

i)   Journalists and photographers must neither obtain nor seek to obtain information or pictures through intimidation, harassment or persistent pursuit.

ii)   They must not photograph individuals in private places (as defined by the Note to clause 3) without their consent; must not persist in telephoning, questioning, pursuing or photographing individuals after having been asked to desist; must not remain on their property after having been asked to leave and must not follow them.

iii) Editors must ensure that those working for them comply with these requirements and must not publish material from other sources which does not meet these requirements.

5   Intrusion into grief or shock

In cases involving personal grief or shock, enquiries should be carried out and approaches made with sympathy and discretion. Publication must be handled sensitively at such times but this should not be interpreted as restricting the right to report judicial proceedings.

6   *Children

i)   Young people should be free to complete their time at school without unnecessary intrusion.

ii)   Journalists must not interview or photograph a child under the age of 16 on subjects involving the welfare of the child or any other child in the absence of or without the consent of a parent or other adult who is responsible for the children.

iii) Pupils must not be approached or photographed while at school without the permission of the school authorities.

iv) There must be no payment to minors for material involving the welfare of children nor payments to parents or guardians for material about their children or wards unless it is demonstrably in the child's interest.

v) Where material about the private life of a child is published, there must be justification for publication other than the fame, notoriety or position of his or her parents or guardian.

7 *Children in sex cases

1. The press must not, even where the law does not prohibit it, identify children under the age of 16 who are involved in cases concerning sexual offences, whether as victims or as witnesses.

2. In any press report of a case involving a sexual offence against a child –

   i) The child must not be identified.

   ii) The adult may be identified.

   iii) The word 'incest' must not be used where a child victim might be identified.

   iv) Care must be taken that nothing in the report implies the relationship between the accused and the child.

8 *Listening Devices

Journalists must not obtain or publish material obtained by using clandestine listening devices or by intercepting private telephone conversations.

9 *Hospitals

i) Journalists or photographers making enquiries at hospitals or similar institutions should identify themselves to a responsible executive and obtain permission before entering non-public areas.

ii) The restrictions on intruding into privacy are particularly relevant to enquiries about individuals in hospitals or similar institutions.

10 *Reporting of crime.

(i) The press must avoid identifying relatives or friends of persons convicted or accused of crime without their consent.

(ii) Particular regard should be paid to the potentially vulnerable position of children who are witnesses to, or victims of, crime. This should not be interpreted as restricting the right to report judicial proceedings.

11 *Misrepresentation

i) Journalists must not generally obtain or seek to obtain information or pictures through misrepresentation or subterfuge.

ii) Documents or photographs should be removed only with the consent of the owner.

iii) Subterfuge can be justified only in the public interest and only when material cannot be obtained by any other means.

12 Victims of sexual assault

The press must not identify victims of sexual assault or publish material likely to contribute to such identification unless there is adequate justification and, by law, they are free to do so.

13 Discrimination

i) The press must avoid prejudicial or pejorative reference to a person's race, colour, religion, sex or sexual orientation or to any physical or mental illness or disability.

ii) It must avoid publishing details of a person's race, colour, religion, sexual orientation, physical or mental illness or disability unless these are directly relevant to the story.

14 Financial journalism

i) Even where the law does not prohibit it, journalists must not use for their own profit financial information they receive in advance of its general publication, nor should they pass such information to others.

ii) They must not write about shares or securities in whose performance they know that they or their close families have a significant financial interest without disclosing the interest to the editor or financial editor.

iii) They must not buy or sell, either directly or through nominees or agents, shares or securities about which they have written recently or about which they intend to write in the near future.

15 Confidential sources

Journalists have a moral obligation to protect confidential sources of information.

16 *Payment for articles

    i)   Payment or offers of payment for stories or information must not be made directly or through agents to witnesses or potential witnesses in current criminal proceedings except where the material concerned ought to be published in the public interest and there is an overriding need to make or promise to make a payment for this to be done. Journalists must take every possible step to ensure that no financial dealings have influence on the evidence that those witnesses may give.

        (An editor authorising such a payment must be prepared to demonstrate that there is a legitimate public interest at stake involving matters that the public has a right to know. The payment or, where accepted, the offer of payment to any witness who is actually cited to give evidence should be disclosed to the prosecution and the defence and the witness should be advised of this).

    ii)   Payment or offers of payment for stories, pictures or information, must not be made directly or through agents to convicted or confessed criminals or to their associates – who may include family, friends and colleagues – except where the material concerned ought to be published in the public interest and payment is necessary for this to be done.

The public interest

There may be exceptions to the clauses marked * where they can be demonstrated to be in the public interest.

1. The public interest includes:
       i)   Detecting or exposing crime or a serious misdemeanour.
       ii)   Protecting public health and safety.
       iii) Preventing the public from being misled by some statement or action of an individual or organisation.

2. In any case where the public interest is invoked, the Press Complaints Commission will require a full explanation by the editor demonstrating how the public interest was served.

3. There is a public interest in freedom of expression itself. The Commission will therefore have regard to the extent to which material has, or is about to, become available to the public.

4. In cases involving children editors must demonstrate an exceptional public interest to over-ride the normally paramount interest of the child.

Bibliography

INTERNET SITES

ABC British circulation figures www.abc.org
Advertising Standards Authority www.asa.org.uk
British Broadcasting Corporation www.bbc.co.uk
Broadcasting Standards Commission www. bsc.org.uk
European codes of conduct www.uta.fi/ethicnet/
French journalism ethics site with useful links www.paris2.fr/ifp/deontologie/ethics/htm
Independent Television Commission www.itc.org.uk
MORI public opinion research www.mori.com
Institute of Global Ethics www.globalethics.org.uk
National Union of Journalists www.nuj.org.uk
Newspaper Society www.newspapersoc.org.uk
Periodical Publications Association www.ppa.co.uk
The Poynter Institute (US ethics forum) www.poynter.org
Press Complaints Commission www.pcc.org.uk
PressWise www.presswise.org.uk
Radio Authority www.radioauthority.org.uk
Reporters sans frontiéres www.rsf.fr
Reporting the World www.reportingtheworld.org
Society of Editors www.societyofeditors.org
Teenage Magazine Arbitration Panel www.tmap.org.uk

Abramson, Jeffrey B. (1995) 'Four criticisms of press ethics,' in *Democracy and the Mass Media*, (ed.) J. Lichtenberg. Cambridge: Cambridge University Press, pp. 229–68.

Aitkenhead, Decca (1999) 'The hunger for "real" sex on the telly has opened the door for hoaxers.' *The Guardian*, 5 February.

Anderson, Peter J. and Anthony Weymouth (1999) *Insulting the Public. The British Press and the European Union*. London and New York: Longman.

Anonymous (1999) 'How to claim a camel on expenses,' in Stephen Glover (ed.) *Secrets of the Press. Journalists on Journalism*. London: Allen Lane, pp. 106–14.

Aquinas, Thomas *Summa Theologiae*. Second and revised edition: the English Dominican Fathers, 1920. Online edition 2000, www.newadvent/org/summa

Archard, David (1998) 'Privacy, the public interest and a prurient public,' in M. Kieran (ed.) *Media Ethics*. London: Routledge, pp. 82–96.

Arendt, Hannah (1958) *The Human Condition*. Chicago: Chicago University Press.

Aristotle *The Nichomachean Ethics*. Oxford: Oxford University Press.

Arnett, Peter (1994) *Live From the Battlefield. From Vietnam to Baghdad: 35 Years in the World's War Zones*. New York: Simon & Schuster.

Bailey, Ric (2002) Seminar at the Department of Journalism, University of Sheffield, 18 April.

Barber, Lynn (1999) 'The Art of the Interview,' in Stephen Glover (ed.) *Secrets of the Press. Journalists on Journalism*. London: Allen Lane, pp. 196–205.

Barnett, Steven (2001) 'Culture watchdogs need a crash course.' The *Observer*, 1 July.

Barnett, Steven and Ivor Gaber (1993) *Changing Patterns in Broadcast News*. London: Voice of the Listener and Viewer.

Barnett, Steven and Emily Seymour (1999) 'A Shrinking Iceberg Travelling South. . .' *Changing Trends in British Television: A Case Study of Drama and Current Affairs*. London: Campaign for Quality Television.

Baumann, Zygmunt (1993) *Postmodern Ethics*. Oxford: Blackwell.

BBC Producers' Guidelines (2001) www.bbc.co.uk/info/editorial/prodgl/

BBC News and Current Affairs (1995) Stylebook and Editorial Guide.

Bell, Martin (1998) 'The journalism of attachment,' in Matthew Kieran (ed.) *Media Ethics*. London: Routledge, pp. 15–22.

Bell, Martin (1999) 'We need TV we can trust.' The *Independent*, 16 February.

Belsey, Andrew (1992) 'Privacy, publicity and politics,' in Andrew Belsey and Ruth Chadwick (eds) *Ethical Issues in Journalism*. London: Routledge, pp. 77–92.

Belsey, Andrew and Ruth Chadwick (eds) (1992) *Ethical Issues in Journalism*. London: Routledge.

Belsey, Andrew and Ruth Chadwick (1995) 'Ethics as a vehicle for media quality.' *European Journal of Communication*, 10 (4), 461–73.

Belsey, Andrew (1998) 'Journalism and ethics: can they co-exist?,' in Matthew Kieran (ed.) *Media Ethics*. London: Routledge, pp. 1–14.

Bentham, Jeremy (1789/1962) 'Introduction to the Principles of Morals and Legislation.' in Mary Warnock (ed.) *Utilitarianism*, London: Fontana.

Berlin, Isaiah (1958/1966) *Two Concepts of Liberty*. Oxford: Clarendon Press.

Berry, David (ed.) (2000) *Ethics and Media Culture. Practices and Representations*. Oxford: Focal Press.

Black, Max (1964/1992) *A Companion to Wittgenstein's 'Tractatus'*. Ithaca/New York: Cornell University Press.

Blair, Tony (2000) 'Statement.' The *Guardian*, 7 March.

Bok, Sissela (1980) *Lying. Moral Choice in Public and Private Life*. London/Melbourne/New York: Quartet Books.

Bok, Sissela (1982) *Secrets. On the Ethics of Concealment and Revelation*. New York: Pantheon Books.

Bok, Sissela (1998) *Mayhem. Violence as Public Entertainment*. Reading, Massachusetts: Addison-Wesley.

Boltanski, Luc (1999) *Distant Suffering. Morality, Media and Politics*. Cambridge: Cambridge University Press.

Bolton, Roger (1990) *Death on the Rock*. London: W.H. Allen/Optomen.

Boorstin, Daniel (1971) *The Image. A Guide to Pseudo-Events in America*. New York: Atheneum.

Boulton, Adam (1997) Interview with author.

Bromley, Michael (1997) 'The End of Journalism? Changes in Workplace Practices in the Press and Broadcasting in the 1990s,' in Michael Bromley and Tom O'Malley (eds), *A Journalism Reader*. London: Routledge, pp. 330–50.

Calcutt, David (1990) *The Report of the Committee on Privacy and Related Matters* (Cm. 1102). London: HMSO.

Calcutt, David (1993) *Review of Press Self-regulation* (Cm. 2135). London: HMSO.

Canel, María José, José Javier Sánchez Aranda and Roberto Rodríguez Andrés (2000)

Opiniones y Actitudes. Periodistas al descubierto. Retrato de los profesionales de la información. Madrid: Centro de Investigaciones Sociológicas.

Carey, John (ed.) (1996) *The Faber Book of Reportage*. London: Faber.

Carruthers, Susan (2000) *The Media at War. Communication and Conflict in the Twentieth Century*. Basingstoke, Hampshire: Macmillan.

Caseby, Jo (1998) Conversation with the author.

Castelló, Fernando (2001) 'Libertad de prensa, para qué?' [Freedom of the press. For what?] *El País*, 3 May.

Castells, Manuel (1996–1998) *The Information Age: Economy, Society and Culture*, 3 volumes. Oxford: Blackwell.

Channel 4 (2001) *Press Release*. 6 September.

Chesterton, G.K. (1906) 'The crimes of journalism,' in *The Illustrated London News*. Volume 27, 300–5.

Chippindale, Peter and Chris Horrie (1999) *Stick It Up Your Punter! The Uncut Story of the Sun Newspaper*. London: Pocket Books.

Christians, Clifford G. (1995) 'Review essay: current trends in media ethics.' *European Journal of Communication*, 10 (4), 545–58

Clark, Alan (1999) 'Why I Hold Journalists in Low Regard,' in Stephen Glover (ed.) *Secrets of the Press. Journalists on Journalism*. London: Allen Lane, pp. 281–8.

Cole, Peter (2000) *The Guardian*, G2, 15 May.

Columbia Journalism Review, March–April 1998.

Commission on the Freedom of the Press (1947) *A Free and Responsible Press*. Chicago: University of Chicago Press.

Comte-Sponville, André (2002) *A Short Treatise on the Great Virtues*. London: William Heinemann.

Curran, James and Jean Seaton (2000) *Power Without Responsibility. The Press and Broadcasting in Britain*. 5th edition. London: Routledge.

Day, Louis A. (1997) *Ethics in Media Communications. Cases and Controversies*. 2nd edition. Belmont, CA: Wadsworth Publishing Company.

Deacon, David and Peter Golding (1994) *Taxation and Representation*. London: John Libbey.

Department of National Heritage (1995a) *Media Ownership. The Government's Proposals*. London: HMSO.

Department of National Heritage (1995b) *Privacy and Media Intrusion. The Government's Response*. London: HMSO.

Department of Trade and Industry and Department of Culture, Media and Sport (2000) *A New Future for Communications*. London: HMSO.

Donsbach, Wolfgang (1997) 'Survey research at the end of the twentieth century: theses and antitheses.' *International Journal of Public Opinion Research*, 9 (1), 17–28.

Eason, David L. (1988) 'On Journalistic Authority: the Janet Cooke Scandal,' in J.W. Carey (ed.) *Media, Myths and Narratives*, London: Sage, pp. 205–27.

Edwards, Robert (1989) *Goodbye Fleet Street*. London: Coronet.

Engel, Matthew (1996) *Tickle the Public: One Hundred Years of the Popular Press*. London: Victor Gollancz.

Epworth, Jennifer and Hanna, Mark (1998) 'Media payments to witnesses – the press faces the first breach of its post-Calcutt defences.' Paper presented to the first annual conference of the Association for Journalism Education, London, 15 May.

Eurobarometer 55 (2000) Brussels: European Commission.

Evans, Harold (1994) *Good Times. Bad Times*. 3rd edition. London: Phoenix.

Fallows, J. (1996) *Breaking the News. How the Media Undermine American Democracy.* New York: Pantheon Books.

Foot, Philippa (2001) *Natural Goodness.* Oxford: Oxford University Press.

Franklin, Bob (1994) *Packaging Politics.* London: Edward Arnold.

Franklin, Bob (1997) *Newszak and News Media.* London: Arnold.

Frost, Chris (2000) *Media Ethics and Self-Regulation.* London: Longman.

Gandy, Oscar (1982) *Beyond Agenda Setting: Information Subsidies and Public Policy.* Norwood, NJ: Ablex.

Geach, Peter (1977) *The Virtues.* Cambridge: Cambridge University Press.

Geach, Peter (1994) *God and the Soul.* Bristol: Thoemmes Press.

Glover, Stephen (ed.) (1999) *Secrets of the Press. Journalists on Journalism.* London: Allen Lane.

Goodwin, Eugene H. (1995) *Groping for Ethics in Journalism.* 3rd edition. Ames: Iowa State University Press.

Greenslade, Roy (1999) 'Is this picture a justifiable image of tragedy? Or a voyeuristic intrusion into private grief?' *The Guardian,* G2, 11 October.

Greenslade, Roy (2001) 'Pure journalism.' *The Guardian,* G2, 17 September.

Grimaldi, Nicolas (2000) *El Trabajo. Comunión y Excomunión.* Pamplona: Eunsa.

Guardian (1998) Editorial, 8 May.

Gunter, Barrie (1999) 'Television news and the audience in Europe: what has been happening and where should we go next?' *Communications,* 24 (1), 5–37.

Hachten, William (1998) *The Troubles of Journalism. A Critical Look at What's Right and Wrong with the Press.* Mahwah, New Jersey: Lawrence Erlbaum Associates.

Hagerty, Bill (2000) Interview with author.

Hall, Stuart, C. Crichter, T. Jefferson, J. Clarke and B. Roberts (1978) *Policing the Crisis.* London: Macmillan.

Hamelink, Cees (1995) 'Ethics for media users.' *European Journal of Communication,* 10 (4), 497–512.

Hann, Michael (2001) 'Media Studies? Do yourself a favour – forget it.' *The Guardian,* 3 September.

Harcup, Tony (2002) 'Journalists and Ethics: the quest for a collective voice.' *Journalism Studies,* 3 (1), 101–114.

Hare, R.M. (1981) *Moral Thinking.* Oxford: Oxford University Press.

Harris, Nigel G.E. (1992) 'Codes of conduct for journalists,' in Andrew Belsey and Ruth Chadwick (eds) *Ethical Issues in Journalism.* London: Routledge, pp. 62–76.

Harris, Robert (1983) *Gotcha! The Media, the Government and the Falklands Crisis.* London: Faber & Faber.

Harrison, Jackie (2000) *Terrestrial TV News in Britain.* Manchester: Manchester University Press.

Hastings, Max (2000) *Going to the Wars.* London: Macmillan.

Hattersley, Roy (1999) Seminar with MA students, University of Sheffield.

Hellen, Nicholas and Judith O'Reilly (1999) 'Television Confessions. How much of what we watch is fake?' The *Sunday Times,* 14 February.

Hencke, David (2001) Interview with author.

Herman, Edward S. and Noam Chomsky (1994) *Manufacturing Consent: The political economy of the mass media.* London: Vintage.

Hodgson, Jessica (2001) 'A gentleman's agreement.' *The Guardian,* 1 October.

Hume, Mick (1997) 'Whose War is it Anyway? The dangers of the journalism of attachment.' *LM Special.* London: LM.

Hursthouse, Rosalind (1999) *On Virtue Ethics*. Oxford: Oxford University Press.

Independent Television Commission (2001) *The ITC Programme Code*, London: ITC.

Independent Television News (2001) *Programme Guidelines*.

International Press Institute (1996) *Dunblane: reflecting tragedy*. A report from the British Executive of the International Press Institute, London.

Jaehnig, Walter (1998) 'Kith and Sin: Press Accountability in the USA,' in Hugh Stephenson and Michael Bromley (eds) *Sex, Lies and Democracy. The Press and the Public*. London and New York: Longman, pp. 97–110.

Jenkins, Simon (2000) 'Top source, low ethics.' *The Times*, 2 February.

Jenkins, Simon (2001) 'Vulgar, crude – and absolutely vital.' *The Times*, 11 April.

Johannesen, Richard L. (1990) 'Virtue Ethics, Character and Political Communication,' in Richard L. Johannesen (ed.) *Ethics in Human Communication*. 3rd edition, Waveland Press: Baton Rouge, pp. 69–90.

John, Danny (2001) 'More eloquent than words.' *The Guardian*, G2, 17 September.

Jones, Nicholas (1996) *Soundbites and Spindoctors: How Politicians Manipulate the Media – and Vice Versa*. London: Indigo.

Keane, Fergal (1996) *Season of Blood. A Rwandan Journey*. Harmondsworth: Penguin.

Kearney, Richard and Mark Dooley (eds) (1999) 'Hospitality, justice and responsibility; a dialogue with Jacques Derrida,' in *Questioning Ethics. Contemporary Debates in Philosophy*. London: Routledge, pp. 65–83.

Keeble, Richard (2001) *Ethics for Journalists*. London: Routledge.

Keenan, Brian (1992) *An Evil Cradling*, London: Hutchinson.

Kelley, David and Roger Donway (1995) 'Liberalism and free press,' in J. Lichtenberg (ed.) *Democracy and the Mass Media*. Cambridge: Cambridge University Press, pp. 66–101.

Kieran, Matthew (1997) *Media Ethics. A Philosophical Approach*. Westport, Connecticut; London: Praeger.

Kieran, Matthew (ed.) (1998) *Media Ethics*. London: Routledge.

Klaidman, Tom and Stephen Beauchamp (1987) *The Virtuous Journalist*. New York and Oxford: Oxford University Press.

Knightley, Philip (2000) *The First Casualty. The War Correspondent as hero and mythmaker from the Crimea to Kosovo*. London: Prion.

Koss Stephen (1981/1984) *The Rise and Fall of the Political Press in Britain*, 2 vols. London: Hamilton.

Lester, Paul (1991) *Photojournalism. An Ethical Approach*. Hillsdale, New Jersey: Lawrence Erlbaum.

Lichtenberg, Judith (1995) 'Foundations and Limits of Freedom of the Press,' in J. Lichtenberg (ed.) *Democracy and the Mass Media*, Cambridge: Cambridge University Press, pp. 102–35.

Lichtenberg, Judith (2000) 'In Defence of Objectivity Revisited,' in J. Curran and M. Gurevitch (eds), *Mass Media and Society*. London: Arnold, pp. 238–54.

Lord Chancellor and the Scottish Office (1993) *Infringement of Privacy*. London: HMSO.

Lynch, Jake (2002) *Reporting the World*. Taplow, Berkshire: Conflict & Peace Forums.

McKay, Peter (1999) 'Gossip,' in Stephen Glover (ed.) *Secrets of the Press. Journalists on Journalism*. London: Allen Lane, pp. 186–95.

MacIntyre, Alasdair (1997) *After Virtue. A Study in Moral Theory*. 2nd edition. London: Duckworth.

MacIntyre, Alasdair (1999) *Dependent Rational Animals. Why Human Beings Need the Virtues*. London: Duckworth.

McLachlan, Shelley and Peter Golding (2000) 'Tabloidisation in the British Press: A Quantitative Investigation into Changes in British Newspapers, 1952–1997,' in C. Sparks, and J. Tulloch (eds) *Tabloid Tales. Global Debates over Media Standards.* Lahman: Rowman and Littlefield.

McQuail, Dennis (1993) *Media Performance. Mass Communication and the Public Interest.* London: Sage.

McQuail, Dennis (2000) *McQuail's mass communication theory.* 4th edition. London: Sage.

Mail on Sunday (2000) 'Gagged: Blairs ban nanny's story,' 5 March.

Major, John (2000) *John Major. The Autobiography.* London: HarperCollins.

Malcolm, Janet (1990) *The Journalist and the Murderer.* New York: Alfred A. Knopf.

Marinovich, Greg (2000) 'The Killing Eye.' The *Sunday Times*, Section 5, 20 August.

Medsger, Betty (1996) *Winds of Change. Challenges Confronting Journalism Education.* Arlington: The Freedom Forum.

Meilaender, Gilbert C. (1984) *The Theory and Practice of Virtue.* Notre Dame: The University of Notre Dame Press.

Mencken, H.L. (1918) 'Newspaper Morals,' in William Grosvenor Bleyer (ed.) *The Profession of Journalism.* Boston: The Atlantic Monthly Press, pp. 52–67.

Merina, Victor (2000) 'Media Plays Fast, Loose with Ethics Online,' www.poynter.org, posted 6 March.

Meyer, Philip (1991) *Ethical Journalism.* Lanham, Maryland/London: University Press of America.

Midgely, Mary (1998) 'The Problem of Humbug,' in M. Kieran (ed.) *Media Ethics.* London: Routledge, pp. 37–48.

Mill, John Stuart (1861/1962) 'Utilitarianism,' in Mary Warnock (ed.) *Utilitarianism.* London: Fontana.

Mill, John Stuart (1859/1982) 'On Liberty,' in *Three Essays.* Oxford: Oxford University Press.

Miller, David (1994) *Don't Mention the War: Northern Ireland, Propaganda and the Media.* London: Pluto Press.

Milton, John (1644/1946) *Areopagitica and other Prose Works.* London: J.M. Dent and Sons.

Mirror (2000) 'Camilla as you have never seen her,' 5 April.

Moeller, Susan D. (1999) *Compassion Fatigue. How the Media Sell Disease, Famine, War and Death.* New York/London: Routledge.

Monk, Raymond (1990) *Ludwig Wittgenstein: The Duty of Genius.* London: Jonathan Cape.

Morrison, David (1992) *Television and the Gulf War.* London: John Libbey.

National Union of Journalists (1996) 'Freelance.' London Freelance Branch. www.gn.apc.org/media/9605mani.html, accessed 10 June 2001.

National Union of Journalists (2001) *NUJ Code of Conduct.* www.gn.apc.org/media/nujcode.html, accessed 10 June 2001.

Negrine, Ralph (1996) *The Communication of Politics.* London: Sage.

Neil, Andrew (1996) *Full Disclosure.* London: Macmillan.

Newman, John Henry (1852/1987) *The Idea of a University.* Chicago: Loyola University Press.

Noelle-Neumann, Elizabeth (1984) *The Spiral of Silence.* Chicago: Chicago University Press.

Nolan Committee (1995) *First Report of the Committee on Standards in Public Life* (Cm. 2850). London: HMSO.

Norris, Pippa (2000) *A Virtuous Circle. Political Communications in Postindustrial Societies*. Cambridge: Cambridge University Press.

O' Malley, Tom (1998) 'Demanding Accountability: The Press, the Royal Commission and the Pressure for Reform, 1945–77,' in Hugh Stephenson and Michael Bromley (eds) (1998) *Sex, Lies and Democracy. The Press and the Public*. London and New York: Longman, pp. 84–96.

O'Neil, Onora (2002) BBC Reith Lectures. Lecture 5: Licence to Deceive. www.bbc.co.uk/radio4/reith2002/lecture5_text.html

Oakeshott, Michael (1991) *Rationalism in Politics and Other Essays*. Indianapolis: Liberty Press.

Oakeshott, Michael (1993) *Religion, Politics and the Moral Life*. New Haven and London: Yale University Press.

Oakley, Justin and Dean Cocking (2001) *Virtue Ethics and Professional Roles*. Cambridge: Cambridge University Press.

Oxford English Dictionary (1989) Oxford: Oxford University Press.

Page, Adrian (1998) 'Interpreting Codes of Conduct,' in Hugh Stephenson and Michael Bromley (eds) *Sex, Lies and Democracy. The Press and the Public*. London and New York: Longman, pp. 127–35.

Parris, Matthew (1998) 'Television's guilty secret: it just can't stop lying.' *The Sunday Telegraph*, 10 May.

Parris, Matthew (2001) 'Stay away from that party, young Will.' *The Times*, 3 February.

Patterson, Philip and Lee Wilkins (1991) *Media Ethics. Issues and Cases*. Dubuque, IA: Wm. C. Brown Publishers.

Patterson, Philip and Lee Wilkins (1998) *Media Ethics. Issues and Cases*, 3rd edition. Boston, Massachussetts: McGraw Hill.

Pearson, Alison (1999) 'Let's be glad that we're bad.' *Evening Standard*. 17 February.

Pieper, Josef (1990) *Las Virtudes Fundamentales*. Madrid: Rialp.

Ponting, Clive (1985) *The Right to Know. The Inside Story of the Belgrano Affair*. London and Sydney: Sphere Books.

Porter, Henry (1999) 'Editors and Egomaniacs,' in Stephen Glover (ed.) *Secrets of the Press. Journalists on Journalism*. London: Allen Lane, pp. 34–47.

Press Complaints Commission (1991) *Annual Report*.

Press Complaints Commission (1992) Report No. 1.

Press Complaints Commission (1992) Report No. 7.

Press Complaints Commission (1992) Report No. 12.

Press Complaints Commission (1993) Report No. 21.

Press Complaints Commission (1993) Report No. 22.

Press Complaints Commission (1994) Report No. 24.

Press Complaints Commission (1994) Report No. 25.

Press Complaints Commission (1995) Report No. 29.

Press Complaints Commission (1995) Report No. 32.

Press Complaints Commission (1995) *Annual Report*. London.

Press Complaints Commission (1996) *Annual Report*. London.

Press Complaints Commission (1997) *Annual Review*. London.

Press Complaints Commission (1997) Report No. 37.

Press Complaints Commission (1999) *Annual Review*. London.

Press Complaints Commission (2000) *Annual Review*. London.

Press Complaints Commission (2000) Report No. 50.

Press Complaints Commission (2001) Report No. 53.

Press Complaints Commission (2001) Report No. 54.

Preston, Peter (1999) Interview with the author.

Private Eye (1997) 'Media to blame.' 2 September.

Purves, Libby (2000) 'We're all voyeurs now.' *The Times*, 7 March.

Purves, Libby (2001) 'We have a right to be sad or sick in private.' *The Times*, 6 February.

Quinn, S. (1999) 'Costs hitting TV quality.' *The Guardian*, 24 May.

Randall, David (1996) *The Universal Journalist*. 1st edition. London: Pluto.

Randall, David (2000) *The Universal Journalist*. 2nd edition. London: Pluto.

Rasaiah, Santha (1998) 'Current legislation, privacy and the media in the UK.' *Communications Law*, 3 (5), 183–91.

Rawls, John (1971) *A Theory of Justice*. Cambridge: Harvard University Press.

Rogers, Ann (1997) *Secrecy and Power in the British State*. London and Chicago, Illinois: Pluto Press.

Rollo, Ogden (1918) 'Some Aspects of Journalism,' in William Grosvenor Bleyer (ed.) *The Profession of Journalism*. Boston: The Atlantic Monthly Press, pp. 1–19.

Routledge, Paul (1999) *Mandy. The Unauthorised Biography of Peter Mandelson*. London: Pocket Books.

Royal Commission on the Press 1947–9 Report (1949) (Cm. 7700), London: HMSO.

Royal Commission on the Press 1961–2 Report (1962) (Cm. 1811), London: HMSO.

Royal Commission on the Press 1974–7 Final Report (1977) (Cm. 6810), London: HMSO.

Rusbridger, Alan (1998) *The Independent*, 8 February.

Sacks, Jonathan (2001) 'In a world run by MTV, nobody has time to think.' *Daily Telegraph*, 6 September.

Sánchez Aranda and Roberto Rodríguez Andrés (1999) 'Profesionalidad y ética. El caso de los periodistas españoles' [Professionalism and ethics. The case of Spanish journalists]. *Comunicación y Sociedad*, 12 (2), 93–114.

Sanders, Karen (1990) *La reforma de la prensa peruana*, 1974 [The Reform of the Peruvian Press, 1974]. Unpublished MA thesis, University of Navarra.

Sanders, Karen, Timothy Bale and Maríe José Canel (1999) 'Managing Sleaze. Prime Ministers and News Management in Conservative Great Britain and Socialist Spain.' *European Journal of Communication*, 14 (4), 461–86.

Schlesinger, Philip and Howard Tumber (1994) *Reporting Crime. The Media Politics of Criminal Justice*. Oxford: Clarendon Press.

Schudson, Michael (1992) *Watergate in American Memory: How We Remember, Forget and Reconstruct the Past*. New York: Basic Books.

Scruton, Roger (1995) *A Short History of Modern Philosophy. From Descartes to Wittgenstein*. London: Routledge.

Scruton, Roger (1997) *Modern Philosophy. A Survey*. London: Arrow Books.

Scruton, Roger (1998) 'Pleasure be damned: to be happy, be good.' *The Sunday Times*, 6 December.

Sedley, Lord (2001) 'Judgement in Michael Douglas, Catherine Zeta-Jones and Northern & Shell plc vs. Hello! Ltd.,' wood.ccta.go.uk/courtser/judgements/nsf/

Shannon, Richard (2001) *A Press Free and Responsible. Self-regulation and the Press Complaints Commission 1991–2001*. London: John Murray.

Simpson, John (1999) *Strange Places, Questionable People*. London: Pan Books.

Simpson, John (2000) *A Mad World, My Masters. Tales from a Traveller's Life*. London: Macmillan.

Skipworth, Mark (1999) Interview with author.

Slote, Michael (1992) *From Morality to Virtue*. New York: Oxford University Press.

Snoddy, Raymond (1992) *The Good, the Bad and the Unacceptable. The Hard News about the British Press*. London: Faber and Faber.

Sokal, Alan and Jean Bricmont (1998) *Intellectual Impostures*. London: Profile Books.

Spaemann, Robert (1987) 'Was ist philosophische Ethik?,' in Robert Spaemann (ed.) *Ethik-Lesebuch. Von Platon bis heute*. Munich/Zurich: Piper.

Spaemann, Robert (1995) *Etica: cuestiones fundamentales* [Ethics: fundamental questions]. Pamplona: Eunsa.

Sparks, Colin (1999) 'The Press,' in Jane Stokes and Anna Reading (eds) *The Media in Britain: Current Debates and Developments*. Basingstoke, Hampshire: Macmillan, pp. 41–60.

Stark, Kenneth (2001) 'What's Right/Wrong with Journalism Ethics Research.' *Journalism Studies*, 2 (1), 133–52.

Stephenson, Hugh (1998) 'Tickle the Public: Consumerism Rules,' in Hugh Stephenson and Michael Bromley (eds) *Sex, Lies and Democracy. The Press and the Public*. London and New York: Longman, pp. 13–24.

Stephenson, Hugh and Michael Bromley (eds) (1998) *Sex, Lies and Democracy. The Press and the Public*. London and New York: Longman.

Stevens, R. (1998) 'For "Dumbing Down" Read Respectable.' *British Journalism Review*, 9 (4), 32–5.

Stevenson, Nick (1999) *The Transformation of the Media: Globalisation, Morality, and Ethics*. London: Longman.

Straw, Jack (1998) *Hansard*, 2 July, col 541.

Sun (2000) Editorial, 6 March.

Sun (2001) 'Islam is not evil religion.' 13 September.

Taylor, Philip (1992) *War and the Media: Propaganda and Persuasion in the Gulf War*. Manchester: Manchester University Press.

Taylor, Susan J. (1991) *Shock! Horror! The Tabloids in Action*. London: Bantam Press.

Teather, David (2001) 'Watchdog demands Brass Eye apology.' *The Guardian*, 7 September.

Tench, Dan (2002) 'Hollow sound of success.' *The Guardian*, 1 April.

Texier, Christophe (1998) 'An Overview of the Current Debate on Press Regulation in France,' in Hugh Stephenson and Michael Bromley (eds) *Sex, Lies and Democracy. The Press and the Public*. London and New York: Longman, pp. 49–60.

Thomaß, Barbara (1998) 'Teaching Ethics to Journalists in the United Kingdom,' in Hugh Stephenson and Michael Bromley (eds) *Sex, Lies and Democracy. The Press and the Public*. London and New York: Longman, pp. 136–46.

Tomalin, Nicholas (1969) 'Stop the press I want to get on.' *The Sunday Times Magazine*, 26 October.

Trelford, Donald (2000a) Conversation with the author.

Trelford, Donald (2000b) 'Foreword,' in Gary Taylor, *Freedom, Responsibility and the Media*. Sheffield: Sheffield Hallam University Press, pp. i–vi.

UNESCO (1996) *Information and Communication Technology in Development: a UNESCO Perspective*. A report prepared for the working group of the UN Commission on Science and Technology for Development: UNESCO.

United Nations (1999) *United Nations Development Report.* United Nations Development Programme. www.undp.org/hdro/99.htm

Urbano, Pilar (2000) *Garzón. El hombre que veía amanecer* [Garzón. The man who saw the dawn]. Barcelona: Plaza y Janés.

Uribe, Rodrigo (2001) *Tabloidisation of Tabloids? Evolution of British Tabloids in the Last Ten Years.* Unpublished MA thesis, University of Sheffield.

Wakeham, John (1998) 'Can self regulation achieve more than the law?' Wynne Baxter lecture, 15 May. www.pcc.org.uk/press/detail.asp?id=30, accessed 25 May, 2001.

Wakeham, John (2000) 'Statement.' *The Times,* 7 March.

Warburton, Nigel (1998) 'Ethical Photojournalism in the age of the electronic darkroom,' in Matthew Kieran (ed.) *Media Ethics.* London: Routledge, pp. 123–34.

Ward, Stephen (1999) 'Pragmatic News Objectivity: Objectivity with a Human Face.' *Discussion Paper D-37.* Harvard: The Joan Shorenstein Center on the Press, Politics and Public Policy.

Warnock, Mary (2001) *An Intelligent Person's Guide to Ethics.* London: Duckbacks.

Waugh, Evelyn (1943) *Scoop. A Novel about Journalists.* Harmondsworth: Penguin.

Weaver, David (ed.) (1998) *The Global Journalist: News People Around the World.* Cresskill, NJ: Hampton Press.

Weightman, Gavin (1999) 'When faking it is the only way.' *Evening Standard,* 17 February.

Wells, Matt (2000) 'It's been a terrible week for newspapers.' *The Guardian,* G2, 15 May.

White, Robert (1995) 'From codes of ethics to public cultural truth. A systemic view of communication ethics.' *European Journal of Communication,* 10 (4), 441–59.

Williams, Bernard (1972/1993) *Morality. An Introduction to Ethics.* Cambridge: Cambridge University Press.

Williams, Bernard (1995) *Ethics and the Limits of Philosophy.* London: Fontana.

Williams, Kevin (1992) 'Something more important than truth: ethical issues in war reporting,' in Andrew Belsey and Ruth Chadwick (eds) *Ethical Issues in Journalism.* London: Routledge, pp. 154–70.

Williams, Kevin (1998) *Get Me a Murder A Day! A History of Mass Communication in Britain.* London: Arnold.

Willis, John (1999) 'The faking of real TV.' *The Guardian,* 18 May.

Wilson, A.N. (1999) 'Reviewers I have known,' in Stephen Glover (ed.) *Secrets of the Press. Journalists on Journalism.* London: Allen Lane, pp. 18–33.

Wilson, A.N. (2000) 'The television camera nearly always lies.' *The Sunday Telegraph,* 19 March.

Winston, Brian (1998) *Media Technology and Society: A History From the Telegraph to the Internet.* London: Routledge.

Younger Committee on Privacy (1972) *The Report of the Committee on Privacy.* London: HMSO.

Zelizer, Barbie (1992) *Covering the Body. The Kennedy Assassination, the Media, and the Shaping of Collective Memory.* Chicago and London: The University of Chicago Press.

Index